PIECES OF ME

PIECES OF ME

RESCUING MY KIDNAPPED DAUGHTERS

LIZBETH MEREDITH

SHE WRITES PRESS

Published 2016
Printed in the United States of America
Print ISBN: 978-1-63152-834-7
E-ISBN: 978-1-63152-835-4
Library of Congress Control Number: 2016938687

For information, address:
She Writes Press
1563 Solano Ave #546
Berkeley, CA 94707

Cover design © Julie Metz, Ltd./metzdesign.com
Interior design by Tabitha Lahr

She Writes Press is a division of SparkPoint Studio, LLC.

Excerpts reprinted with permission from the *Anchorage Daily News We Alaskans* 1994 © Alaska Dispatch Publishing.

For my daughters,
Marianthi and Meredith.
I love you forever.

CONTENTS

Prologue:

AFTERMATH

2016

Sometimes I'm asked if I feel lucky. Usually, it's after I've given a presentation about domestic violence or the Adverse Childhood Experiences Study, and in the context of "Aren't you glad all the bad stuff happened when your kids were little?"

As though prebirth and early childhood experiences are any less impactful.

The truth is, I do feel lucky, but not because my kids were little when their father tried to kill me. I feel lucky because I survived, and so did they. I feel lucky because when he stole them years later and took them to Greece, I was still a young adult, with all the energy and optimism I needed to risk bringing them home. I feel lucky because I knew from living through my own kidnapping how important it was to right this wrong, and was adept at developing a support network that would make doing so possible. I feel lucky that I recognized how much support the girls needed when they returned, and I often did my best to get it for them. And I feel lucky that my daughters have forgiven me for the decisions, large and small, that I've made that were not in their best interests.

But there are times when I don't feel so lucky. When I take one of my daughters to the hospital for a trauma-related illness. When I am the only parent to hear their joys and sorrows. When I must reassure them, now in their late twenties, that I'm all right and I'm still here for them after they become panicked when I've taken too long to return a text or call. When I'm on a date and I'm asked anything about my marriage or how involved my kids' dad is in their lives.

I never wanted to be one of those crime victims whose identity revolves around victimization. Then last year, I filled out a grant application and listed my passions. Budget travel in foreign countries. Writing. Volunteering with literacy projects. All directly connected to surviving my victimization.

I have my daughters. I have my passions. And, all things considered, I guess that makes me better off than lucky.

Chapter 1

LAST VISIT

I brush Marianthi's hair as fast as I can without upsetting her. My oldest daughter, like so many firstborn children, seems in tune with my every mood since her birth. Just six years old now, she senses my wave of anxiety about her father's impending weekly visitation.

"Are you scared, Mommy?" Marianthi's voice sounds like a Munchkin's from *The Wizard of Oz*, as small and sweet as she is.

"No, sweetie." I smile. "I just don't want to keep Daddy waiting. You look *beautiful*."

And she does. She's wearing her blue dress with the floral collar that matches her ocean-blue eyes. A barrette holds her straight brown hair back neatly. I direct her to her coat and boots while I work on getting her little sister ready.

I push Meredith's plump calf into her boot. She groans.

"Point your foot down, baby." Slowly, the boot slides on. I run my fingers through her wispy brown ringlets and inspect her round face for remnants of Rice Krispies.

Meredith is the antithesis of her sister. At two, she lost her grasp on a helium balloon. She silently watched it float toward the clouds, then announced, "God stole my balloon." At three, she told a bald man that he had a baby head. And now, at four, Meredith has learned she can belch as loudly as a college boy at a frat party.

My daughters are absurdly cute. I'm not the only one who thinks so; I get requests for them to be flower girls at weddings from people I hardly know.

"Ready just in time," I tell them, as their father, Grigorios, Gregory for short, pulls up in his dented, bright-blue Jeep Cherokee. A male passenger I don't recognize is sitting next to him. I try to get a closer look. The passenger catches me, and I avert my eyes immediately. What guy would ride along with Gregory to pick up the girls? And why?

"Momma, will you pick us up tomowoh?" Meredith asks. I dread the day she's able to pronounce her R's.

"I'll pick you up on the tomorrow after tomorrow, remember?" But of course Meredith can't remember the court-appointed visitation schedule. She's only four, and her father's visits are irregular. She doesn't know that the court only recently lifted the supervised-visitation requirement that had been imposed during a restraining order, or that I pick her and her sister up at their day care for the express purpose of avoiding unnecessary contact with him. And she shouldn't have to. Neither of them should have to know the grim details of their parents' divorce. They're still little girls, after all.

I feel as if I have spent my entire twenty-nine years of life walking on eggshells. It's March 13, 1994, and I'm four years out of my violent marriage. But despite the passage of time, my fear of Gregory is as strong as it was the day in March 1990 when I got back up off the floor, collected my baby girls, and fled in a taxi. The scratches and strangulation marks healed after several days, but his parting threats haunt me: "I would rather kill you than let you leave. That way, you'll die knowing the girls will have no mother and their father will be in jail. Leave and you'll never see them again—I'll take them home to Greece. I have nothing to lose."

That was by no means the first time Gregory had threatened to harm or kill me. Not even close. In our marriage, he'd isolated me from friends, taken my car, and, at the lowest point, limited my access to food while I was pregnant. Eventually, he wrung my neck. All the while, he delivered the same message over and over: *You are worthless, stupid, and helpless. I am the only person you have to rely on. Without me, you are nothing.*

But it was his threat to take the children and disappear to his native home in Greece if I left him that got to me. He knew I could never live without my children.

I remind myself that our circumstances are different now. Yes, things are still hard. I have no family around to help with the girls or with the house. We live in Alaska, a place where one battles ice and snow and long periods of continual darkness followed by short periods of constant light. It's a place best suited for those with money. Money to buy a four-wheel drive. Money to buy lots of insulation for the house, fancy winter boots and coats, and airline tickets to leave the state once or twice a year for a warmer climate. All of the things I don't have.

But what I do have are two smart and healthy little girls who know how to respond if anyone, including their father, attempts to take them away from me. I have my long-fought divorce that includes provisions in our custody arrangement to prevent Gregory from making good on his threats. I've earned my journalism degree. I have a promising job, and I'm determined not to feign independence through remarriage and further dependence. We are out of low-income housing and off food stamps. There is no reason to be afraid.

"Don't forget your blankie, baby," I remind Meredith. I hand her the paper-thin quilted blanket with red teddy bear print and red fringe that she's loved since birth. Life for everyone around Meredith goes better when she has the comfort of her security blanket. While her sister is the sensitive, pleasing child, Meredith's attitude is that if she has to suffer, then so should the entire community.

The doorbell rings. I hug the girls and open the door. Gregory is standing there in his hooded blue jacket and baggy khakis. His dirty-blond hair looks even thinner than it was the last time I saw him, and his cheeks more hollow. Though he's a half inch taller than I am, I outweigh my former husband by an easy fifteen pounds, despite my frequent crash diets. This stupid fact has pissed me off over the years as much as the legitimate reasons I have to hate him. And yet his gaunt look makes him appear more scary and desperate to me somehow.

Gregory wordlessly takes Meredith's hand. She in turn grabs Marianthi's hand. They carefully step over the ice and snow that have yet to melt in the extended Alaskan winter, and Gregory lifts them into his Jeep. They both look back at me before he shuts the rear passenger door.

"Good-bye! I love you," I call out.

"Bye, Mommy!" they say in unison.

Gregory glares hard at me before getting into the driver's seat. I return his gaze and smile brightly, refusing to defer to his intimidation tactics, and then shudder as the Jeep disappears from view. I close the door, chiding myself. I hate being paranoid, but who is that guy with him? *None of your busi-*

ness, Liz, I tell myself. Bad things always seem to happen when I question Gregory about anything, and it isn't illegal for him to have someone I don't know in the car. *Just get over it.*

Time to prepare for the day ahead. I plan to take my friend Julie to lunch at a new restaurant for her thirtieth birthday and will force myself to enjoy the quiet time without the girls. It should be fun, except there is a palpable feeling of unrest in the pit of my stomach today. I don't know why.

The climate between Gregory and me has cooled again in the last few weeks. I had always hoped we could be on civil terms for the sake of the children. Occasionally, I was encouraged when time passed without any hint of coarse language or bullying as we exchanged the girls for a visitation. But the peace has been short-lived. In general, it seems that the passage of time has only increased their father's intentions to possess or destroy me, whichever comes first. And although I'm too scared to cross Gregory unless the girls' and my safety is at stake, the state of Alaska boldly dipped into his bank account to collect child support a few weeks ago. Gregory is livid. I can't help but worry about repercussions. He has strong feelings about paying child support.

"If you need diapers, call me," he told me after our daughters and I got settled into low-income housing four years earlier. "If you and the girls run out of food, you have my number. I'll do what I can. But don't ever let some government agency tell me how much I need to pay you to support my children. I will decide this."

And, true to his word, Gregory has not bowed to the government mandate of paying child support. Instead, I have learned to manage the financial struggles of supporting two little girls on next to nothing. I have learned how to manage his threatening phone calls and the image of him in my rearview mirror. I have even learned to parlay my fear of his killing me into an inspiration to live each day with my daughters as if it might be my last. Because it really might be.

Yet I know I can never learn to live without my daughters, and my ex-husband knows it, too.

1969

I wince as my mother slams the hairbrush into my head, pushing the bristles through my scalp. At five years old, I know that the only time Mother brushes my hair is when there's trouble. The brush trails down my back, until she lifts it again.

"You want Larry to be your father, right?" I nod quickly, but the brush still crashes down hard on my head. "Because he wants to be your father, and he's been your father all along, so you'll need to tell that to the nice judge we see today." She pushes the bristles more deeply into my scalp this time. Tears spring to my eyes. "I will, Mother. I promise."

And I do. I assure the nice judge that I am happy to have Larry as my father. Little do I know that I will be rewarded with a new last name. No longer am I Lizbeth Meredith. I am now Lizbeth Ponder. Libby for short. Libby Ponder. And, just like that, I unwittingly become my mother's accomplice in her abduction of me. It will now be impossible for my country-simple father to find his only daughter, who disappeared three years earlier from Kentucky with his ex-wife and three of her five other children from a previous marriage. All evidence of the real me vanishes, and I learn to find comfort by becoming invisible.

Sometimes I dare to inventory the people around me, my family. Uneven. Uneducated. Unreliable. *When I grow up, I will not be like them*, I tell myself.

❖ ❖ ❖

I am older and stronger now. I am no longer the little girl who longs to be invisible. And I am no longer the young wife who attempts to iron the wrinkles out of her husband's life so that he might be kind to her.

At least, that's what I'd like to think. Yet even though it's now been four years since I left Gregory, I still give careful attention to sending my daughters to their father looking perfect so they can attend church with him, a church that he reviled during our marriage.

"Why should I go there?" he said about the church during a heated argument after Marianthi was born. "What did they ever do for me? I needed money to attend college in this country, and nothing!"

"But it's the Greek Orthodox Church. Don't you want your daughter knowing her culture, being raised in the same church you were?" As a woman without a traceable past, I find the very idea that my girls growing up disconnected from their Greek heritage unthinkable. Gregory refused to attend, until a conveniently timed spiritual renewal occurred moments after I got my first restraining order. He convinced the magistrate he needed to worship at the Greek Orthodox church once he realized I still attended services there. And he won.

I decided at the time it was not a battle worth fighting, after parishioners called to express their support of my husband's apparent turnaround and encouraged me to forgive and forget the past and remember only my marriage vows. "Look how sad he is," a female parishioner named Betty told me after services. She motioned to my despondent-looking husband, who had miraculously appeared at church after the separation. "He's sorry, Liz."

I had looked up to Betty as a kind older woman whose marriage to an even older Greek man survived many hard times. Early on, I confided in her at church when Gregory's behavior went off the rails. "I know he loves me," I told her. "But is that enough?"

"Look," she said, a bit more directly, "I understand your feelings completely. I married my husband twenty-five years ago. If I could do it again, I wouldn't. But it's done. I made my vow before God. And you've made yours, too."

I took Betty and the other parishioners' advice for the entire four and a half years of my marriage, and it didn't change a thing. So I finally gathered my courage and my daughters and left my husband. That changed a lot of things. Few of the changes were the ones I wanted, but I remain hopeful that the passage of time will bring the children and me safety and financial security. I just want my happily ever after.

Yet I still can't define for myself what that will look like. What kind of job do I want for myself one day? What will my hobbies and interests be, once I have the time to develop them?

Sometimes I feel like I've been set free. I can do what I want. I can neglect the phone bill and order pizza instead. But other times, usually after I've bounced a string of checks or received a shut-off notice from the electric company, I feel swallowed up by the enormity of having to make my own decisions. I don't know what I want out of life for myself.

What I want for my daughters became crystal clear to me as I began my new life as a single parent. I want their lives to be free from the impediments I experienced as the child of two hot-tempered high school dropouts. I want my girls to know who they are and have strong family connections. I want them to be educated. I want them to travel the world. I want them to be able to support themselves, and if they choose to be in a long-term relationship, it will be based on their strengths, not their weaknesses. And I know that in order for them to get there, it is important that I take more than a surface glance at my unhealthy and unsafe relationship with their father. Only then will I ever have any hope of keeping history from repeating itself in their future.

As I walk back into the kitchen, I bend down to pick up Meredith's blanket. She forgot it anyhow. I smile to myself as I place it on her bed. This will be a long couple of days for us all.

Chapter 2

KIDNAPPING

Visitations have been just another way for my ex-husband to manipulate me. During our divorce proceedings, Gregory asked that he be allowed to see the girls each Sunday afternoon to Tuesday afternoon, as well as a four-hour block of time on Thursdays. When I asked him why he did not request weekends or every other weekend, as is more typical, his response was automatic. "That's easy. You won't be able to date if you have the girls on the weekends."

Perhaps he didn't realize that things like coffee shops and movie theaters are open on weekdays. But when he found out that I managed to sneak in a date on a weeknight, he failed to arrive the next Sunday night and pick up our little girls.

"Mommy," Marianthi asked at age three, shifting uncomfortably in the starched dress her father had bought her for his visits, "how long do we have to wait?" Both girls were dressed and ready to go and watched anxiously at the window as the minutes turned into an hour, and then another. And another. I was helpless to fix this for them. And from that Sunday forward, Gregory visited whenever he pleased. If I hoped to make plans with friends on a Sunday night, I would need to be home at just the right time in case he decided to appear. If he did not appear, I needed to have someone handy to step in and take care of them. It wasn't easy, but we managed. Sometimes, weeks and months in a row, Gregory arrived on time and ready to go. Other times, he was nowhere to be found. I spoke to my divorce attorney, who assured me there was no recourse if Gregory chose not to exercise his right to visit. I, on the other hand, could be fined $200 if I did not have the girls ready to go at the appointed time. So they were ready and waiting, every week, whether their father showed up or not.

When Gregory did show up, I was quietly overjoyed. I needed the break.

In the past, I had to use every available childless moment to study. But since I completed my degree in journalism, I now have time for fun. I almost feel guilty.

But the girls are gone now. I watched them drive off. The timer is ticking.

After surveying the house, I quickly toss their stray toys into the toy box and start the dishwasher and a load of laundry. Good enough. Housekeeping has never been my strong point.

I drop off my dry cleaning, return phone calls, and pick up Julie for lunch. Friends since high school, Julie and I have no problem burning an afternoon visiting. By the time our conversation winds down, it is after dinnertime and the restaurant is closing. I get the last half of my spicy tuna roll boxed up to go. Reluctantly, I drop her off at her place and head back to my empty home, where I read and watch television until it is time for bed.

I cannot fall asleep. My mind wanders to the girls. Did their dad remember to read them a story before bed? Are they having fun? Then I think about the day ahead at work. I used to sleep more soundly when our roommate Barbara lived in the downstairs basement bedroom. A six-foot, muscular redhead in her fifties, Barbara filled a grandmotherly role for my kids for the year that we lived with her. And she scared Gregory senseless. But Barbara moved back to California to be closer to her grown daughters at Christmastime. Now I have the whole creaky house to myself.

Rest hasn't come easily to me since I married Gregory. Starting the first week of our marriage, I found out that he often forgot his way home. One day. Two days. Several days at a time. Just disappeared without explanation. When our babies were born, it was just me who rocked them to sleep. Marianthi had colic; twenty months later, Meredith's squalling made Marianthi's efforts seem amateurish. When I finally left Gregory, the girls and I moved from couch to couch to shelter to low-income housing. As I protected us from random weirdos and their father-turned-stalker, my hypervigilance ruled. I learned to shut my eyes and work on relaxing, counting sheep, praying, listening to relaxation tapes. Five hours for me was a good night's rest.

At the first sound of footsteps coming from the hallway, my heartbeat quickens. *Deep breath. You're fine*, I tell myself. After a few quiet seconds, I hear the footsteps coming toward me again. I pull the blankets over my head, but the steps get louder, closer. Gregory is rumored to have bought another handgun. *Who's watching the girls if he's here?* I pull the pillow over my head on top of the blankets and squeeze my eyes shut. I wait for the inevitable. The steps are rhythmic, becoming louder and louder as he gets closer. Trembling now, I clamp my hand over my mouth to keep my teeth from chattering. *At least dying by gunfire will be quick.* Step, step, step. *Unless I don't die right away but slowly bleed to death. I hope he doesn't shoot me in the face.* I have always imagined that I will have an open-casket funeral, so my friends can see me one last time before saying good-bye.

Around fifty steps later, I realize that Gregory should have reached me by now. My house isn't that big. I pull the pillow and quilt off and open my eyes. I am alone. I have been listening to the sound of my own frenzied heartbeat.

For two years I've worked as a battered women's advocate at Abused Women's Aid in Crisis (AWAIC)—the same shelter the kids and I fled to in 1990. While the salary is pitiful and I don't make enough to afford health insurance for the girls, my income is offset by working with a group of talented professionals committed to making a difference in the lives of people affected by domestic violence.

Most days, I see an average of three to five women presenting for their intake appointment. Often the appointment has been scheduled in advance, but sometimes a woman at her wits' end simply walks in unannounced and says, "I just need someone to talk to." I love being that someone. I get to listen to her tell her story, without expressing the judgment or hope that a family member or friend might have about whether she should stay in or leave the relationship. I ask questions in order to spur thought and give general information about safety and emergency planning. Why do you think he did that? What did he gain from the situation? How does he show you he's sorry afterward? How do you feel after the apology? Has he threatened to hurt you before? Are there weapons in the home? Do you know where they are? Has he threatened to use them on you or on himself?

Never is it okay to tell a woman what I think she should do. It is simply too dangerous a gamble—most battered women that are killed by their partners are murdered just after they've left an abusive relationship or while they are planning to leave. Instead, I refer her to information and support groups we facilitate, where she will meet other victims of emotional, physical, or sexual abuse by an intimate partner. And, week by week, she will muscle up emotionally by meeting with women in similar circumstances and hearing their stories of survival. She will learn to tell her own story.

A year or two later, that same woman who once walked timidly through the door returns transformed. She is making a life for herself without abuse and proudly volunteers her skills or makes a donation to the center. The bonus for me is obvious: I inhale secondhand strength.

Mondays I cofacilitate one of the support groups, which ends at 8:30 P.M. I am tuckered out once I get home, and sleep easily afterward. The next day flies by also, and after work it is time for me to pick up the girls at their day care. Heavy snow carpets the ground, and I agree to drive an elderly Filipina foster grandma home on the way to the day care so she won't be stuck waiting outside for the city bus. She inquires politely about my marital status, offering me her oldest son once she hears that I am a single parent. "What you need is a nice Filipino man," she says, and chuckles. I smile back, enjoying her hard *p* on the word *Filipino*, but keep my focus on the slippery road ahead. My old Ford sedan wobbles when braking, and the back of the car fishtails twice before we arrive at our destination.

My passenger stays in the idling car while I go inside the day care to retrieve the girls. I go to Meredith's class but don't find her. Maybe she's waiting in Marianthi's classroom. I go there and don't find either of them. The daycare director shrugs when I inquire at the front office. "He didn't come by today. He didn't call, either. Strange."

My stomach churns. This is more than strange; Gregory knows the visitation routine well and in the past has enjoyed keeping us guessing about whether or not he would arrive to pick up the girls. But he's rarely late to return them.

I'm distracted as I drive my passenger home. She continues to prattle about her son, and I nearly push her out the door when we arrive at her apartment. As soon as I get home, I call Gregory. No answer. I call again. And again. And again. And I wait. Finally, an hour later, I call the police and report the girls missing.

The dispatcher gives me a lukewarm reception and asks me how long the girls have been missing. Two hours or more, I tell her. Not long enough to evoke this panicked response, I imagine she's thinking. And why haven't I gone and checked his house myself? That's a natural question that begs a few answers, which I'll save for the responding officer.

Half an hour later, an officer responds. Officer Gansel is a hair past middle age, and his casual demeanor tells me he has seen much in his career. He is initially unmoved by my panic. "Ma'am, he is the father. He's probably just lost track of time. Can't you just agree to let him keep the girls a little longer?"

Allegations of international child abduction are not part of the daily diet of a beat cop in Anchorage, Alaska. And it shows.

I have to convince him that I am not a spiteful former spouse trying to screw her ex out of time with the kids. "My relationship with my ex-husband isn't typical. He's threatened to take the girls and leave the country before. I have no reason to think he would do the right thing."

He looks at me blankly.

"Check your records," I continue. "I've gotten restraining orders in the past."

It takes some coaxing before he looks a little further. I tell the officer of Gregory's and my volatile history—in marriage and afterward—including all of the provisions made in our divorce to prevent the abduction he has repeatedly threatened. "He's just discontinued his supervised visits," I tell him. "He's not even allowed to take the girls out of the state until next year, and even then it has to be with my written permission. I'm supposed to get a copy of the itinerary in advance. He can take them to Greece with my permission after that, so long as he's posted a big, fat bond so that I can cash it in if he attempts not to return with them. He's even posted on the children's passport issuance alert system."

"Okay, okay," he says. "Let me make a few phone calls, all right?"

Using his connections at a Greek-owned deli he frequents, Officer Gansel calls a renowned entrepreneur in the Greek community, who dresses like Liberace and keeps his businesses listed under other people's names. He tells the officer to call Dorothy Paul, an elderly former coworker of Gregory's who is now Gregory's landlord. The call is brief, and he hangs up the phone smiling.

"Your ex-husband is simply moving across town to a new place," he says, clearly pleased with himself. "See, it's not so bad. The landlady's husband gave me a new address for him. The phone's probably not even connected yet, but he gave me the number of a friend of his to chat with."

I want to believe him, but I know better. Gregory would never accidentally overlook such a detail. If he were moving, I would know about it in advance, unless he was up to something shady. There has to be more to this story.

Officer Gansel's third phone call is equally brief, but now his smile fades. He places the phone back on the receiver and says nothing for a couple of beats. I watch him processing the new information he won't share as the color drains from his face.

"I hate to say this," he says finally, inhaling deeply, "but you may be right. There are allegations now that your husband flew out of Alaska two days ago with the girls. Your daughters are with him in Greece."

He looks at me and waits for my response. I have none. I cannot cry or scream. I'm not even sure I am surprised. I am frozen.

Officer Gansel proceeds to calmly outline law enforcement's response to parental child abductions while I stare at him blankly. He stops and slips me a pen and a sticky note. I take his cue and begin to write. The case will be assigned to a detective, who will put the children's information into the National Crime Information Center (NCIC) database. On the off chance that Gregory is picked up on a new offense or citation, it will alert law enforcement in that jurisdiction to the child abduction. Federal law requires law enforcement officers to input the information into NCIC's system without delay after a report of child abduction. The detective will complete an investigation and get assistance from the FBI to deal with the international aspect of the child abduction. Other agencies, such as Interpol, the international crime policing organization, will be contacted to provide extra assistance if necessary.

"Ma'am, I'm so sorry about all of this. I really am." He squeezes my hand, which is clammy now. "But your case will be assigned to the Crimes Against Children Unit tomorrow, and they're some of our best. You're in good hands."

After I thank him and escort him out the front door, I return to my empty house. Marianthi's bed is covered with rows of Barbies and trolls, lined up perfectly. Her nearly five-month-old Halloween candy remains untouched in a jar on a nearby shelf so she can inventory her goods at will. In the next room, pajama bottoms peek out from Meredith's unmade bed, and her collection of ponies spills out of her toy bucket. I pick up her security blanket from the top of her bed and inhale her scent. She still smells like a little baby. How scared and confused the girls must now feel.

I realize it is strange that I don't flounce on the bed crying or let out a bloodcurdling scream after the news of the girls' disappearance is confirmed. Early life experiences have discouraged big displays of emotion.

1972

"Lizbeth Anne!"

There is only one kind of situation when my mother uses my middle name. I am an eight-year-old girl facing big trouble.

"Lizbeth Anne! Get your ass down here! *Now!*"

I put my Midge doll face down on the floor of my attic bedroom and begin the death march down three long flights of stairs. By the time I reach Mother, her face is red and her fists are clenched.

"Sit down!"

I quickly sit on the chair that she motions me toward. I am truly bewildered.

"Did you open the shades in the living room after I vacuumed and dusted?"

"No." I am telling her the truth, yet I know I am not telling her all that she needs to hear. Mother requires that we kids call her Ma'am. Not Mommy or Mama or Mother. Only Ma'am will do.

I see her open hand coming at me before I feel it strike my right cheek. Tears spring to my eyes, but I do not move.

"No, what?" she growls.

"No, Mother." I brace myself for what comes next, inwardly pleased with my own defiance. Her right hand connects again with my right cheek. This time, I keep my eyes fixed directly on hers.

"This is your last chance, young lady. Think hard before you answer this time, because you don't want to get it wrong," she warns. "No, what?"

Though it appears that I am looking up at Mother's face, in truth I am looking through her. I turn down the volume in my ears so that her shouting is merely background noise for the dialogue in my head: *Do not cry. This isn't really happening. Be strong.*

Throughout my life, these words replay in my head many times and help me achieve a detached state when crises arise. Like when Mother placed my wet mattress in our front yard, certain that my bed-wetting could be stopped when my fifth-grade classmates viewed my shame while they walked to the bus stop. "Whose mattress is that, anyway?" my next-door neighbor Lawrence asked, as he slid into his desk beside mine at school, grinning. He knew only too well that I was the youngest child in the household; my next-oldest sibling was in her early teens.

"My mom's at it again." I shrugged. "She's nuts."

What can I say about my mother? It is true that she left both emotional and sometimes physical scars on her children. It is true that she ripped her children from their respective fathers and from one another before finally leaving them all behind herself. First, she ditched my brothers when they were ten and eleven, assuring them they would have a boys' weekend with their father. Instead, she fled to Alaska with her daughters and new beau without notice, never to call, visit, or support them in any way again. In a flash, my brothers lost their mom and their sisters without explanation. A few years after that, Mother tossed her oldest daughter, a pregnant fifteen-year-old, onto the streets of Anchorage, hurled her clothes at her, and told her she was now released to be with the "other prostitutes."

Next daughter in line to leave was Mother's nemesis. If our mom said so, we kids were not allowed to speak to Sister Number Two, who was prettier than Mother and never in her favor. Mother said so a lot when that sister became a teenager and began living in forced isolation for days at a time. "Tell Her Highness to pass the carrots," Mother would say at the dinner table, refusing to look at my sister, sitting right next to her. When the effects of emotional and physical abuse took a toll on my sister's mental health in her mid-teens, Mother was more than happy to give her a one-way ticket to visit relatives many states away. "I'm so glad Her Highness has left this family. Aren't you?" Mother smiled happily at we remainders at the dinner table. We said nothing.

Sister Number Three got caught in the crossfire at fifteen when she shielded herself from our final stepfather's drunken advances, locking us in the bathroom after he gave us too many rum and Cokes while Mother was out of town. I was ten years old and heard his pleas to my sister: "I want to fuck you!" Mother appeared to be upset with him upon her return but quickly changed her target to my sister. "Why are you trying to come between me and Larry?" Seeing the handwriting on the wall, Sister Number Three graduated early from high school and moved to the big city of Anchorage from Chugiak the next year, at sixteen.

Leaving me. Just me and Mother and Larry.

At first, I thought things were improving with Mother. I lay low, didn't ask much, and went along with anything she wanted. She seemed happier. But within a year, she was making her getaway plans with Larry, and they didn't include me.

Despite her physical and emotional aggression toward us, to dismiss her as simply abusive or nuts ignores other truths. The time she spent the better part of a day excavating the Anchorage city dump when I was five to find Pinky, my beloved stuffed toy rabbit that accidentally ended up in the garbage. Or the time she kept a constant bedside watch over a dragonfly she placed on her pillow after accidentally swatting him in a heated game of badminton. Or the time she intervened at my Episcopalian kindergarten when the nuns insisted on paddling the devil out of my left hand.

Anticipating her moods, good or bad, was impossible.

My sisters found different ways to cope. When the oldest was in her early teens, she reached for alcohol and older men for comfort. The next oldest withdrew inside herself and built a social life exclusively with imaginary friends. She became irretrievably unstitched when she was fifteen and I was nine. The last sister, five years older than I, was sickly and became conflicted when she received extra attention from Mother. How could she call out our mom for being abusive when she was the recipient of Mother's kindness? So she did her best to be a loyal daughter and distanced herself from the rest of us when we talked plainly about the violence in our home.

I desperately needed them to be strong so that I could have someone to hold on to, but instead I watched them marching further into danger. It was as though they were walking on train tracks, oblivious to the oncoming train half a mile behind them. An onlooker to their impending doom, I wanted to scream out a warning to them, but it was no use. We were each on our own trajectory.

Later, I would understand that my refusal to cry when hurt was not a victory over pain. It was a training program by

Mother, an attempt to teach me to suppress my unimportant emotions in order not to inconvenience anyone else with them. Still, there was no denying that withholding my anguish troubled her. It was worth my effort.

1972

Mother increases her volume. "No, what?"

Enough already, I tell myself. Mother's raised voice is evidence enough that I have already won this battle. I can abort this exercise.

I look at her evenly.

"No, Ma'am."

It is more than my years at trauma boot camp that keep me from falling apart after I first learn my daughters have been stolen. I also have a growing sense of relief.

A friend of mine once told me about getting the call at work that his wife had finally died of breast cancer. He had been her caretaker for the five-year period after her initial diagnosis and told himself daily how lucky he was to still have her to care for. He believed that so long as she lived, he could deal with whatever happened along the way, no matter how hard it was to provide care or how crushing it was to acknowledge her impending demise. "But when she finally died," he said, "I actually felt liberated instead."

I understand.

The worst thing, the very event I have dreaded for so long, has really happened. Nothing worse ever can.

My daughters have been kidnapped. It doesn't seem real. I feel like I am watching an overdramatized made-for-TV movie. Maybe I just need to find my remote and change the channel.

Chapter 3

FINDING HELP

I need to call someone immediately. It is eleven at night already, but it doesn't matter. I have to share the news. I am too stunned to cry myself, so I need to hear the emotion of a friend. A surrogate crier. "Hello?" my childhood friend Marti whispers. Before I can say anything, I hear the crash of breaking glass on her end of the phone. "That's weird," she says, returning after a pause. "The picture of your girls just fell off the wall and shattered in the living room."

"He's taken the girls."

It's all I need to say. Anyone who knows me understands exactly what that means.

The next few calls are a blur. I call my friend Ann Kreider, whose brother, Jim, and husband, Michael, are both successful Anchorage attorneys.

What a lucky day it was when I met Ann. We were both at a park in 1989, pushing our two-year-olds on the swings. I stared ahead and stole an occasional sideways glace at her. She was around forty, petite, with shoulder-length brown hair. She wore no makeup, except for bright-red lipstick, and she talked incessantly: "It's my anniversary today. Michael and I met at ... I moved to Alaska in ..."

My world had become void of adult conversations, and her constant chatter was equal parts welcome and overwhelming. Ann paid no mind to my silence, and eventually she wore me down. I held my own in our conversation. When an hour or more had passed, Ann motioned toward an ominous-looking dark van with few windows and asked if the girls and I wanted a ride to her place. *My husband would be livid*, I considered telling her. Instead, I accepted her invitation to share a box of macaroni and cheese, the powdered kind, and a beer. We talked like lifelong friends while her son and my daughter played and little Meredith fussed in her snuggly.

I learned that Ann and I were from different worlds. She was smarter, sunnier, and wealthier than I. I felt like a stray puppy she had rescued from the pound and proudly brought home to her family. If her family felt the same way, they never let on. Ann became one of the few friends my husband allowed me to see during our marriage. When I slipped into the AWAIC shelter in 1990 with the girls, I was surprised to get a message from the staff that a woman named Ann had called and left: *Lizzie, I heard you had to come to the shelter. I'm going to Bermuda. Do you want my house?*

The offer was appealing. By then I knew that staying anywhere other than the secure shelter would not be safe, but I appreciated that Ann was willing to share anything and everything she had without hesitation, including her husband's and her brother's billable hours. Throughout the divorce process and beyond, she gave generously of their time.

The news of the abduction doesn't surprise Ann, but she

sounds devastated. She instructs me to call her brother, Jim, the next day. "He'll work with Michael. They'll do all they can to help, Lizzie. We'll get 'em back." I can tell by the pitch of her voice that she only half believes herself. Michael talks over her in the background. "Tell her to call me tomorrow. Tell her not to panic."

I call my older sister Kim in Arizona and make a to-do list for tomorrow. I should have known better. My sister has always tried to protect me from harm, and though I'm almost thirty years old, she still thinks of me as a child. Delivering the news to her only makes her feel helpless and miserable, and I find myself having to talk her off a ledge. "No, please don't call Interpol now. There's a whole process we have to go through to get to them. I don't need you to get involved in the process; I just need your emotional support. I'll be fine."

I hang up the phone and lie on top of my bed, still fully dressed. I'm not fine. I'm deeply tired, but sleep does not come. Hours later, I haven't moved and I haven't slept, so I turn on the radio to catch the chorus to a Toni Braxton song on the radio. She's crooning about the possibility of never seeing her loved one's face again. It feels like she's talking to me, warning me about never seeing the girls' faces again.

I slam my fist over the power button and sit straight up in bed. It is four in the morning. Of course I will see their faces again. To even consider the contrary is unbearable. Meredith's round face and supple cheeks; Marianthi's delicate features, her pointed nose and sharp chin. I watch time tick by on the clock until it is time to go to work. I don't bother to brush my teeth or wash my face. I run a comb through my hair and put my contact lenses back in, and I'm off.

At work, I stare at my computer screen and listen for my coworkers to arrive. I need to make this announcement only once.

First in is Jennifer, our accountant, who has the office next to me. She peeks her head in my door and feigns shock since I've finally beat her to work. Her smile quickly fades when she sees what I imagine is my stricken look.

"What's wrong?"

Jennifer isn't just one of my favorite coworkers; she's one of my dearest friends. A transplant from rural Kentucky, she tends to underreact, like I do, in a crisis. When Gregory slashed my tires last year, Jennifer arrived at my home to give me a ride. No tears. No conversation. Just quiet support, the kind I trust over the inevitable histrionics I'll surely experience with others.

Before I can answer Jennifer, in comes Sara from the front desk, followed by Mary from the maintenance department and my fellow advocates Susan and Sally. My work family is nearly complete. It's time to tell them.

I open my mouth to speak and promptly feel my throat close. I inhale deeply and wait a beat. The room is scarily quiet.

"Gregory took the girls and went to Greece."

No response. They look frozen. I'm not sure what I was expecting, exactly, but I didn't expect a roomful of my female coworkers to stare at me and have no reaction to my crisis.

I wait for what feels like five minutes but is more likely thirty seconds. "Gregory's kidnapped my daughters. They're probably already in Greece."

All at once, the tears, the hugs, the patting come. I feel like a small child. That's better.

"We're here for you, Liz. We'll do this together."

I've known these women long enough to know that they're each strong willed and believe deeply in the power of connection.

"Does Heather know?" Jennifer asks immediately.

Heather Flynn is our executive director at AWAIC. She's on leave while she runs for mayor, and she's expecting my daughters to be in her mayoral commercial, which starts filming at lunch hour today.

Heather is the reason I came to work in the same battered-women's shelter the girls and I fled to when I left Gregory. She is a longtime politician, instrumental in the local Democratic Party's efforts to advance the status of women and children in Alaska, and she serves on the local city council. Mouthy and passionate, Heather does not hesitate to cut a wide swath when necessary. And she adores my children. I know that she will be a source of strength.

I drive to her headquarters, a rented warehouse in midtown Anchorage. Heather is dressed to the nines in a navy-blue suit, and her hair, usually a wild, curly mop, has been tamed. Is this how the distortions begin? I hardly recognize her and feel bad when her glance darts behind me, looking for my daughters.

"Gregory's disappeared with the girls." I've said it too many times already, and for some reason, seeing Heather connects me briefly with my emotions. I start to whimper, and I feel like a toddler who has fallen on the ground and gotten quietly back up until the sight of her mother inspires wailing. It's ridiculous, but I have a hard time regaining my composure.

Heather looks miserable, too, and I know it's not just because she's lost the two cutest extras her mayoral campaign will ever see. The fact that she loves my daughters makes me feel good because she's not typically a kid person. I've brought the girls to holiday parties and occasional fundraisers at AWAIC, and they've always been a hit, equal parts polite and unruly, just like Heather herself.

She gives me a quick hug as I leave her office. "Get ready for the fight of your life, kid. There won't be a quick fix for this one." I know she's right, but I'm not ready to hear it.

Next stop: the law office of Michael Kreider, husband of my friend Ann. Her brother, Jim, joins us from his law office across the street. While Michael has found success as a personal-injury attorney, Jim has the municipal contract to serve indigent misdemeanants. Michael is serious and sensitive; Jim is aggressive and direct. Together, the two make a perfect team. "Don't worry about the money," Michael says to me, knowing I have none. "At least not for us. But when you're rich and famous, see us then."

I am so fortunate. They have consulted with law enforcement and the district attorney's office already, and they're all in.

Like Heather did, Michael reminds me of the long path ahead. He explains that Jim will understand the criminal justice aspects of the situation, and he will work with the civil aspects of the abduction. "Chin up, kiddo. We'll get those girls yet," he says, as he hugs me good-bye.

Returning to my empty house is dreadful. Everywhere I look, there are reminders of my daughters: a birthday party invitation for Meredith, a pink hairbrush full of Marianthi's thick brown hairs, a gift certificate on the refrigerator for a new indoor playground. It is murder.

What little sleep I have is disturbed, not by bad dreams but by no dreams at all. I have always dreamed with great regularity. My dreams are in color, and I review and analyze them each morning as I brush my teeth. I feel sure that in my dreams, I will get to see the girls. But they vanish there, too.

Within three days, I am running on fumes. I can't eat. I can't sleep. In my fog, I also can't keep up with my calendar, or I would have already thought to cancel my semiannual dental cleaning with my forever dentist, Dr. McBratney. The girls have always loved getting their teeth cleaned at the same time as I do, and it's morphed into a sacred ritual. There are dentists who have toys and puzzles and specially colored toothpastes for kids to enjoy. Not our dentist. Dr. McBratney is more of an introvert, so when little Meredith first saw him at age two, she fussed so much that he told her, "I'll have to refer you out if you keep this up!" It worked. She quieted down.

The girls also have appointments to get their teeth cleaned. I haven't canceled them. *I'd like to postpone the children's appointments indefinitely. They've been abducted.* So I go alone to my appointment. By now, the news of the girls' disappearance has made it in to the local newspaper, and I wonder if my dentist has read about it.

I sit in the lobby and read magazines for what feels like twenty minutes without seeing a soul. It's unnaturally quiet. The receptionist hardly looks at me. I scan *Ladies' Home Journal* and find recipes I'll never make. Then I read *People* magazine's twentieth-anniversary edition, with Mia Farrow on the cover. *Did I brush my teeth this morning? Did I brush them yesterday? I wonder if Dr. McBratney is sick.* I ask the receptionist where he is. She says he's in the bathroom. *He must have diarrhea.*

Finally, the bathroom door opens.

When Dr. McBratney—a big moose of a man—comes toward me with his arms outstretched, the dam breaks. He hugs me tightly as I sob, leaving mascara stains and snot all over his white overcoat. I know I'm a mess and I'm making a spectacle of myself, but I can't stop.

"It's okay," he says, patting me with uncharacteristic tenderness. "I get it." After I compose myself, he tells me that he's been depressed and has been seeing a therapist weekly for months, without making progress. "Then one day, I went to get a physical and started to cry when I was talking to my doctor. He hugged me. Later, I told my therapist about it, and she was jealous."

Dr. McBratney assures me that he believes the girls will return. "They have to come back," he teases gently, giving me a final squeeze, "so your movie will have a happy ending. Who do you think will play my part?"

His tactic works. I smile back at him. "Donald Sutherland," I tell him. "No question."

After my appointment, I learn that my case has been assigned to a detective named Karen Rose. I'm excited to meet with her. She's a woman. She might be a mother. Surely she'll care about my situation. I drive to the police station for a preliminary interview. There are no magazines to read in the lobby, where three or four other people are sitting in hard chairs, but the wait is much faster than it was at my dentist's office.

"Lizbeth Meredith?"

I look up from my seat to see the detective for the first time. She looks to be in her fifties and sports a long blond wig and ten bright-red, clawlike fingernails, which match her red stiletto heels perfectly. Detective Rose is easily a size 16 stuffed into a 12, her pants so tight I can count the change in her pocket. Eighty-five cents—three quarters and a dime. I have watched enough true-crime shows on television to know that she has to be in costume for a prostitution sting. My estimation of her increases. What an adventurous job she must have.

She walks me back to an interview room, stopping by her office cubicle to answer the phone. Her voice takes on a flirty tone, and I can tell she's speaking with a love interest.

"I know, just one more interview. How 'bout I meet you at the restaurant right afterward?" Then it hits me. These are her work clothes, not a hooker costume. My positive regard for her plummets.

After her call, Detective Rose tells me that she has investigated crimes against young children exclusively for many years. I don't feel reassured.

She leads me into a small interview room, turns on a tape recorder, and begins the interrogation.

I know that as a parent-victim I will be a potential suspect to law enforcement. Still, I'm not prepared for the hostility the detective directs at me as she peppers me with questions: "Where were *you*, exactly, between the time Gregory collected the girls and when you went to pick them up again? Do you have a boyfriend? Have you said or done anything that might make Greg think he needed to hide the girls from you? I see, looking at your records, that you've called the police more than a few times over the past few years; can you tell me about that?"

In truth, I have called the police far less often over the years than I should have. The first time I called was to get a protective order served against Gregory after I left him in March 1990. I called again a week or more later so the police would help me safely get clothes for the kids and me out of the apartment Gregory still lived in. I called them in 1993 when he keyed my car and slashed my tires, and again after that to serve him with a new protective order. And I called the police to report the girls' abduction. Five times total.

But I did not call them the times during our marriage when Gregory threatened to kill me. The time he actually tried to kill me. The time he grabbed a loaded shotgun while in a drunken rage and promised to kill himself, then drove away to do it. And the many times after our marriage when he followed me in a vehicle. Harassed my friends. Broke into my home. No, I cannot legitimately be accused of being the woman who cried wolf.

I come by my distrust for police honestly. Until the Violence Against Women Act of 1994, law enforcement officers had limited arrest authority when dealing with domestic disputes. Calling police back then could make things worse. Battered women told me this every day. There were no mandatory arrest laws. Victims were interviewed in the presence of their perpetrators. It reminded me of the time a police officer came to our trailer home in Anchorage after a concerned teacher reported that my fifteen-year-old sister had bruises all over her body. He lined up all four girls in a row in front of Mother for questioning. "Has anyone hurt you?" I was only five but still remember the warning glare Mother shot us over the officer's shoulder. We shook our heads no in unison but got in trouble as soon as the officer left. I learned then that the arrival of law enforcement compromised, rather than ensured, safety.

After Detective Rose questions me for thirty minutes, I burst into tears. She instantly appears relieved. Satisfied, even. Mission accomplished. I imagine her lighting a cigarette after the climax, taking a big drag and inhaling deeply. But I am shaken. I repeat to her what Officer Gansel told me to expect from law enforcement. This seems to annoy her further.

"We can't prove Greg went to Greece," she tells me. "He could be in Oregon, for all we know."

And without knowing his whereabouts, Detective Rose says, she cannot get a warrant for his arrest and therefore cannot enter the kids into the NCIC database. But I should follow up with the State Department and be heartened by the fact that Greece signed an extradition treaty recently that promises a speedy return of children abducted and taken there. "The State Department can explain it best," she says. "I'll be in touch soon."

I don't get the feeling this woman will be in touch soon, but I've got a list of things to keep me busy. I head back to my empty house and open the refrigerator. I'm finally hungry. All I find is a past-due carton of milk and my to-go container of spicy tuna rolls from my friend Julie's birthday lunch, now several days old. It's all I have. I quickly pick at it before tossing it out and starting down my to-do list.

I call the National Center for Missing & Exploited Children (NCMEC), the agency that turned milk cartons into missing-children billboards. NCMEC is the nonprofit organization established a decade ago when crime victims like John Walsh were screwed by the lack of coordination between key players in abduction cases. I'm assigned to case manager Ron Jones. The sound of his voice makes me feel like I've been served a steaming bowl of macaroni and cheese just out of the oven. After I stammer out my first sentence ("My ex-husband has taken my girls to Greece!"), I am calmed by his steady support. Mr. Jones is part knowledgeable counselor and part fearless advocate. "It's up to you to keep track of your case. You're one of five hundred parents a day who call about their missing kids. We'll be here for you."

I call the State Department and am bounced from person to person until I finally reach a male staff member in the Office of Children's Issues. He gives me a dry, historical overview of the Hague Convention as it pertains to child abduction:

In 1980, more than twenty countries signed the treaty to prevent international child abductions—necessary since a growing number of international marriages had led to a growing number of international divorces, which had often resulted in conflict about which country the children of such unions should call home. Many more countries continued to become signatories as the problem of international abductions increased. The treaty was meant to prevent parents in unhappy relationships from fleeing the country with their children as though they were refugees. Protections should not exist for such parents, who need to return to the country of the child's habitual residence and seek legal relief from the courts.

In lay terms, if a parent breaks a custody agreement and flees with his or her child to another country that is a signatory of the Hague Convention, the left-behind parent can apply for relief. Then the signatory country will expedite the return of the child to the country the original custody agreement was made in, unless it can be established that serious harm will occur to the child upon his or her return.

It's kind of like how if a brother and sister get in a fight at school, they'll be sent home, where their parents, who know their dynamics best, will decide on the appropriate consequences for them.

"So, how do I get help?" I ask, imagining that this situation, like everything else I've heard about, won't be cut and dry.

"You'll need a lawyer in Greece," he says. "He alone will know how this works there. I'm just telling you what I've read."

I appreciate the honesty—someone who knows the limits of the law and won't get my hopes up.

The plan sounds kind of weak, but it's clear that if I am to get the support of the State Department, I will need to set aside my doubts and apply for relief.

Four days later, I receive a booklet from the State Department on responding to international child abduction, with step-by-step instructions for parents in crisis.

To apply for relief from the Hague Convention, my lawyers and I will need to fill out the forty-page application, get it translated into Greek, and submit it, as soon as possible.

I call my friend Maria, who teaches Greek lessons at the Orthodox church. "I can try to do it for you," she says sympathetically, "and you won't have to pay me."

But I insist on paying her the going rate. How bad can it be, after all?

"It's going to cost you two thousand dollars for a document this size," Maria says.

Two thousand dollars? Two thousand dollars! I make ten dollars an hour. It will take me over a month to get that kind of money together, and that's if I stop paying for other expenses, like food and rent.

"There are a couple of us at the church who do translation services. We want to help, Liz. I'm happy to do as much as I can."

And just like that, I'm back to begging mode. I might as well be the lady in a pitiful frock, pleading for donations on the street. I've just graduated from a life of begging. I signed up for public assistance when I left Gregory. I hated doing it, but I didn't have other resources to tap. I asked the government to subsidize my rent and my day care. I asked for a scholarship of sorts to get milk and cheese and cereal for the girls. The paperwork was both exhausting and intrusive, and I promised myself that once I got a degree, I would never again ask for a handout.

But here I am, begging like a vagrant, and there's not a thing I can do about it just now. Moving on:

File a missing-persons report with the local police. *Check.*

Report the abduction to the National Center for Missing & Exploited Children. *Check.*

Enter my children's names in the US passport name-check system. *Check.*

The booklet explains that the children should be entered into NCIC's database immediately, and that the process is not contingent on whether a warrant has been issued.

I call Detective Rose back and leave a message. I wait until the second half of my workday before I leave her another. Nothing. I call her again the next morning. I leave another message and decide to go visit her at work on my lunch hour. I put on a nice pair of khakis and a red sweater and some red lipstick. Red makes me feel fierce, and I'll need that for this impromptu trip. I spend at least fifteen minutes waiting in the long line in the police station lobby before I reach the clerk, who tells me that the detective is on annual leave.

"So can I see her supervisor, please?" I surprise myself

by asking. This feels weird, like I'm going to squeal on the detective. I'm young and poor and don't have a lot of weight to throw around, but these are my little girls.

The lieutenant is a pleasant-looking, unassuming man in his early fifties. He takes me back to his small office with a large window overlooking rows of cubicles and listens to my concerns politely with a half smile on his face. I tell him I don't feel listened to by the detective, and that from what I've heard from other sources, she's not following the proper protocols. He lets me finish without interruption and then speaks.

"The district attorney's office needs to have proof that Gregory left Alaska," he tells me.

"So, didn't the police request airline flight schedules or interview the airline employees on duty the night of the abduction?"

"No. It would have been too time-consuming," he tells me. "We just don't have those kinds of resources at our disposal."

Yet the one thing that the police department and the district attorney's office seem to agree on is that Alaska law necessitates direct evidence that Gregory left the state before a felony warrant can be issued.

"So that's it, then?" I ask the lieutenant. "There's nothing more you all can do?"

He nods, looking secretly pleased, as though he's helped me make progress in accepting the hopelessness of the situation.

I don't accept it, but I won't waste any more of my time with the police just now. I don't have enough energy to waste.

When I get back to work, I call the State Department again. The voice on the other end of the line tells me, "Just continue to cooperate with your local law enforcement. And be patient."

Be patient. My little daughters are half a world away with the person who will stop at nothing to destroy me, even if it means destroying them in the process, and I should be patient?

I'm not the patient kind. To me, patience is built on faith

that a person or an agency will do what they've promised. It's built on positive experiences that create assurances, and so far I have not banked enough of these to result in patience.

When I arrive home from work, I find a large manila envelope inside the mail. The National Center for Missing & Exploited Children has sent thirty or more black-and-white fliers of the girls that I can hang up around town. My daughter Marianthi is wearing her wide-collared pink dress and has perfectly combed hair. Meredith's wearing her vivid polka-dot dress, and her wavy hair is held back with a barrette.

It is official. My daughters are missing kids. Milk-carton kids. And if my daughters are the milk-carton kids, then I am the most pitiful mother of all: the Mother of the Missing. I don't know how to feel. I'm not sure I want to feel. So instead I make a mental note to avoid the reminders. My daughters are missing. I will never again go to Walmart, where an entire wall is dedicated to missing-children posters. I will never drive by the girls' day care, even though it is on the most direct path to my work from home. I will never drive by the movie marquis where children's movies play—always Disney films in which the main characters are separated from their mothers.

One day, I will have my girls again. Until then, I cannot come unhinged. It is better to swallow my tears and aim to feel nothing.

❖ ❖ ❖

Another missing-children's agency sends literature advising that left-behind parents should open and maintain communication with the abductor, if at all possible. "If the children return, it will be because the abductor allows them to."

This is impossible. I don't have Gregory's address or

phone number in Greece, for one. And two, though I have been to Greece once with Gregory, six years ago, to baptize Marianthi, I don't have command of the Greek language or close enough relationships with his family to expect any cooperation from them.

I hear from some of the women at the Orthodox church that the Greek police might be a source of help, so I ask a Greek friend to phone her brother—a police officer in Greece. He tells her that the Greek authorities won't look for Gregory and the girls without being asked by Interpol. And Interpol won't initiate action without state and federal warrants being issued for Gregory. And the detective isn't exactly breaking her back to get the evidence necessary for a warrant.

Amid all the snafus I've hit in the legal system during these past couple of weeks, I find myself becoming increasingly desperate. If the justice system in America is too complex for law enforcement to understand its own protocols, I can only imagine what lies ahead when I get to rely on a cooperative pact between two government justice systems. How will I ever get my children back? I begin to look for any kind of sign that a higher power will prevail.

The sign comes while I watch the local news about the death of a man I recognize from my work at the battered-women's shelter.

Ashton Smith battered his wife for years. I saw Cynthia arrive at the shelter, their two tiny children in tow, with worse and worse injuries. Once, Ashton beat Cynthia's front windshield with a bat while she tried to back out of their driveway, and shards of glass cut their infant son, who was strapped in his car seat. Cynthia shared her husband's addiction to crack cocaine and kept them both supplied with it by selling herself. After each beating by her husband, I made the cursory referrals to child protective services, transitional housing, and substance-abuse programs. Cynthia's injuries would heal, and she'd bank several days of sobriety as she put together a plan of action for her and her children. The plan was always interrupted by her posting bail and becoming Ashton's third-party custodian—followed by another beating. We as staff felt helpless to empower Cynthia to make choices that could interrupt the cycle of domestic violence.

But now, many days after the girls' disappearance and almost instantly after I pray for a sign of their return, the news reports that Ashton snatched the purse of an elderly woman and ran with it tucked under his arm through downtown Anchorage. He was then chased by a passerby and fled into the street, where he was struck by an off-duty police dispatcher, sailed high into the air, and plunged to his death. Problem solved.

I am gleeful. The universe has spoken. My children will return.

Chapter 4

HELPING THE HELP

After many days of little progress to speak of, I realize the justice system needs a boost.

I promised Detective Rose I would not contact the press as quickly as my instincts directed me to. "Wait a couple of weeks," she said. "You don't want to mess up any leads we might get by telling too much."

Two weeks go by. Nothing. A month. More. Now it's April 18, Meredith's fifth birthday. My baby girl is turning five without me. Is she safe? Will anyone bother to make her a cake? Do the girls think I've abandoned them? The pain is more than I can bear—I have to do something.

Despite Detective Rose's objections, I call the *Anchorage Daily News* Metro section to run a piece on the girls' abduction. The idea is flatly rejected. "How can the newspaper write a fair and balanced story about parental abduction when only one parent is present to be interviewed?" the editor asks. Good point for them. Bad point for me.

Time for plan B. I call Doug O'Harra at the *Daily News*, who writes feature stories for the Sunday newsmagazine insert called *We Alaskans*. It reminds me of Alaska's version of *People* magazine.

Doug first contacted me six months ago, when he was writing a feature story on the topic of stalking. He wanted some composite information about the clients AWAIC served and had heard in his initial conversation with AWAIC's program director that I had had my own experiences as a victim after leaving my husband in 1990. I developed an easy trust with Doug, and though the stalking story was never published, I have read enough of his work at the *Daily News* to admire his gift of storytelling. Plus, he's a parent. If the newspaper covers the girls' disappearance, maybe enough information will pour in from readers for police to cobble together a case. I'll also need a support system, especially when it comes to having a base to approach for money—a comprehensive story in *We Alaskans* could pull on a lot of heartstrings.

"Don't quote me," Doug says, "but my editor is a guy with a lot of soul, and he's got three daughters of his own. I think this might fly."

The editor not only agrees that my missing daughters would make a great cover story but adds that it will be more heart-rending to run it on Mother's Day. A childless mother on Mother's Day. I like it.

Any hopes that the newspaper story will be a simple tool to access fades as soon as I get a call back from Doug. A photographer is assigned to follow me for two weeks, and Doug will be chained to my side for hours at a stretch to follow my day-to-day happenings. From Marianthi's classroom to the Greek Orthodox church, no place will be off limits.

Friends from high school, from my job—even of Gregory's—are interviewed.

Doug visits Marianthi's first-grade classmates, who have written letters to President Clinton and colored pictures to illustrate their pain. *Dear President Clinton, I miss Marianthi. I wish she was here.*

On May 8, Mother's Day 1994, the *We Alaskans* article goes to print. The cover picture is of me at the Greek Orthodox church, looking into the distance, with religious icons in the background and a caption that reads: "He took my children." I look pale; my too-red lipstick makes me appear just that much more tragic. Pictures of the girls' artwork around my living room, and pictures of the girls' classmates' letters to the president, are all gut-wrenching. Phone numbers for readers to call and share any tips are listed at the end. Perfect.

As I read the article, I become more outraged at the justice system's response. Ron Jones, from the National Center for Missing & Exploited Children, scoffs at the police's explanation that they can't issue a warrant for Gregory without proof he's left the state.

"Let's use some common sense here," he says. "Here goes a woman who has custody through the courts, and here comes a man who takes the kids in violation of that custody—and the police are saying we can't do anything because we don't know where he is. Now that's stupid.

"You know, that means if I come rob a bank in Alaska, just because you don't know where I am, you're not going to issue a warrant for my arrest. That's crazy."

Detective Rose sounds like an idiot when defending her actions and inactions. "We honestly thought we had to have a warrant first," she says in an interview, when asked why the girls weren't entered into NCIC system until after Ron Jones faxed her a copy of the federal law. She says the investigation was further stymied by police attempts to interpret thoroughly the conditions adopted in our divorce outlining custody and visitation. And she blames the girls' mother for attempting to investigate the abduction. *She's blaming me? This crazy hooker wannabe is blaming me?*

Attorney Michael Kreider comes to my defense, telling the reporter, "I'm extremely frustrated with the response of the local police. We have more than a hysterical woman in a domestic situation. We have independent confirmation from sources unrelated to Liz that he may have taken them out of the country. And you've got everybody camping on their thumbs. Why is that?"

My other lawyer, Jim Swanson, echoes Michael's sentiments, saying he is shocked police didn't move more quickly on Gregory's disappearing with the girls. "It's clear that he's gone. It's clear from everything that we can tell that he's left the country and gone to Greece. You don't have to prove a case beyond a reasonable doubt to get it over to the DA's office."

Heather Flynn, my supervisor and outspoken ally, agrees with the lawyers. "This is a case where a bit more advocacy and a little less doubt would have made the trail of information more available. The trail gets cold very fast."

It's surreal reading about the girls and me in the paper. *That poor mother. Those poor girls. That bad man.* I find myself wondering how it will all end for these people. And it hits me that the story is mine. My daughters' story and mine. It's Mother's Day, and I am a motherless child who is now a childless mother, who will celebrate by waiting for tips from the Anchorage public on how to find her daughters.

My phone begins ringing at 7:00 A.M. Every time I complete a call and return the phone to its cradle, it rings again. Friends, acquaintances, concerned strangers, and miscellaneous lunatics call my listed phone number with support, information, or criticism. A woman from her cell phone: "I'm driving behind Gregory," she says, her voice quaking. "Call the police, will you? Tell them I'm on the hillside next to Abbott Loop Church." I can tell by her tone that she believes herself. I can also tell that she's nuts. She becomes outraged when I don't bite. "You need to call the police *now*! Do you hear me?"

I hang up. Shortly afterward, neighbors knock on my door. I'm sitting on the kitchen floor with the phone in my lap, dodging the windows. Next, they begin peeking through my windows. *Do they think I've offed myself? Should I off myself?*

The kind thing to do would be to reassure my neighbors that I'm fine. The trouble is, I'm not fine, and I haven't the energy to reassure them of anything.

I need to eat, but there is nothing in the refrigerator. Stealthily, in case my neighbors are still creeping about, I crawl over to my bedroom and throw on some sweats, then dash to my car and drive to the store.

The quick trip for food turns into a lengthy ordeal as people approach me to ask questions and offer sympathies in the parking lot and then all throughout the store, as I grab Weight Watchers frozen meals, wheat tortillas, and Cheetos. The checker blinks away tears as she counts my change back to me, and I feel guilty.

For as long as I can remember, I have been keenly aware of the emotions of people in my surroundings. I have to work to keep their emotions from becoming my own. So while I'm numb when it comes to experiencing the loss of my daughters, I'm engulfed by the pain I read on the faces of those around me. By the time I get back home to microwave my dinner, I'm wrung out. I ignore the ringing phone and devour my dinner.

After I eat, I receive a call from a local attorney. A Greek man whom he once represented in a civil suit has called him to report that Gregory called him long distance, needing money.

A second call, from a second lawyer, indicates Gregory left Alaska with tens of thousands of dollars he won in a lawsuit against his former landlords at the pizza restaurant he once owned. More callers offer stories of custody battles gone wrong. A male caller tells me I am likely to blame for my children's disappearance. He is my last call of the day, at almost eleven o'clock. I pull the phone cord from the wall to get some peace.

The momentum the *We Alaskans* story creates is astounding. Who would have thought a news story could turn me into a local reality star? For the next few days, my children are the star feature of coffee-shop conversations around Anchorage. Partly because of the dramatic topic, child kidnapping, and partly because of the vivid pictures, and mostly because the story ran on Mother's Day, the community around me is interested and ready to help.

Alaskans as a whole are always ready to help. Most people who move to Alaska have left family behind in the contiguous states to pursue opportunities and are sort of orphaned because of it. The weather and the layout of the land force Alaska residents to rely on one another, and family-type relationships are forged. When one person has a crisis, all kinds of people step up to help.

Within a week, Heather and AWAIC staff members begin to plan fundraising events, and the response generated from the article translates into the ability to create a support base.

I find that my well-wishers fall into four distinct categories: (1) those who love the girls, (2) those who love or feel sorry for me, (3) those who care about human suffering in general and feel compelled to join our efforts, and (4) those attracted to drama who want to become a part of ours.

Before the abduction, I hadn't needed to keep in contact with those who fell in the fourth category. But now I have a number of people, mostly women, who seem unsatisfied enough with their own lives that they seek to attach themselves to me and feed on my agony. Emotional vampires. Tragedy whores. Whatever you name them, these parasites consume my pain until their bellies are bloated, before looking around for their next meal. I notice that one of my coworkers circles me closely when my pain is obvious. She is quick to give a hug or send a card. "Call me anytime, day or night," she says with tears in her eyes. There are others who give of themselves and expect nothing in return, so I think nothing of it except for how lucky I am. I attend my first counseling session since the girls' disappearance and return to work with more focus and hope. But my coworker is angry at me, almost as if I've cheated on her. She needs me to be needy and then drops me like a hot potato when a better bit of live theater comes within her reach.

With the passage of time, I learn not to personalize anyone's agendas. They're getting their needs met, just like I am. I'll take any help I can get. And if some people are hard up for horror, I have plenty to go around. I have a full-on Greek tragedy.

An unexpected phone call from one particular drama queen introduces a familiar voice back into my world. As soon as I pick up the phone, she starts right in.

"You have no idea how hard this has been on me," she says.

"Mother?"

"I have the entire community in Seward praying for me," she continues. "I've developed hives, it's been so stressful."

What am I supposed to say to that? I'm sorry? To the grandmother who never once changed a diaper or sent a birthday or Christmas present to my daughters? To the grandmother who sniped at my tiny, traumatized children shortly after they witnessed their father assault me? To the grand-mother who has met her granddaughters on three occasions total? I haven't heard from her since she shanghaied my college graduation nearly two years ago. Still, she is my mother, and I know I ought to try to forgive her, warts and all. Maybe time has changed her. Unlikely, but it's a nice thought.

Reluctantly, I agree to meet my mother for coffee the next time she's shopping in Anchorage, which is in a few short days. I choose a dive appropriately called Mea Culpa. My fault. Everything wrong with our relationship, at least according to her, is my fault.

The days pass too quickly. My stomach flip-flops as I park my car. Inside the dark, dirty coffeehouse, Mother is hard to miss. At age sixty-two, she looks remarkably older since our last encounter, but her brightly dyed red hair is the same. She's leaning over the counter, looking closely at the young male barista. "Well? What do you suggest?" she asks coyly. I stop in my tracks. My mother is flirting with a boy too young even for me. Any hopes that she's changed are quickly dashed.

"Honey? Is that you? Look at you, so thin and pale now!" she says, opening her arms when I get in line behind her. I freeze when she hugs and squeezes me. I feel nothing. After she releases me, I buy myself a latte, remembering that the last time I saw Mother, at my college graduation, she refused to buy me the lunch she'd promised when I said something that upset her. This is not a woman to whom I wish to be indebted.

I follow her to a booth. There is only one other customer nearby, so it's as good a place as any to air our dirty laundry. Mother wastes no time.

"Those girls need me, and you need to make it a point for them to know me when they get back. I can give you the key to my trailer so you can be there sometimes, waiting for me when I get off work."

I could argue the point. I could remind her how clenched she was during the three times she spent with her granddaughters when they played too loudly or wanted to climb onto her lap. I had to intervene so that Mother wasn't tempted to dispense her special type of discipline, which leaves bruises. But why bother? I have bigger fish to fry. My daughters are missing. While Mother launches into another rant about how troubling my daughters' absence has been to her, I silently write her off forever. Nothing has changed or ever will change with her. Maybe Mother can't help herself, but I can. When I excuse myself from our meeting, I feel like I have been set free. A weight has been lifted. I have been polite. I haven't argued with her. And I now understand I can conserve my energy and be okay without a relationship with my mother.

It's Sunday morning, seven days since the Mother's Day article was published, and I get a call. The caller identifies herself as Lynn. "I dated your ex-husband," she tells me, "I hadn't seen him in several years, until he came into my travel agency."

Lynn tells me she's the lead travel agent at US Travel and saw Gregory enter the agency a few months back. She says she heard he was married and divorced and had two little girls. "I don't think he saw me that day, the day he came in to buy tickets to Greece. I was in my last month of pregnancy, and I didn't want to talk to him or to anyone else, for that matter. I noticed later he'd bought one-way tickets to Greece for him and the girls, and it bothered me. There's nothing illegal about that, but it bugged me. A lot."

My heart is racing. This is it. It's the news I've been waiting for. The State Department's actions hinge on this evidence that will help local police get a warrant. I can't believe my luck.

"Thank you" is all I can stammer out. "Thank you. Did you happen to call the police with this information?"

"That's just it. I have called the police. I've called them repeatedly. No one will call me back. I even reached the detective and left a message confirming Gregory's whereabouts. I got nothing. So I took my baby to his pediatrician this week for his checkup, and your daughters' missing-children's poster is on the wall there. I felt like it was a sign. I knew I had to talk to you."

I calmly thank Lynn for the information and get her contact information before I hang up. I pick up the nearest Barbie I can find and pull the long, blond, Detective Rose–like hair, snapping the head off its shoulders. The Barbie becomes a voodoo doll, and I prick the poor thing many times with a safety pin in honor of the many impediments the detective has created in the recovery process. I'd like to claw her eyes out, if only I had claws. Instead, I have fingertips that are swollen from biting my nails to the quick.

Who would have imagined that Gregory's ex could be the key to solving my problems? I'm lucky that she is caring and compassionate. Indeed, I may be the luckiest unlucky woman ever.

But what about the girls? Are they experiencing any grace while going through their crisis? Is Gregory's family around to fill in the gaps created by the loss of their mother, their friends, and their routine? I hope more than anything that they know I did not, that I would not ever, abandon them. Because there is nothing worse than being discarded by one's mother. No one is shocked when a father opts out of a child's life, but a mother is universally recognized as a necessity. This I know for sure.

❖ ❖ ❖

1977

"Larry and I are leaving," says my mother.

I look to see if she is dressed for the trip to the city. I am thirteen. Chugiak is the place we have called home for five years, and it is a twenty-mile ride on a dirt road to Anchorage, where the best shopping malls are found.

Mother is still wearing her muumuu. Her face is unmade, a clear sign that she isn't budging from the house.

She sees my confusion. "We are. Moving. From Alaska. Larry and I."

I am the last child in the home, and I'm at the height of my awkwardness. Change doesn't come easily, and the only things I have going for me are my good grades and a few good friends I've made in school. I can't believe what I'm hearing.

"We're going in the motor home," she scrambles to explain. "There's not a lot of room. But your sister has volunteered to take you with her to Washington when she leaves for college. Or you can stay in a foster home."

I'm not liking my options. My sister will soon turn eighteen and has been living in Anchorage with a roommate for many months, doing what unattended teenagers do.

And a foster home? Seriously? My introduction to foster care standards came the year before, when Mother applied for a license. The investigating social worker never asked Mother about the time the Anchorage police questioned her regarding the injuries on my oldest sister's back. Our well water, however, was thoroughly tested before four very sad children were made even sadder by being placed in Mother's loving care. Mother kept them as long as she could tolerate—less than a month, to be exact. No thanks.

Three months later, my sister and I are alone in Seattle. She cannot find work. Without work, we cannot find a home. Without a home, I cannot enroll in school.

We are stuck.

Until an Alaska Native family in Tacoma, transplanted from Anchorage, who are distantly acquainted with my mother, hear of our troubles and offer us a place to stay while we get our feet on the ground. Soon we become the guests of Stuart and Emma Johns. Our host family delights in sharing their traditional foods with me—Eskimo ice cream made with berries and seal oil, and fry bread—while my sister is away, looking for a job.

If only I could be a gracious guest. Instead, I close off from everyone. I don't eat. I don't speak. I just exist.

Painful welts rise on my skin. In a few days, I am covered with them. Worse, my eyebrows fall out, and the hair on my head also begins to leave me. Though I am certain death is near, a doctor assures me that it is really only shingles and stress-induced hair loss.

Lying on the top bunk in the Johns' spare room, curled in the fetal position, I am dreading my first day at Jason Lee Junior High. My outdated clothes and shingled face are sure to make an impression. I straighten up and dangle my head off the bed, watching my long hair fall out, strand by strand. I am unlovable and increasingly unattractive.

I miss my mother. Without her, I feel naked in this big, new world.

Chapter 5

REDUCED EXPECTATION

I call Detective Rose, armed with the evidence I need to prove her dereliction of duty. She responds without apology or explanation. "I'll contact the district attorney's office right away." One quick call later, the district attorney's office issues a warrant for Gregory's arrest. Finally I am getting somewhere. I can't wait to call the State Department with the news of the warrant. I feel a lump in my throat as I dial the number, anticipating a shared happy moment with the government official at the end of the line.

"They did *what?* Now you'll never get your kids back," Barb Diaz says, sounding angry. She explains that the Hague Convention is designed for friendly interactions between the abducting parent and the one left behind. A warrant inevitably locks them into contentious interactions.

My joy turns into anger. I'm in no mood to play. "May I remind you that it was you who told me to cooperate with local law enforcement? That it was you who assured me you couldn't help further until I did?"

Ms. Diaz does not engage but wishes me well as I attempt to find my way through the process.

"Call us before you go to Greece," she urges. "And don't do anything stupid or illegal. We can't help you then."

"Fine, I will, and I won't," I respond, though I have the sinking feeling that the State Department knows as little as I do about resolving international child abductions.

This is crazy. I do as I'm told and am blamed for unforeseen consequences. How do people survive this mess? What do I expect, anyhow? For the government officials to admit they are as clueless as I am about the abduction recovery process? For the detective and the State Department staff to cry for me? With me? I'm not sure.

I have to reframe and focus on the things that I do know. My problems obviously won't be solved overnight. There will be no meaningful help from law enforcement. Interpol and the FBI will not be jumping in to rescue my girls. The people in the system who know the most have no definite answers. Yet many strangers I meet who know virtually nothing about such matters confidently offer a steady stream of advice:

"You should read *Not Without My Daughter*. It's just like your story."

"Why don't you write *America's Most Wanted*?"

"Why don't you hire one of those militia teams?"

"Have you thought about getting remarried and starting a new family?"

"Have you ever thought about writing Oprah?"

Some days, I appreciate their words. Other days, not so much.

In truth, I consider all of these options and more, dashing off letters to Oprah and John Walsh, of *America's Most*

Wanted, that first sleepless week after the girls' disappearance. I read about militias. It seems like hiring bar bouncers who would attempt to forcibly grab my kids and escape from Greece. A lawyer I know said that his client had hired militia for $60,000 to get his son out of South Africa, and another parent I read about spent $100,000, only for one of the militia members to be shot and the recovery effort foiled. The danger and the price would make it a last resort. Besides, I have a strong legal case. The girls were in my custody for years before the abduction, and Greece is a signatory of the extradition treaty. My daughters will return home safely and lawfully. It will just take time.

Clearly, if I want to survive the crisis at hand, I will need to pace myself. I don't want to become a drunk or a prescription drug addict by the time the girls return. I want to be in better shape, both professionally and personally, so I have more to offer them.

Lucky for me, I have experience in overcoming adversity. Gregory saw to it when he married me, after the briefest of courtships, and began chipping away at my already frail self-esteem.

I am twenty years old and new to my job as a maid at the only five-star hotel in Anchorage. Frequenting the dean's list of academic probationers for the past two years at Western Washington University has made it impossible to get student loans, and the money I've made at my nursing home job barely covers rent and food, no matter how many double shifts I take. My efforts at independence have failed. Deflated, I call my mom and ask her if I can live at her new house in the spare bedroom until I can find work and get my own place.

"Of course, love," she coos. "I'll just ask that you pay $300 a month for your room."

It's 1985, and $300 a month feels like a lot of money, but I agree.

So here I am, wearing a black polyester uniform, with my hair in a bandanna, doing what I do worst—cleaning and organizing—for eight hours a day. But at least this is a union job. When it's clear how badly I perform as a maid, I get a clerical position in Food and Beverage Control within a month— finally I have medical benefits and some hope of job security. In no time, I should have enough money to attend community college at night. It'll be a new start.

Returning to Alaska is a good idea in theory, but the reality quickly begins kicking my ass. I am soon tiptoeing around Mother's dark moods. I have to take the city bus to work, since I still don't have my driver's license, and I get lost. A lot. Any old friends from my childhood moved away to attend college out of state. I'm broke, easily intimidated, and alone.

I am twenty, going on sixteen, when I meet a dazzling older coworker from another department while taking inventory in the food warehouse. He is a little taller than I am with light-brown hair, a receding hairline, and green eyes. When he smiles, I see a flash of perfectly straight teeth.

"My name is Grigorios, but people here call me Greg, or Gregory," he says, extending his hand to shake mine. He lingers to make small talk and then disappears.

My boss notices my brightened mood after he leaves. "Watch out for that one," she tells me. "He's trouble." When I press her for details, she tells me rumors she's heard about possible drug use but admits that it's all hearsay. I shrug it off as gossip.

The next day, I glimpse an employee newsletter. Gregory is the employee of the month in the Banquet Department.

A druggie can't be an employee of the month, right? In his brief bio, it's clear Gregory is from Greece and came to the United States to attend college and become a pilot. He moved to Alaska after getting a two-year degree and worked as a bush pilot before getting a job at the Captain Cook. He sounds perfect. Worldly. Smart. Adventurous. Hard-working. Reliable.

Maybe someday we can have coffee at one of the hotel's cafés and get to know each other. If I see him, maybe I'll ask.

"Do you think you have daddy issues?" my boss asks me when I tell her about my coffee-date idea. It's not like her to get this personal with me, but she's taken a keen interest in this potential romance.

I've just turned seventeen, and I get a call from Larry. "Hey, kid, want to grab a pizza after I get off work?"

My mother is away on a work trip. We've only recently moved back into our house, rebuilt after a mysterious fire consumed it while Larry and my mother were on an overnight excursion.

"Sure." I hang up the phone gingerly. I can't remember a time when he's ever taken me to pizza or a burger alone, just because.

This is the same man who has spoken with a boozy slur immediately after dinner every night for as long as I can remember. The same man who let his erect penis run free underneath his bathrobe when I was little, while we watched evening television, and invited us girls to sit on his lap. The same man who has hurt pets and siblings and who slipped rum in our Cokes when our mother was out of town. The same man who fled Alaska and left me behind to dodge his child-support payments, and the same man whom I nursed for nearly a year after his roofing accident, changing out his bedpans and making sure he had food.

It makes no sense how happy I am to have his attention.

A few hours later, Larry picks me up at our house in his Datsun pickup. We're not even out of our neighborhood when my hope for father-daughter time is dashed. "I don't know if your mother told you, but I'm moving to my own place."

I look out the passenger-side window as we head toward the nearest pizza joint. My eyes fill with tears, but I will hold on to them, no matter what.

Yes, I found the note Larry intended for his girlfriend at our house. I've heard his and mother's loud fights, but none of this is new. Why now?

He natters on about this and that. I say nothing. I feel like such a fool, thinking he was actually taking me to dinner for no particular reason. When we get to the restaurant, he leaves me in the idling car while he pays for the pizza. No time to waste eating inside, apparently.

When he returns, he hands me the pizza box. "Cheese okay?"

I shrug.

"When are you moving?" I finally ask him.

"Just after I drop you off." He looks happy. I want to punch him. "Look in the back of the truck."

I turn around and look through the back window to see his belongings piled high, covered by a tarp.

He's been planning this speedy exit for a long time.

The tears begin to spill quietly at first, and I feel silly when the trickle turns into a gush and I begin hiccupping. Mascara runs down my cheeks. Everything hurts.

❖ ❖ ❖

Three weeks after Gregory and I first meet, he offers to buy me a cup of coffee, and I take this as a sign—*there, he asked me out on a real date.* When we meet up two days later at a real sit-down restaurant, he wears a pale-green silk shirt with the top three buttons unfastened to reveal fancy gold necklaces. When it's time to pay, Gregory opens his wallet and I see a string of credit cards. A sign of wealth, I think. I am impressed. One date turns into another, and soon we are inseparable.

Everything I do, everything I say, seems perfect to Gregory. I love the attention. I love the way he charms my mother. He agrees with my opinions on anything from politics and religion to child-rearing theories. I am hooked. And for his part, he seems more than equally smitten with me. I hardly notice that he demands all of my time. Soon there is no time to make new friendships or develop hobbies; my new beau is practically a full-time job. Any differences that begin to surface don't bother me either: I carefully count my groceries before getting into the express lane at the supermarket, while Gregory strides to the front of any line with a full cart, smiling at those already waiting, and nudges his way in. "Do you mind?"

I am a twenty-year-old virgin. At thirty-two, Gregory has been around.

Less than two months after our first date, Gregory, armed with a dozen roses, makes an impromptu appearance at my mother's house and nervously asks if he can speak to her. Touched by his deference, my mother gives her blessing right away when Gregory asks her permission to marry me. "But can you do it quickly?" she says. God has called her to report to Oral Roberts University in Oklahoma for a job, and since I am a fatherless child, it is her job to give me away at the wedding.

Who am I to argue with God? Who am I to argue with Mother, for that matter? Clearly, I can't invite my biological father, and Larry is out of the question.

Gregory and I marry three months after meeting. It is a Greek wedding that he and my mother plan and that I mostly pay for. I'm twenty-one now, old enough to drink wine, and I even get my driver's license before the nuptials.

And this wedding ends love as I know it.

It starts small enough, with his jokes about my abilities: to cook, to clean—anything the average wife should know how to do. And his claims are not unfounded. I dye a load of his underwear pink and serve him half-cooked chicken during our first week of marital bliss. So I try to remember to separate the whites from the colors when laundering my new husband's clothes, and to bake his favorite pound cake for him twice a week. But then he uncovers another flaw. "Have you gained weight?"

I can only imagine my horrified expression, because he responds to it quickly. "*What?* Don't look at me like that. I'm just curious."

When I assure my curious husband that I'm not technically overweight, his response buoys me. "I know you're not. You're beautiful." But then he continues. "It's just that you look bad for your age. Under your clothes, I mean."

Given that he is the only person who has seen me under my clothes, I assume he's got a point.

So I go on a diet.

My eating habits aren't the only thing to change.

"Are you watching this?" he asks, one day when he returns home from work and turns the channel on the show I am clearly watching. No response is needed. He slides down on the love seat to enjoy a *M*A*S*H* rerun.

Before I met my husband, I volunteered as a mentor to troubled youth and read books for the local library for the blind. He loved this about me when we were dating. Now, a few months into our marriage, he changes his tune.

"Why do you do that? It's a waste of time. What does

it do for you? Or for me, for that matter? I think you need to spend your time off work learning to be a wife, don't you?"

I let my wants and needs take a backseat to Gregory's wishes. His insults only shift to other things: my intelligence, or lack thereof; my unusual family background; my figure; my friends. His disappearances compound the insults. During our first week of marriage, Gregory vanishes after his catering shifts, only to return at four in the morning, defensive and smelling of alcohol and cigarettes. "Where *were* you?" I ask. He repeats the behavior at least three times a week. *Where were you?* becomes my new mantra. The answer is always different. Playing cards. At the bar. At a postwork party. When he does return, the smell of alcohol permeates our 580-square-foot home and seems to seep from his pores. It is the first I learn of his substance-abuse problem.

At first, I try to lure him home by donning the lingerie I bought before our wedding and staying awake to greet him, no matter how late his return, no matter how early I have to work the next day. I tell myself that if I am pretty enough and alluring enough, that'll do the trick. When that doesn't work, I try crying. When that doesn't work, I try raging at him and threatening to leave. And when that doesn't work, I give up and realize that I have made a fatal error in marrying him, but it is a commitment I will not break. I simply have to make the best of it. So I enroll in classes at the community college and drop my already-limited contact with my friends and family. I do this partly because my new husband prefers it, and partly because I am embarrassed at the mess I have made of my life by marrying him. But this has unintended consequences. Now when Gregory insults me or threatens to leave me, I believe him. There is no one else left in my life to tell me that despite my human frailties, I still possess strengths and abilities. So he just keeps chipping away. "You know if I left you, no one else would have you, right? You don't have a mother or father who would take you. I'm all you've got."

He strikes a nerve with that comment. The home I come from isn't just broken; it was smashed to bits long before I was born.

Chapter 6

ROOTS

My mother's kin are from Louisiana. Mother tells me that her mom married at sixteen and had her first child (my mother) the next year. Four years later, she had three more kids in rapid succession—a son named Ron, a daughter named Wanda, and a final daughter named Ann. When my mom was a teenager, her father disappeared, leaving her to be the caregiver for her siblings while my grandmother scrambled to support her brood with money from housekeeping jobs. My mother eventually quit high school to work and help out her family.

Years later, my grandfather resurfaced. He had left the county after abandoning his family, married again without first divorcing my grandmother, and produced two more children: a second Ron and another Ann.

My mother also married as a teenager, a union she had annulled for reasons unknown to me. Not much later, around

1953, she married a struggling accountant named Bill. They moved around with his job, to Oklahoma and eventually to Kentucky. Together they produced five children in four years: two boys and three girls. This would have been a lot for anyone to handle, but for Mother, who was quick-tempered and still bitter about raising her own siblings, it proved insufferable. She wanted to experience the finer things in life and needed the recognition that beauty had brought her sisters, who by now had found jobs modeling and acting in local television shows. My mother was uncommonly beautiful, with auburn hair and green eyes and pouty lips that she carefully penciled in, but her children didn't care about her looks. They just wanted what they wanted, and she wanted what she wanted. And what she wanted most was out.

She found her way out when Bill's client Kova Meredith came to their home for dinner. Kova was a simple man from a small town in Kentucky. He was nearly fifty years old and made his living working as a machinist for the government. He owned a small upholstery shop in Elizabethtown. He was in the middle of a heated divorce in the early 1960s, a time when simple men from Kentucky were not having heated divorces.

Kova saw Mother. Mother saw Opportunity. She easily convinced him that she was a battered woman with five children and no way out. Kova loved children and he'd had less contact with his own sons since his divorce had begun. He saw that my mother had it rough. And he understood rough all too well.

Kova's mother, Grace, was the love of his life. A petite woman from Edmonson County, Kentucky, she was just thirteen when she married Felix, a local man much older, taller, and meaner than she was, who had become a legend in his small town in the early 1900s when he sewed the eyes of one of his pigs shut because it escaped from its pen one too many times.

Felix and Grace moved into a small house in Bee Spring and had thirteen children while developing a successful farm and family store. They were not rich but had more than enough money to feed their family. Felix demanded his boys quit grammar school so they could help with the family farm. His daughters continued with their education, wearing dresses made from burlap bags that Felix's older sister made, since Felix refused to buy material. Felix also thought that an outhouse was a luxury his wife and family did not need, insisting instead they walk barefoot through acres of long grass filled with snakes and spiders when nature called, so as not to soil the area around their home.

But the worst damage Felix did to his family was to abuse Grace in front of his children. Kova later talked about his failure to protect his tiny mother, and the grief he and his siblings felt after seeing her mistreated, when she deserved so much better.

Kova saw in my mother a chance to make past wrongs right. My mother left Bill for Kova and took her five children with her. In turn, she allowed Kova to put his upholstery business in her name so it wouldn't be counted as an asset to be divided in his divorce. Mother married Kova as soon as their respective divorces were final. They barely knew each other, and their union became volatile. Several months later, and for reasons I'll never know, they divorced. Soon after, they learned that my mother was pregnant with me. They remarried immediately so that their offspring—me—would not be a bastard.

What does extreme stress on a mother do to the developing baby inside the womb? Decades after my birth, scientists confirmed that stress is transmitted from mother to baby before birth. The umbilical cord is like a telephone line. I don't remember how I felt before birth. What I do know is that as a baby, I was inconsolable. Siblings and babysitters have confirmed this. Toddlers are egocentric by nature, and as such, I became convinced I was the cause of my parents' misery.

Throughout my life, I have done everything I can to neutralize my impact on the world around me. I have asked for nothing. I expect nothing. When I learned that the two people who hated each other had reunited on my behalf, I vowed to avoid becoming a further inconvenience.

My parents divorced a final time before my first birthday. The stress of single parenting must have become too much for my mother. She wouldn't do it for long before unloading. She unloaded her stress on the children before she began unloading the children themselves.

I have no memory of how I came to lose my father and my brothers. I was only two when it happened. It was only later, when relatives who had never met before told me the same story that I knew I had found the truth.

Somewhere between her second divorce from my father and her union with her final husband, my mother lined up her oldest five children and delivered an especially harsh beating. It wasn't as though the kids were unaccustomed to her violence, but now the beatings were becoming more severe and occasionally occurred in public. The kids, ages seven to twelve, met together to come up with a coordinated response.

"Mom," my ten-year-old brother said, "we can't keep taking this. We just can't. If you don't stop hurting us, we won't be able to live with you anymore." He didn't duck fast enough to avoid being hit in the face with a belt buckle, which cut open the skin in the corner of his left eye.

"You'll get your wish sooner than you think," she hissed.

A week later, Mother prepared the boys for a weekend visitation with their father. "This is a boys-only weekend. You get to do guy stuff with your dad this time. The girls will stay with me," she said brightly.

Of course I had to stay with her. I was little, and their dad wasn't my dad.

The boys' father, Bill, told them later that there would be no return to Mother's home. She had simply disappeared, taking their sisters, and it wasn't nice to talk about, so they didn't.

❀ ❀ ❀

Good men become harder to find as a woman's family size and age increase. Her glamour fading, my mother settled on a younger man to be her final husband and my adoptive father. Eight years her junior, Larry shared Mother's Louisiana roots, as well as her lack of education and lack of interest in caring for the house full of hungry mouths he had created with his own wife. He was a truck driver. After a long day of work, he couldn't wait to put on his bathrobe and watch *The Tonight Show* with his feet propped up on the recliner, balancing his beer and a tub of popcorn on his lap. Mother could be found in the back of our trailer, primping in the mirror, checking for signs of new wrinkles or age spots. Still high-fashioned. Jackie O. meets *Hee Haw*.

All I knew as a youngster was that my mother had a house full of mismatched children in a trailer in Alaska. I knew that I was supposed to call her last pick of a husband Daddy, even though she later told me that I had a real daddy somewhere in another state, but he didn't want me and had tried to kill her, so she was forced to grab up her girls and run. It didn't seem right. I seethed when I looked at my siblings, how different they looked from me, how different they were from me. I despised our tin-box home. And I was embarrassed by my mother and her ridiculous husband and their bellowing matches, which echoed off the other tin homes in our neighborhood. I thought that if my real daddy had tried to kill her, then Mother probably deserved it.

In the close environment of an Alaskan trailer park, gossip spread like a drop of grape juice on a Sunday blouse. But never mind the world outside the trailer; my worst tormentors were locked inside—my three older, towheaded half sisters.

They teased and called me Indian. And they were right. My father was rumored to be some part Indian. I disappointed them by refusing to respond to their verbal jabs, choosing instead to consider their words a compliment.

It was easy, because I had a special secret: Indians have gifts and magical powers. And one day I would use them and prove it.

The chance came in the summer of '68, when I was four years old. It was an unusually dry season in Anchorage, Alaska, on this late-August afternoon, and my mother was discouraged by the lack of rain. A woman who lived in a world of her choice but not of her design, she found herself frustrated by the tedium of running a household and tending to her children's needs. Being stuck in a trailer full of their unending demands threatened to choke the life right out of her. She fancied herself a Hollywood starlet waiting to be discovered. But the discovery never happened, and her home became littered with ungrateful children. Her one escape was working in the small garden she had created in the park space, where she tenderly nurtured plants and flowers that helped her forget her pedestrian life. They were her salvation, and now they were dying.

Maybe she didn't know that Indians could command the elements with a dance. But her Indian daughter did. And I was ready to set my powers free. So outside in the bright Alaskan sun, I began. Unabashedly dancing and chanting, I released my energy to the universe. I believed with all my might I could summon the rain. When I saw my sisters laughing through the windows of our trailer, I shut my eyes, threw my head back, and focused. I visualized the joy the rain would bring my mother and, more important, the horror it will bring my sisters. I held the images in my mind, and danced and chanted my way through the first hour and well into the second, taking breaks as I needed. As the sun went down, I continued to dance.

I felt the first drops on my forehead. Maybe it was sweat. But as the drops came down more steadily, I dared to open my eyes and see the glorious rain, which fell through the night, through the next day, through the month. My mother later complained that her garden was flooded. No matter. The raindrops collected in a cup, and now, I heard a Sunday preacher say, my cup runneth over. This Indian had demonstrated her power. She—I—was untouchable.

So how did my cup, once brimming with hope and strength, drain away until it was empty?

It was a gradual process, occurring in increments, drop by drop.

It emptied partly with the realization that I caused some of Mother's unhappiness—I was a stifling agent, rather than the source of pride I longed to be. My cup emptied more as my siblings disappeared one by one, their absence an unspoken threat that I might be next. Most of my Indian powers drained away in times of high family drama, like after a beating by Mother, or when my oldest sister's bloody back peeled like an onion as Mother's belt buckle struck it again and again. My Indian self saw that she could no longer control the elements.

Wobbling through the remains of childhood, that defiant Indian was finally reduced to me, a painfully awkward little girl who never raised my hand in class, no matter how sure I was of my knowledge. A tempting target for school bullies. A dateless high schooler who joined the junior varsity basketball team without learning the rules of the game, tucking the first ball passed to me under my arm and running the length of the court, to the distress of the coach. All signs of strength had evaporated.

Mother also lost her power as the years marched on. Her good looks and dreams for adulation slipped away. Mother lashed out even more at the root causes of her misery: her children. We had ruined her life, and since turnabout is fair play, she effectively used her energies on responding in kind. She found creative solutions so that she could get out from under us, once and for all.

Chapter 7

THE BABIES COME

My husband is right—I don't have family in my corner. I'm twenty-one. I've only just learned to drive. I have an entry-level job. I am in no position to make idle threats about leaving him.

"You're just like your mother," he tells me. "You'll probably marry over and over if I leave you."

The very idea that I am anything like my mother is terrifying. I cling harder to my marriage to prove that I am different. Being unhappily married forever is better than being like her.

Just as we reach our first anniversary and I get used to the flow of my awful marriage, another flow stops. I've missed my period.

"What?" Gregory asks with disbelief as I show him the pregnancy test. "But you're only twenty-two. You can't raise a child."

"Yes, I can," I tell him. "I can work my job and you can be with the baby, and I'll come home and you can go to work. It will be fine."

I am as shocked as he is. Kids were not in my plan for at least another five years, but I am pregnant. We've talked about having kids before, and both of us like them. I see this as merely an adjustment to the plan, an early gift.

A few days later, Gregory announces that he will be sending the baby to his mother in Greece to raise. "We'll send her a little money for it. It's just until we're ready to be parents."

No way. There is no way I am sending my baby anywhere. We argue the point, and then drop it, and I notice that the further my pregnancy progresses, the more excited Gregory is to be a father. Sometimes he even seems to like me better, smiling affectionately at my expanding waistline.

Picking our baby's name is a no-brainer. Gregory is the eldest son in his family. In keeping with Greek tradition, the firstborn son names a child after each of his parents. Discretion is given only if the son has two children of the same gender. Gregory's parents were Marianthi and Giorgios. If by chance we one day have two daughters, we've agreed that we will name our second daughter Meredith in honor of my father's side of the family.

The birth of our baby girl, Marianthi Cassandra, in July 1987 changes the balance of power in our marriage. I am buoyed by my new status as a mother. Someone in the world needs me now. My life has importance. And when Gregory returns to his old habits of drinking too much and staying out all night just days after Marianthi's birth, I am no longer anxious but disgusted instead. I let him know about it loud and clear, and it doesn't go over well with him, but his opinion matters less to me suddenly.

I leave Gregory the first time when Marianthi is just three

months old. He disappears for a couple of days in a row, calling finally in a boozy stupor. I pack her up in my 1976 Monte Carlo, and away we go to a cheap hotel in a seedy part of the city. In my mind, I am bravely breaking away. But Anchorage is a small town, and he knows I have little money, which narrows his search. Gregory finds me easily and knocks on the hotel door. Through the peephole, I see that he's brought me flowers. "I need you, Liz. I swear I'm going to change. I'm going to stop drinking. I'll stay home more." He has tears in his eyes, which I chalk up to sincerity. I return to him.

You just focus too much on the bad stuff, I chide myself. *Get a hobby. Make yourself happy.* I decide that what I really need is to do some volunteer work. Get my mind off me and my minuscule problems. Get me around some other grown-ups.

I don't have a babysitter, so I find volunteer work answering a suicide crisis line for a local nonprofit. After I attend the volunteer orientation, I sign up for one shift per week. The crisis line will be forwarded to my home.

At first it is easy. Mostly lonely people call, which is perfect, because I am lonelier than they are. I can empathize. But they don't know that. I can rock my daughter with one arm while holding the phone with the other. It's nice to make a difference.

For her part, little Marianthi cooperates and often sleeps peacefully on my lap while I hold the phone—until one fateful evening, when a painful bout of colic hits her.

The phone rings. Marianthi wails. A male caller speaks, but my crying baby drowns out his words.

"Would you repeat yourself, please?" I shout through Marianthi's screams. "I'm sorry about this."

Again, the caller speaks.

Again, Marianthi bellows into the phone, muting the message on the other line.

"I'm so sorry, sir," I apologize. "I'm having a hard time here. Please repeat yourself one more time."

"I'm thinking about killing myself!" he yells. *Me, too*, I think back. My caller stays on the phone, listening patiently, as I confide in him the details of my miserable existence while I pace the floor with Marianthi screaming and writhing over my shoulder. After twenty minutes, both Marianthi and I are properly soothed.

"I think things will improve with time for you," the caller tells me. "Don't lose hope."

After that, I trade in volunteer work for romance novels to distract me from my pain. I find a few Harlequin romances at a used bookstore and buy them with the same measure of sheepishness as a pastor buying porn. I know they are simple and ridiculous. I am addicted almost immediately. Will Colton ever return from battle to reunite with Tiffany, who has loved him so long from afar? Will Veronica ever hook up with her brooding supervisor, Hunter? Sure she will.

All these happy endings keep me from noticing a pattern that is developing in my relationship with Gregory. His disappearances, insults, and threats get me to think about leaving him. I can raise the baby alone. I can get an apartment and start life over again. I feel empowered just thinking about it.

But then comes Gregory's apology. "I love you so much. I would never act like this if I didn't love you." Or his sudden loving attention. A gift of flowers. A compliment. A promise of a better future. It is just enough for me to remember the good side of Gregory, and to stay put. Time to forgive and forget. After all, I'm not perfect. Maybe his disappearances, his drinking too much, his sharp words are my fault. I don't want my daughter growing up in a broken home like I did.

So I don't leave. And for a while, things are better. Gregory's home more. He helps with Marianthi and makes a wonderful Greek dinner. But after the passage of time, tensions build again, and I feel like a knife is twisting in my stomach. I begin tiptoeing around land mines, waiting for the bad thing to happen again. That bad thing at the beginning of our marriage was an insult. Later on, that bad thing became a threat of harm or death. That bad thing has now become losing all of our money on lottery tickets and booze and hard-porn magazines that I find stockpiled in our storage shed, which necessitates that I babysit a lawyer's three kids for food money. That bad thing becomes Gregory's withholding money for food during my second pregnancy, forcing me to choose which baby to feed: the one in my arms or the one in my growing belly. Then the bad thing becomes Gregory's withholding my own vehicle from me so he can use it in a business venture whenever he pleases, thus cutting me off from the outside world entirely and sending me spiraling into depression. The bad thing becomes a weeklong disappearance by Gregory that tantalizes me with the hope that he might have died in a tragic accident, until he returns without explanation. And now, ten months after our second daughter, Meredith, is born in the spring of 1989, the bad thing becomes something so bad that it cannot be apologized away.

Chapter 8

BREATHLESS

Gregory has disappeared again. No call. No note. He is gone. I don't think much about it over the weekend. I'm used to it. I put an X on the calendar of the date of his disappearance: Friday, March 2, 1990. A second X on Saturday, and a third X on Sunday. But on Monday, between fixing meals for the girls and laying Meredith down for her afternoon nap, I begin considering the possibilities.

Has he been murdered, maybe shot by a random drug dealer in the night as he got off work late at the hotel? Is he clinging to life somewhere in his crashed vehicle, deep in a ditch and too hidden by snow to be rescued? Or is he drinking with friends and playing poker, betting what little money he's made in tips at work, while I open the fridge repeatedly to see if any groceries have magically appeared?

I should have known that Gregory isn't dead. God doesn't love me that much. But when I hear the phone ring at one in the afternoon on March 5, I run to the phone, full of great expectations. "Leez, it's Greg."

And down they go. Gregory is alive. I can tell that he has been drinking hard. His accent is always thicker, his tongue heavier when he is drunk.

"Look, before you get really peesed off at me, I want you to talk to someone here."

It is too late. I'm not just pissed. I am murderous.

"Hi." A woman's voice comes on the line. "I'm Gregory's friend. He just wanted me to let you know he's been with me the past two days."

"Excuse me? Why are you on the phone? Put him back on the phone!"

"It's not like that," she continues. "My car got stuck in the ditch a couple of nights ago, and he helped push it out. Then he hurt his back, so I gave him my muscle relaxants, and he's been asleep ever since. . . . We didn't do anything."

"What a relief that is," I say acidly. "He's a real gentleman, leaving his wife and two kids behind for days to help you out. Put Greg on the phone. Now!"

Injuring my husband's ego in front of this woman is a mistake I will come to regret, but in the moment, I'm too upset to think about it. When Gregory walks into the apartment a half hour later, I'm madder still.

Our argument quickly turns to shouting. Two-year-old Marianthi is standing on the couch, looking like she's dressed for church. Gregory and I sit across from each other and continue our verbal battle while her gaze moves side to side as though she is watching a tennis match.

"I'm leaving this time," I tell Gregory. "I'm not kidding. I've done the math. The girls and I can live on child support and my babysitting money. We don't need this. We don't need you."

"Don't think you're taking my kids, Leez. I'll get a good

lawyer. I'll quit my job before you get child support. You won't get a dime. Do you hear me?"

I hate this man. I've lost all sense now. Rising out of my chair, I give Gregory a vigorous air kick. Big mistake. In seconds, I am on the floor, with his hands wrapped around my neck and his long fingernails clawing into my skin.

"I'll kill you, and you'll die knowing the girls won't ever be with you or me again. I have nothing to lose. You'll never see these girls again."

Marianthi's screams wake her sister, who starts wailing from her crib on the second floor.

As he squeezes, I struggle to push him off me and grab at his heavy gold necklace. He hits me on the ear and then squeezes harder. Things move in slow motion.

Being choked is not unfamiliar to me. My next-oldest sister's hands appeared to have a magnetic charge with my neck while growing up. Given that I was younger than her by five years, I was an easy target whenever she needed an outlet from our family life. But this throttling is different: as Gregory squeezes my neck, my weakness, my passivity, escapes my body as the air is wrung out. Gregory releases his grip and moves away.

I stare into his eyes.

Are they his? I feel myself slipping out of consciousness. I open my eyes wider. My sister is looking down at me, her teeth clenched as she grips my neck. I blink hard. My red-faced mother is now the strangler.

I close my eyes and reopen them. It is Gregory. Definitely Gregory.

My lungs begin to burn.

Will the distance between my first breath and my last provide no feeling of safety and security? Is this my only inheritance? Perhaps this is my punishment for years of quietly believing that my mother deserved to be beaten by my father.

I cover the left side of my neck with my hand and start to get up. Gregory is back on top of me again in no time. Choking. Squeezing. Threatening. Over and over and over.

He doesn't know that with each inhalation I draw power and determination.

Someone once told me that I alone will know when enough is enough. Now I understand. And while it is clearly Gregory who is squeezing the life out of me, my resolve covers so much more.

If I live through this, I'm done. I'm really done. Done being hurt. Physically. Emotionally. In front of my daughters. Done. No more living in fear. No more living to please. No more eating the children's leftovers and living a life that doesn't matter. No more being stifled.

Gregory releases his grip one final time and walks out of the apartment. I grab Marianthi and go to the phone but decide against calling the police. I have heard tales of the police driving the abusing spouse around the block for a cooldown, only to then let him walk home after. No thanks.

I see Gregory drive off, so I grab anything I can think of and throw it in a garbage bag. A few diapers, a Bambi video, Meredith's favorite blanket. Good enough. It is still cold enough outside to merit warming up the car in advance, so I leave the girls in the apartment and dash to the carport to start the car. Nothing. No clicking sound whatsoever. My car is dead. I search for my wallet to see if I have cash for a cab. My wallet is suddenly missing. Gregory has outsmarted me again.

I phone Tina, the lawyer I babysit for. She works at the Office of Special Prosecutions and Appeals. Surely she will know what to do. Tina directs me to take a taxi with the kids and ride downtown to her law office, where she will then pay the driver to take us to a different friend's home to spend the night. From there, I can figure out what to do next. Gregory walks in as we're mapping out the plan.

"If anyone hangs up the phone, I'm calling the police," she says calmly. "Do not let that happen, Liz. Put the phone down and get what you need to leave, but don't hang up."

The taxi arrives a few minutes later. Gregory watches as I gather up our whimpering daughters and the garbage bag of belongings, and head out in the snow into the taxi, toward safety. I refuse to look back.

Chapter 9

NEW BEGINNING

A call to the local battered-women's shelter initiates the process of leaving behind my life as the intimidated wife.

It is no easy call to make. I feel like a phony. All of the other residents probably have it much worse than I do, but there is no safe place for the girls and me. Gregory quickly tracked us to my friend's home, and I didn't want to put her at further risk.

It turns out that Tina doesn't want further risk either. After Gregory makes an impromptu visit to her law office—a bold move, considering she is a prosecutor for the state—she can see that things are getting out of hand. She tells me that she can't risk harm to her own children by having me around. "You know it's nothing personal, Liz. You're like family to us. I just can't be sitting at my desk at work, worried that Gregory will show up at my place while you're with my kids . . . It's too dangerous."

So there goes my ability to make money while taking care of the girls. It is the right choice for her to make as a mother. The only choice. But it sure doesn't make life any easier for me.

Tina tells me to apply for public assistance. "You're going to need medical coverage for the kids," she says, adding that I will have to learn to convince strangers that while there are many needy people in the world, the girls and I are special. "Make them believe in you. Make them think that your story is unique. Make them want to help you." I thank her, knowing there is no way in the world I will let Gregory make me a welfare mother.

My counselor at the shelter also tells me that I need to apply for public assistance. After we look at my budget together and subtract the cost of day care for my daughters from the paltry salary I qualify for, I reluctantly agree. My mother married over and over to avoid becoming a welfare mother, and if her husbands were anything like mine, then being a welfare mother must have been worse than death.

Standing in the welfare line, looking down at my tired, dirty daughters, I don't believe I can sell anyone on our being special or unique. The eligibility technician, a fiftyish woman, glances up at us occasionally as she reads through our paperwork, frowning when Marianthi sits on the floor and begins to cry. She asks a litany of questions while I bounce Marianthi on my lap and Meredith crawls around my legs.

"Why do you need help? Do you have money in the bank? Are you married? Are you working? Why not? Do you have any skills? Education? Who can I call to verify this?"

It isn't until she phones my references and grills them about my sorry state of affairs right in front of us that I begin to cry. Of course she is only doing her job, but it is more than I can take.

Her expression softens, and after she completes the reference check, she explains that the girls and I are eligible for food stamps, a monthly stipend, and Medicaid. "You can apply for housing assistance, and since you're at the battered-women's shelter, you'll quickly get to the top of the waiting list."

As I gather the girls to leave, she asks if I have ever considered finishing my bachelor's degree. I tell her it would likely take three more years of college before I graduate. "I would be twenty-eight by then," I explain.

She smiles at me for the first time. "I hate to break it to you, but how old do you think you'll be in three years if you don't go to back to college?"

I pick up a schedule for summer school at the university on the way back to the shelter. By the end of my first week at the shelter, I have applied for a restraining order, gone to my local legal aid office for help filing for a divorce, and gotten my name on the housing assistance waiting list. One day, I tell myself, I will never ask anyone for help again. I just need time to regroup.

Naively, I believe that leaving my husband is the key to safety for the girls and me. If I paid attention to what experts in the field of domestic violence report, information shared at the shelter by advocates there in the mandatory information and support groups, I would know that the riskiest choice I could make is to leave my husband. It has toppled his sense of control.

It's good that we don't know what the future holds. If I had had a crystal ball, I would have never left my husband. The next few months and years prove that it's possible to be more miserable living away from an abuser than with him.

When I move across town, Gregory moves nearby. When I tell the judge during a restraining order hearing that I'm on food stamps, Gregory calls public assistance and tells them that I am living with a man and working but not reporting the income. Workers come to my apartment for a surprise visit. One rifles through my closets and drawers, looking for evidence of cash or a man. Upon spotting my size 9 blue ski boots in the closet, she turns to me. "Are you sure these belong to you? They look awfully large."

After Gregory returns the girls from a two-day visitation, Meredith wants me to take her to the bathroom immediately, and it's there that I see two unusually large bruises. I ask him if she's taken a spill. Gregory takes her and Marianthi from me and takes them to the pediatrician, reporting that I must have harmed my youngest daughter. Social workers are dispatched to my apartment; they strip search the girls and ask them a battery of questions.

I go out on a limb once and ask Gregory why he puts so much energy into making things a living hell for me. "Maybe if you get good and miserable enough, you and the kids will come back to me." As though abuse is some sort of sick foreplay.

When I have a date—three years after our marriage has ended—he follows us, slashes my vehicle's tires, and leaves obscene messages on my answering machine. "Leez, do you know what you are? You are a cunt. K-u-n-t. Cunt." And, days later, he sends me a message through the girls. "Mommy, Daddy says you're going to leave us forever."

I don't know how to interpret this one. Is Gregory trying to convince the girls that I will abandon them, or is there an even more sinister message that he is passing on?

At first, the constant stress of the unknown gnaws at me, interfering with my sleep and focus, and giving me chronic stomachaches. A friend who has listened to my complaints one time too many offers a piece of advice.

"You have to schedule your worry, Liz. You can't possibly let your thoughts run wild with all the 'what ifs.' Take control of it. Say to yourself, *I'll give myself an hour a day after the kids are tucked in to think about all the things that can go wrong.* And after that, get on with your life. Don't let him win by taking over your mind."

She is right. I can't possibly allow myself to obsess about what might happen, to the exclusion of everything else. I have a life to figure out. Children to raise. I have a future to create. So I take her superb advice and give myself over to my many concerns once a day. I worry that Gregory will steal the girls. I worry that he will kill me. I worry that I will be alone forever. I worry that we will always live in poverty. And I take time to catalog the losses the kids and I have already experienced by leaving Gregory: the loss of financial independence and the ensuing loss of pride while on government assistance, the loss of our home, the loss of raising the girls in a two-parent family. It is not my actual marriage that I miss; it is the loss of the ideal marriage that I always longed for.

And, sure enough, the Worry Hour means that I have twenty-three more hours a day to get on with my life. I fill these hours by getting some counseling for the girls and me, by going to parenting classes, and by attending college part-time. I sleep in the space between. Little by little, I reach out to re-create my social network. It takes time, but my life—our lives—begin to take form. By the time Gregory abducts our girls in March 1994, the years of psychological calisthenics have me in tip-top shape for the marathon ahead.

Chapter 10

SUPPORT TRICKLES IN

I feign interest as my friend Lauree speaks to me from across the table. We're at my favorite coffee shop, Café del Mundo, in midtown Anchorage. I love the heavy wood tables and the world map that covers an entire wall. I take a drink of my Americano with cream and steal a look at Greece over her shoulder, hoping Lauree doesn't notice my distractedness. I feel a pang of guilt for being out in public just for the fun of it. *My daughters have been kidnapped, and I'm having coffee at my favorite spot.*

Lauree's lips keep moving steadily. "And Matt loved the rides at Epcot. I know it's a park for kids, but it was such a romantic trip."

Jesus, is she really saying this? Maybe no one's mentioned to her that my kids disappeared.

My friends just can't win. I have plenty of them, and most of them make their best efforts to envelop me with love. But if they speak about their own happier lives, I am resentful. And if they insist on downplaying their own happiness and needs because my girls are gone, I am even more resentful.

Mary, another old friend, phones me to complain about her teenage son, only to stop herself and apologize. "Nothing I'm going through could compare to your situation. How can I complain?" *Can't we have regular conversations where I can support my friend once in a while?*

But by far the worst discussions include a heavy dose of reality. "Do you ever think of getting married and having more kids?" Translation: *Can you imagine yourself giving up on your daughters and just getting on with life?*

I have to admire the brutal honesty of it. For every person who asks the question, there are ten more friends and acquaintances wanting to.

Some days I hate everybody. At least I am smart enough to keep most of my thoughts to myself, because the truth is, I need my friends. And I need to remember to be a friend and realize that their lives and stressors are important to me, too, just as mine are to them.

My sister Kim is the only family member who calls regularly. Kim is the sister who let me live with her after my mother took off when I was thirteen. She had just turned eighteen at the time. I called her shortly after the girls were abducted. Big mistake. She still thinks of me as her baby sister who is in constant need of saving and inserted herself right in the middle of the crisis. She called Interpol and the FBI, providing them with the only information she knew. Those calls took her but a few minutes to make and took me an hour apiece to address and correct, since it appeared to the agencies that I was attempting to circumvent the system.

"But I'm only trying to help," Kim protested when I shared my frustrations.

"When I need your help, I'll let you know," I told her firmly. "I just want to be able to lean on you for support." So we agreed to instant message or talk by phone weekly.

After work one Friday night, I brace myself for the forty-eight hours of aloneness that weekends now offer. I go online to block out the deadly quiet, happy to have a distraction. The Internet is now accessible to plain folks like me, and I'm just getting comfortable with instant messaging.

How are you tonight? Kim instant messages.

Great. I reply sarcastically. *Just staving off feelings of suicide and baking some cookies.*

Then the conversation turns to the daily grind. She gives me her update about her daughter, her schooling, and her small-town life in Arizona. I'm equal parts irritable and pre-occupied. All day, I've eaten nothing but popcorn and cookie batter, and I can't wait for the cookies to finish baking.

Kim, I have to go now. The oven buzzer is ringing—my cookies are done. Be right back.

I remove the cookies. They're perfect—not too crisp, not too doughy. I put the cookie sheet on a hot pad so they can cool off and race back to the computer.

A message from America Online tells me that my live session has ended. Kim has left our chat. I shoot her a quick e-mail promising to call her tomorrow; then I unplug my phone and settle in for a quiet evening.

On Saturday, I wake up to a call from my office. "Liz, I hate to bother you at home, but the police just called about you," the shelter advocate says. *Oh my God. What now?* "There was a concern that you might self-harm, and they wanted to make sure you're okay."

It seems Kim called them to report that I am suicidal. My staff is panicked.

My work is the only place left where I am more than a

woman in crisis. I need the routine and the structure my job provides me. Besides, I told her last night that I was coming right back. Suicidal? Absolutely not. Homicidal is more like it now.

I am furious. I can't tell whether this is an attention-seeking behavior or whether a sudden bout of angst set in, and I'm too upset to call her and find out right now. Whatever the case, I will have to limit my contact with my sister to avoid more crisis-driven interactions. I simply don't have the energy.

My father, Kova, now old and frail, seems disinterested in regular contact. The siblings on my father's side of the family don't know what's going on, and I do nothing to change that. My maternal siblings have their own chaotic lives. My eleven brothers and sisters are too poor, too distant, or too young to be helpful. And my contact with my mother has served only to remind me that our relationship has to be all about her.

It's strange how a new loss brings the old ones to the forefront. I had already experienced so much of it by the time the children were abducted, and now those losses are the ones that seem to form the lump in my throat.

I give myself permission to think of my missing siblings from my mother's side of the family. I miss my two brothers, from whom I was separated as a toddler, who disappeared out of my world without warning. I miss my three older sisters, who left my mother's home prematurely, one by one, and my little sister and my brothers on my father's side of the family, whom I met only months before I married and dropped contact with when my life hit the skids. I miss everyone. I reach for no one.

My melancholy doesn't end with my siblings. It extends to homes I've lost because of my mother. The house that burned to the ground when I was seventeen, which netted Mother a handy sum of cash from the insurance company, and the next home, which was foreclosed on while Mother threw her cash at televangelists instead of paying her mortgage. It extends to the father I barely knew before he died, and to my wacky mother.

I avoid thinking of Marianthi and Meredith for long periods of time. What will happen if I let myself cry and cannot stop? It feels much safer to indulge my grief about the old losses than to acknowledge the possible permanence of the new ones.

One night after work, I drive to Elderberry Park, a scenic playground by the ocean I frequented as a child and where I later took my girls when weather permitted. I get on the swing set and pump my legs as hard as they can go. I remember the first time, two years ago, I had a trial run at losing a child. I was with the girls at Elderberry Park. We had gathered along with a swarm of tourists to wave at the train going by. Meredith was in my arms and Marianthi stood next to me. When the crowd dissipated, Marianthi was gone. I walked up and down the trail, calling her name, and fell to pieces after repeated searches of the area failed to produce any sign of her.

"Are you Liz?"

I nodded, and a man told me that Marianthi was with his girlfriend, just down the trail. Marianthi had wisely gathered a team of volunteers and had given them a precise description of me. "Your little girl said you had long brown hair and were wearing a pink shirt with a muscleman on it," the volunteer told me when she brought me my daughter, who said, "Mommy, where were you? I was looking everywhere!"

I am brought back to present day 1994 earth when I hear a familiar little voice.

"Liz!"

I look down in disbelief. Gina, Meredith's best friend

from day care, is staring up at me, with her hands on her tiny hips. I scan the park and playground. Her parents are nowhere in sight, but five-year-old Gina is not to be intimidated.

"Where's Meredith?" she demands, pushing her stringy hair out of her eyes with dirty fingers.

I notice that Gina has grown taller. The girls have been gone only a couple of months. Has Meredith grown, too?

"Sweetie, she's still in Greece with her dad, I think," I say, coming to a stop on the swing as I realize how strange I must look to Gina.

"When is she coming back?"

"I'm doing the best I can, Gina. I promise I'm trying to bring her home."

Gina glares at me, clearly unsatisfied. She looks me in the eye and then appraises me on the swing set. "Are you even looking for her?"

Human contact diminishes me, even if it is with the humans I adore.

So I distance myself from them, and from anyone else who stands to deplete me of my limited energy and offers no tangible support for my mission. It is a move that smarts for some of my family and friends, but I feel like I have to protect myself and create a safe haven from any added drama.

My focused strategy pays off. Not only do I avoid doing time at the local psych ward but I also apply for and receive a promotion at work. I'm now in charge of the nonresidential/community education portion of the battered-women's agency, the largest one in the state of Alaska. I'll get to use my experiences to inform how programs are developed and grants are administered to assist victims and families affected by domestic violence. I am ecstatic. Through work, I take a sign language class and travel to the Alaskan bush to give presentations when requested. And because my rent is too steep, I begin the process of buying a fixer-upper townhouse that will cut my living expenses in half. I go cross-country skiing most days after work to increase my stamina and enroll in some graduate preparatory courses at the university for the next semester. All of those support groups I've cofacilitated about self-care have finally begun to take hold—with two childless months behind me, I've at least made some progress on the personal front.

Progress reuniting with my daughters is much trickier.

I retained a Greek law firm in Chicago after receiving a referral. They have affiliates in Greece, brothers Michael and Panayiotis Pappas, who are recognized by the US State Department as international abduction experts. The local lawyers agree that we'll let Michael Kreider be the liaison with them, and Michael will keep Jim and me in the loop. They'll take the translated documents I got from the State Department and become familiar with our standing custody decree in Alaska before filing anything in Greece or hiring a private investigator.

"Pace yourself, kiddo," Michael tells me. "It's going to take a while yet."

This I know. What I don't know is how I'm going to pace myself but continue to push toward my goal. There aren't any good step-by-step workbooks on the subject. And whom can I talk to about it? Yes, I'm a bit of a therapy junkie, but this is different. I need support from someone who's been there.

When the girls were babies and I floundered with mothering basics like bedtime schedules and feeding problems, I joined a new-mothers' group at a local church. I liked it so well that peer-led groups became my go-to crutch in times of crisis—groups on single parenting, getting off welfare, surviving abuse. I like slogging through the trenches with someone who's in my shoes, or who has been. But there aren't a lot of left-behind parents of internationally abducted children in Anchorage, Alaska.

❧ ❧ ❧

The phone rings one May evening. A silky voice is on the other line. "Lizbeth? This is Ron Jones, with the National Center for Missing and Exploited Children. How are you?"

There's not a lot that he can do for me now that I'm in a waiting period, but it's still nice to hear from him.

"You've heard of Betty Mahmoody, right?" he asks.

Have I heard of Betty Mahmoody? Anyone with a foreign partner knows who she is. Betty wrote her harrowing account of escaping from Iran, titled *Not Without My Daughter*, which was published in 1987, and she's still a clearinghouse of information on how to recover an internationally abducted child. She runs a small nonprofit now, One World: For Children, that's given me some tips on surviving the mountain of paperwork that the American and Greek governments require. Ron Jones told me about them earlier.

"Indeed I have," I tell him now. "They've been very helpful to me."

Mr. Jones assures me that while he can't make any promises, the One World staff is working with the Justice Department to coordinate research with left-behind parents of internationally abducted children. He thought I might be interested so he put in a good word for me.

Not long afterward, a staff member from One World: For Children calls. He's to the point.

"I have a question. What would you think about meeting with eleven other parents whose kids were stolen and taken to different parts of the world?"

The goal, he explains, is to learn about international abduction by comparing incidents that occurred in Hague and non-Hague countries. Are the parents whose children have been taken to Hague countries really any better off than those whose kids are in non-Hague countries? We will weigh in as the experts, based on our individual experiences. While only twelve people will meet face to face in Washington, DC, to be in focus groups, many more parents of abducted children will answer questionnaires by mail and by telephone, and will participate in the study from their locations.

It sounds perfect. I can find my new tribe. And it sounds expensive.

As if he hears my thoughts, he adds, "It will be no cost to you. The entire trip will be sponsored by the Justice Department."

This seems too good to be true. I jump at the opportunity.

Chapter 11

PARTNERS IN SUFFERING

So, less than three months after my daughters are stolen, I am making the trip to Washington, DC. I have never been to a city this size and have much more on my agenda than to simply participate in the study.

To prepare, I've spent the past two weeks scheduling appointments with Alaska's senators and congressman. AWAIC board member Louann Cutler speaks with her father, general counsel to President Clinton, who agrees to make time to meet with me at the White House.

The White House. I'm going to the White House. My girls are missing, and I get to go on an all-expenses-paid trip and see things I never would have otherwise. I know it's a positive move, but I feel guilty about my excitement all the same. What are the girls doing right now while I'm on vacation?

Just before I leave, a national tragedy in California rocks the nation and its aftershocks change my work life forever. The slaying of Nicole Brown Simpson and Ronald Goldman turns the spotlight on our nation's problem with domestic violence. The 911 calls Ms. Simpson made during and after her marriage to sports star O. J. Simpson, as well as images of her bloody corpse, are all over the television. AWAIC's crisis line is inundated with callers frantic to address the violence in their own relationships. Local television and radio stations want interviews immediately. And who better to interview than a local battered-women's advocate, still suffering years after leaving? In a twisted way, I feel a sense of importance. I'm in a great position to be the face of domestic violence.

I put in some long hours before my trip, squeezing in interviews and community panels on domestic violence and preparing my staff for the weeks ahead. I feel guilty for leaving during the hysteria that's become our lives.

The flight from Anchorage to Washington, DC, takes thirteen hours with a layover. My calves swell to the size of tree trunks on the plane because I refuse to eat or drink. If I do, I'll have to pee or do something even more involved, and to do that, I will have to get out of my seat and walk around. I haven't flown much the past few years, and my anxiety is in high gear.

Big cities make me nervous. So many people squished together competing for space and resources makes me feel unsafe. Although dread tempers my excitement, I can breathe again as soon as I get off the plane. The people seem friendly in the snack shop. The public transportation is easy to navigate. In no time, I've eaten an apple and some biscotti, downed a twenty-four-ounce bottle of water, taxied to my hotel, and jumped in the shower to wash off the effects that my nerves, plus the heavy, warm DC air have had on me.

To most people, the hotel might not seem like much, but to me, it's a mini castle. I have my own room with a large bathroom that includes a Jacuzzi, and an allowance for food. I can't help it; I'm giddy. I order room service, a burger and fries with a Diet Coke, and peruse the itinerary that was tucked under my door when I arrived.

Tomorrow, I'll meet the whole group of kidless parents and we'll have a brief orientation before splitting up into Hague and non-Hague groups. I wonder what they'll be like. I wonder if I will be the only emotionless parent. I wonder if my kids are the most recently abducted. I wonder if anyone's been successful in getting their children back yet, and if I'll need to be careful not to laugh or smile around the others. What shall I say to them?

My dinner arrives, and as soon as I scarf it down, I'm beat and fall asleep. The next morning, I meet up with the group of parents, who range in age from their twenties to their forties. Regular people, just like me.

Our repartee is instant. Soon we're talking about topics much deeper than frustrations with government agencies: strain on relationships with partners or friends, antidepressants. "I don't think I can manage more than two years like this," I hear myself saying. The room gets quiet.

Or then what? I'll kill myself? Or give up on the kids altogether? Sometimes I wish I had a filter. I can't imagine how this sounds to my new friends, some who have kids that have been missing much longer than two years.

But the group talk continues soon afterward, on to other taboo topics, like having more children or using various illegal means to get our kids back.

I'm not sure why I've been worried. Within fifteen minutes, I feel more like I'm at a family reunion than involved in a government study. The other parents' children have been taken to Canada, England, Germany, Ireland, Israel, Iran, Lebanon, Jordan (two separate cases), and Mexico. And, of course, Greece.

Once we are divided into the Hague and non-Hague focus groups, the facilitators are naturals at making us feel comfortable and getting us to open up.

My kids have been missing only three months. Another woman's children have been missing the longest, eight years. Three parents have already recovered their children, and I wonder if they have survivor's guilt when they're with the rest of us.

There's a redhead named Sam who just got his three children back by invoking the Hague Convention in England after his former wife had abducted them months earlier. He says that the British government made the process smooth and efficient, paid for his hotel and his attorney, and ensured that justice was enacted swiftly and fairly. The British courts refused to entertain allegations by the children's British mother of the father's wrongdoings, since the premise of the Hague Convention is that custody arguments should be heard in the place of the children's habitual residence. (Trouble at home? Fix it at home, not here, in a strange place.) The kids returned with Sam to the States, where he and their mother civilly ironed out the details. It's a perfect example of how well the treaty can work.

It's the only one. Other parents have been far less fortunate. A black man named Robert finally speaks up when called upon. He is a soldier who served a leg of his military duty in Germany and fell in love with a tall, willowy German woman. They married and eventually relocated to the United States and had a son. Their marriage, unlike those of most of the participants, was a happy one. He describes them as having common interests, common friends, and common goals. "We had a barbecue with friends over the night before. Everything was fine," he says. "I mean, we had no arguing, fighting, nothing. We had it all."

The next night, Robert says, he returned home from work to find his house empty. His wife had prepared his dinner and set the table for one, so he assumed she and their son had already eaten. When his family didn't return home after a couple of hours, Robert worried that they must have had a car accident. He placed one call after another—to hospitals, to friends, to relatives—but came up with nothing. He heard nothing for a day and a half. Finally, he got the call. His wife told him matter-of-factly that she and their son were in Germany. "We're not coming back. Ever."

Robert says that at first he thought the circumstances might reverse themselves naturally. But when phone calls weren't returned, he recognized the finality of the situation and began to slump into depression. He decided to go to Germany to fight for the return of his son. He filed for protection under the Hague Convention and was assigned an attorney, who advised him to capitalize on his history as the protector of Germany. "Wear your army fatigues to court. Don't let the court forget how you came to meet your wife."

Robert complied. But his wife's attorney brought a black male Ken doll wearing army fatigues. "It looked just like me," Robert says. "He used the exhibit to show the judge what a violence-riddled culture America was, full of dangers for the children raised there."

The court ruled against him. Robert describes his despair—despair over so unexpectedly losing the family he loved, despair over trusting the legal system in a country he once protected, and, finally, despair that the rest of his life would likely go on without his little boy. He wanted so much to see his son before he left Germany. His wife agreed to arrange a visit on one condition: Robert had to agree to sign away all of his custody rights in exchange for the final visit. He guiltily admitted that he took the bait. Robert described in painful detail his final farewell to his beautiful son, how he drank in every feature of his child, his scent, his voice, attempting to create a mental photograph that would last him his lifetime. Then he returned home alone to what was left of his life in America.

Something shady between the lawyers must have gone down behind the scenes. I imagine Robert's wife's lawyer treating Robert's lawyer to a post-hearing steak dinner for getting Robert to agree to wear his army fatigues. If Robert has similar suspicions, he doesn't let on. I hope that the lawyers in Greece are more aboveboard.

We sit in silence for what feels like an eternity while Robert regains his composure, drawing a deep breath and wiping his eyes. Collectively, we exhale.

The non-Hague parents seem to have had as much (or as little) success in recovering their abducted children as the Hague parents. One woman, an immigrant from Egypt, who works as an engineer in Michigan, says she was told the Jordanian government would arrest and extradite her husband to the United States when he and their children are located. It may be only lip service, but it promises more hope than I have received thus far, and I'm envious. Another woman, an attractive blond nurse from Michigan, who develops red blotches on her neck as she talks, says that her Iranian ex-husband took her sons to Australia. She quickly recovered them using mercenaries. "It was worth every penny of the $50,000 I paid them," she says.

I wonder why she doesn't look happier, since she got her kids back. Life returned to normal, she explains, and she finally began to relax close to a year after her sons' retrieval. Then her former husband stole her boys again. This time, he took them to Iran. She spent as much money after the second abduction on mercenaries, but this time she did not get her sons back.

"I give up," she says quietly, looking down at her feet. "There's nothing more I can do."

"Well, I wondered where you wuz."

This is my father's first conversation with me. It is 1985, and I am twenty years old, a few months shy of my twenty-first birthday and I've called him from my dorm in Washington. He is in Bee Spring, Kentucky.

Several days later, when we have our first in-person moment alone together after he's wired me an airline ticket to meet him, he recalls my disappearance as a toddler.

"I looked for you. . . . I hired an investigator."

And then? I want to ask him. *And then what happened?* But I can't because the family has already let me know how hard it was on him, having his only daughter at the time kidnapped by her mother, how men didn't usually get custody of their small children back in the '60s and '70s anyhow.

Besides, I can see what happened. My father married a third time and had four more children. He got busy.

"The kids all know about you," my stepmom tells me proudly. "We raised them to know about you." And for this, I am grateful. I need to be grateful, because any ingratitude could make my father disappear from my life again, taking with him all of the siblings and aunts and uncles I've just met, the family I've wanted.

Did you know I was in danger? I want to ask. *Did you know I was taken and then left behind? Did you know how scary my life got in Alaska? Did you think about me on my birthdays? Do you remember when my birthday is?*

"Thank you," I tell him, meaning *thank you for wanting me.* "That must have been hard."

❧ ❧ ❧

I'm not prepared for this level of honesty and despair in the focus group. I don't want any of us to give up, ever. The others look equally sad, but no one tries to talk the Egyptian woman out of her feelings. We sit quietly and share in her misery.

Life after the abduction goes differently for each of us. Some of the parents admit they have isolated themselves from their support systems so they can focus intently on their abducted children. They seem warped. Others have remarried and had additional children or acquired stepchildren, so their focus is now divided. That seems odd to me, too. How can they possibly leave a young family behind in the States to locate an abducted child? Every choice comes with its own consequence.

But no matter our choices, we have shared problems. We are all up to our eyeballs in expenses, paperwork, and emotional devastation. Some of us have close families to rely on for support; others have wealth and influence. A few of the parents who have means feel they cannot justify holding fundraisers in their communities to offset the costs to get their children back, though we all agree that not one of us created a rainy-day fund to cover the $100,000 that an abduction recovery can cost. In some ways, I feel glad to be among those who have nothing to offer but good intentions.

"What are the signs you can now see, in retrospect, that the abduction was about to occur?" one of the facilitators asks.

Most of the abducting parents began contacting their home countries more frequently in the months before the abductions. They began detaching from their American lives in subtle or dramatic ways—withdrawing from friendships, quitting their jobs, or taking trips to their homelands. They sent money to relatives or received cash settlements before the abduction. Gregory received two cash settlements and then went on a shopping spree, writing a host of bad checks on a closed account before he left. Some abductors liquidated their assets. Some had relatives from their home countries visit in advance of the kidnapping. Some parents did not return their children from a visitation prior to the abduction, almost like a practice run. Phone calls and faxes to extended family members increased in frequency. While several of us had recently separated from the abducting parents, Robert believed he was happily married at the time of his son's abduction. (I had been apart from my husband for four years.) Every parent, with the exception of me, was contacted by the abducting parent shortly after the kidnapping and told some variation on, "If you don't report this to the authorities, I'll bring our child home soon." Then time passed, and more promises to return the child (or children) were made in subsequent phone calls. And by the time the left-behind parents realized their children would not be brought home voluntarily, it was too late to effectively ask for help from law enforcement or the court system.

Our initial responses as left-behind parents also varied. Some chose not to contact law enforcement, for fear of driving the abductor away forever. Some chose not to because of suspicions that it wouldn't help. Some told anyone who would listen about it. Others kept the abduction a secret, hoping the situation would resolve before family and friends entered the picture.

We are all trying the best we can, but we are walking in the dark.

Emotionally, the experience has gutted us. Sleeplessness, an inability to eat or to concentrate, and a disconnect from previously close relationships make us feel like the walking dead. We may be stuck in this purgatory forever. There will be no closure that a death would provide; instead we will wonder whether our children are safe. We will wonder whether our missing children continue to remember us. And we will always wonder what the children think of us, the parents who couldn't keep them safe from this disaster.

By the end of the first day, we have more than a bond— we have fused. We tour the famous sites of DC, from JFK's gravesite to the Smithsonian, and at every meal in between, I feel as if I have a new family. There's nothing I can't say to the other participants, and I feel freer than I have in a long time.

This new freedom is due only in part to our common struggle. The truth is, I always open up easily to people I have little investment in. Though I fully plan to get my new friends' physical and e-mail addresses and keep in touch, I know that I won't have to see them again. I can show them my fears, my tears, my anger. They won't leave. They'll just return to their lives, and it won't be personal.

As the days fly by, I learn about the challenges that lie ahead from my new friends' experiences. I hear about negotiating with abducting parents. I hear about failed attempts at using the courts and the militia. I will need to assume that the best-laid plans can go to shit. I will need plans A and B to be on speed-dial simultaneously. I'll need to keep my wits about me. I'll need to hold my tongue if I'm insulted by Gregory's family or by any member of the public. I'll need to manage my emotions, and I'll need to retain good friendships and not wear them out with my tale of woe. I need. I need. I need.

More than half the kids taken out of the country by a parent never return. Failure to bring my daughters back may be the one thing I can't endure.

On my last day in DC, I meet with the Alaskan senator Ted Stevens, who gives me his full attention and promises to be my advocate with the State Department. Senator Frank Murkowski, on the other hand, is brisk and bothered, displaying the warmth I would normally use to greet a phone solicitor who interrupts my dinner. Congressman Don Young is not in Washington but agrees through his aide to meet with me later, in Alaska, for lunch. I'm still in my twenties, and I don't know what these political figureheads can do for me, if anything, but somehow it seems like a good idea to talk to them.

And now it's time for the best meeting yet: the one with President Clinton's attorney. Lloyd Cutler, general counsel to President Clinton, gives me the better part of his afternoon at the White House. He shows me around the White House and even gives me a peek into the Oval Office. I am sad to hear that the president is away, but as I enjoy the majestic setting and see the artwork that documents our country's history, I can't help but think how fortunate I am to have earned a spot on the calendar of this important man. There are worldly matters of much more significance than my two missing children, but you wouldn't know it by how attentively he listens to me. He offers to call a Greek lawyer he knows who works for the prime minister of Greece. I can't believe my ears. For a moment, I feel as though a magic wand has been waved and that the whole mess that has become my life will be straightened out in no time.

I come back to earth when I return to the hotel. It's time to say good-bye. To DC. To my fancy hotel room. To the other parents.

We pose for one last picture together in the hotel lobby. Two rows of smiling faces. Who knows what the future holds for us and our children?

As I board the plane to return to Anchorage, I think about my takeaways. What matters doesn't seem to be the amount of money people have, or whether their children are in a Hague or non-Hague country. A bit of luck and a lot of perseverance are what parents need to recover their kidnapped child from a foreign country.

I give a polite nod to the passenger to my right, a grand-motherly-looking woman who takes the acknowledgment as a green light for conversation.

"What brought you to DC?" she asks. I imagine that this nice woman with the decaled sweater lives a life much kinder than mine currently is. She shouldn't be subjected to my lousy truth.

"I've never been before," I tell her. I pull the thin airline blanket over me and face the window.

One day, I will tell the story of why I went to DC. It will be an amazing story for my girls. I only hope that I can tell them sooner rather than later.

Chapter 12

STRIKE ONE

I return from DC with renewed hope and energy, ready to resume the business of finding my daughters. On my first day back at work, Michael Kreider calls me.

"The attorneys in Greece are on strike."

"*What?*" I've never heard of such a thing. "How many of them? Why? How can this happen?"

All Michael can tell me is that all of the lawyers in Greece, including ours, are on strike and until it ends, all progress is stalled. He gives me some variation of his "keep your chin up, kiddo" speech and encourages me to keep working on getting information and support in Anchorage.

I don't want to get information and support. I want to choke someone. Isn't it bad enough that the abduction requires everything I don't have? Patience. Money. The ability to travel. Isn't it enough that I've had to break out of my quiet life and operate as a live exhibit in a museum, answering penetrating questions from strangers in order to increase my panhandling success? That I am pushing the boundaries with my friends in high places to help me out? And now, for reasons unknown to me, the lawyers are on strike? What next?

After fuming for several hours, I push myself beyond my feelings and do what Michael suggests: I will find support. After all, Michael isn't on strike, and he isn't being paid. I suspect if I can just get over being self-conscious about my neediness, asking for more support will go a long way toward accomplishing the near impossible.

Despite my reluctance to ask for it, I soon find that support is abundant.

One of my work benefits is free therapy. I make getting back into counseling a priority after I meet the other left-behind parents in DC and witness firsthand the collateral damage unaddressed trauma can inflict.

Going to counseling remains a taboo for many otherwise intelligent people. But for me, it has been practically a way of life since age thirteen, when my mother moved away from me, and through the early years of my separation from Gregory, when I needed a neutral trained professional to school me on how to best heal, parent my daughters, and continue to put one foot in front of the other.

This particular therapist looks like a displaced fifty-something flower child and listens to me, teaching me to acknowledge my worries, accept them, and breathe anyway. She doesn't judge me or pressure me to attend sessions regularly. "Come as often or as little as you need," she says. "No stress." And with that, pressure that's been quietly building releases.

Heather, my supervisor at work and member of the Anchorage Assembly, continues to introduce me to her friends at dinner parties, work functions, and Rotary meetings. "This is my friend Liz—the one whose kids were kidnapped and taken to Greece." She tells me to keep talking about the girls, whether I'm at work, giving a presentation on domestic abuse to a business or church group, or at the gym, answering questions from the woman on the treadmill next to mine. "Keep the story alive in the community. Memories are short, and there's always another crisis to focus resources on. It's your job to keep that from happening."

The children's day care mobilizes its troops immediately.

Faith Daycare & Learning Center, the girls' day care since I began working at AWAIC, is as every bit as conservative as it sounds. Because of its Baptist roots, I approached the staff reluctantly when enrolling the children. I wanted my daughters to respect people of all faiths, cultures, and ways of life, and worried the staff's fundamentalism would interfere. And I was, after all, a divorcée and a single mother. Not exactly Baptist material.

The first day, my fears seemed to be confirmed. When I went to five-year-old Marianthi's classroom to pick her up after her first day there, she grilled me on my religious leanings. "Mommy, do you love Jesus?" she asked, as I readied her sister to go home. I gave her a halfhearted yes. "No, Mommy, I *mean* it. Do you love Jesus?"

"Yes, Marianthi," I groaned, "I love Jesus. Let's go home." Picking up three-year-old Meredith, I began walking down the hall to leave.

"No, Mommy." Marianthi stopped walking. "I mean it! *Do you love Jesus?*"

"Yes, Marianthi, I *love* Jesus!" I said, turning back to look at her. Other parents were watching us now.

She looked at me doubtfully. "Are you lying?"

That night, as I tucked the girls in bed, Meredith surprised me by folding her pudgy hands together and closing her eyes. "What are you doing, sweetie?" I asked.

"Praying my sister goes down to the debil," she answered.

But now, after more than a year of caring for my children, the staff have become like family. Through sickness and in health, for better or worse, they have been the other coparent for me. After learning of the girls' abduction, Leesa, one of the directors, calls to let me know the church is solidly behind my recovery efforts. "Call us, Liz," Leesa says. "We can help with fundraisers. We can get people together, bring food, help set up. Whatever you need."

Mona, the other director, echoes her sentiments. "And stay in touch. We want to know how it's going. We miss them, too."

Coworkers offer to donate their leave if I need it, their sympathetic ear if I want it, and even financial resources. Most of them make little more than I do and live just above the poverty level, but whatever they have, they are willing to share.

Support is covered. And while support flows in a continuous stream, news about Gregory and the kids has to be hunted.

I contact a police detective I met through work last year, hoping to get an outsider's take on how my case is progressing; what is happening versus what should be happening. He was so excited last year about his work in the Crimes Against Children Unit that he spent extra time with a coworker and me, giving us tips on how we could become police officers. He is the only personal connection I have at the police department and he works in the same unit as the detective assigned to my children's case, so I call and ask him if he has any insight into how the investigation is going. He tells me he doesn't feel comfortable talking to me while he's at work and offers to meet me for coffee on a lunch break soon.

We meet at a crowded coffee shop. I scan the room, hoping I will still recognize him. He stands up as I approach the table, hugging me tightly as if I were an old friend. I pull back and then take my seat. If I had to pick an animal that he resembles, it would definitely be a beaver. A beaver with glasses who whistles through his buckteeth when he speaks. A chubby, whistling beaver in his late forties. "So, how are you holding up?"

He listens without interrupting about my impression of the police investigation, placing his hand over mine and enclosing it with his doughy fingers. I feel a pang of guilt for critiquing his looks. He tells me he's watched Detective Rose sit on the information she's received about the case. He agrees that it seems personal, rather than legitimate ignorance, and offers to watch a little more closely and fill me in regularly if I make the time for him. "But don't tell anyone about this meeting, or that we've spoken at all. This could have negative implications for my career, not to mention your case. Don't tell anyone we've spoken, or I can't help you."

I agree to keep our communication secret. He releases my hand and skims my thigh before resting his own hand inches from my lap. Then he starts whining about his unhappy marriage. "I can't afford to divorce my wife," he says, "but I'd really like to spend time with you."

A wave of nausea runs through me, and I want to slap him for attempting to exploit my misfortune. It is an obvious abuse of power. Still, I can't ignore that he's the only person who can provide me with checks and balances in the police department. "Marriage takes a lot of work," I respond. "I think you're smart to stick with it." He frowns, and I promise I'll keep our communications private. "Thank you for caring about my daughters," I say, giving him an air hug, before sliding out of my seat and getting back to my office.

A few days later, he calls me. "I'm on the way to your house to check on you," he says.

"Why?" I feel my heartbeat increase. "I'm fine," I say, mortified at the potential invasion. "You don't even know where I live."

"Sure I do," he responds. "I'm a cop, remember? We have ways. . . ."

A detective not assigned to my case—a man wearing a gun, who has promised to help—is on his way to my home.

"Don't bother," I hear myself say curtly. "I'll let you know if I need anything. *Thanks.*"

This is not the help I need.

Every few weeks, I force myself to attend the Greek Orthodox church to get a read on what the Greek community knows about Gregory. I still have some friends at the church, and one by one, they pull me aside after the liturgy to tell me what they know. "He's called, asking for money again. He's asked for $1,000 this time." I also learn that Greg's gambling, drug use, and attempts at drug dealing caused some of his friends to distance themselves from him before he left the States.

Some knew about the abduction of my daughters when it was in the planning stages and do nothing to assist with the investigation. I tell myself a thousand times not to personalize the situation. They are Greek. Greeks stand by one another, no matter what. But I feel my cheeks get hot whenever I catch a glimpse of one of them, and my thoughts become dark and vengeful.

The worst of the worst is the Brubaker clan. Fotini Brubaker was a Greek national who moved to Alaska in the '60s. She wasted no time in marrying a promising law student, who later became a renowned legal eagle in Anchorage. Word had it their marriage was rocky from the start, laced with infidelities on both sides and held together loosely by the births of their four children and the potential humiliation associated with divorce. However, they were divorced by the time I began dating Gregory, and Fotini openly lamented that she had wanted him for her oldest daughter. "He would be a great son-in-law," she explained at the time, "and I want a Greek for my daughter."

After Meredith was born, Gregory asked me if Fotini could be Meredith's godmother. In the Greek Orthodox custom, a baby is usually baptized anytime after its first forty days, within its first year of life, and the godparents—known as the *koumbara* and *koumbaro*—remain close to the baby and the parents. I could not imagine a life with Fotini on the periphery, but Gregory wouldn't budge. "She's got money. Don't you see how much property she owns? Come on—think! Don't you think she'd share her money if we'd bestow such an honor upon her?"

I contested the idea with determination that was uncharacteristic for me at the time. After the demise of our marriage only a few months later, it appeared that the matter would remain permanently tabled and Meredith would not be baptized in the first year of her life. But three years later, when she returned from a visit with her father, it all came back. "Mama, I was bath-tized yesterday with Daddy, but I'm not supposed to tell you, 'cause it's a secwet." When confronted later, Gregory proudly admitted that he and Fotini had covertly planned the baptism, tricking the priest into believing that I didn't want to be part of it.

Greek Orthodox parishioners now tell me that Fotini's son was the getaway driver who took my children and their father to the airport at the time of the abduction. How much her son knew about Gregory's plan to keep the girls in Greece can never be proven.

How can I resist giving in to my feelings of hatred? She is a mother, after all. I sit in the church toward the back, glaring at the back of her head, imagining lighting Fotini's house on fire while she is sleeping, hoping she wakes to realize that she is engulfed in flames. I decide against taking Holy Communion because I know I will spontaneously combust for all of my murderous thoughts.

Still, I have more friends than enemies at the Orthodox church, and I have only to look into their eyes to see my sadness reflected in theirs.

One Sunday, a stunning parishioner whom I have noticed for years approaches me; she embraces me warmly and offers to help in any way she can.

Dina is a tall blonde from northern Greece and tells me that she grew up close to Gregory's family. She is stylish and gregarious, and I privately wished during my lonely married years that we could be friends. Dina and her husband own a popular restaurant in a nearby town, and their two teenagers are nearly grown. She tells me that she loves the life she's lived but secretly wishes she could have been a private investigator.

"Let me help you, Liz. Please. In two weeks I'm going to visit my family in Thessaloniki, where Greg's family is. My brother-in-law there is a police officer. I can find your children for you. I know it!"

No arm twisting necessary—I need her help. Dina promises to call me with any news.

Almost three weeks later, she calls from Greece. She's speaking so fast that I can barely understand her. "I found them, Liz! I found your girls!" Dina says that she called the number I gave her for Gregory's younger brother, Costas, and told him she was an old friend of Greg's from high school. Costas said Greg wasn't at the residence but the girls would be there until Greg returned.

"Thank you so much for this," I tell her. "I can never repay you."

My spirits soar. They plummet just as quickly when I realize there is nothing I can do with the information. My lawyers aren't in a position to act—the abduction expert Mr. Pappas has told me they're still on strike. If I fly to Greece, I'll have no way of getting the kids away from Gregory. I can't grab the girls out of his arms and make it out of the country safely.

After I spend the next few minutes calming Dina, who is as heartbroken by the mess as I am, I hang up. What if I'm not getting the truth from the people I've hired? How many times can lawyers go on strike, anyhow? I'm relying on people across the world whom I have never even met to help me with the single most important event in my life. It requires a lot of blind faith, to say the least.

I decide to visit a friend of Gregory's whom I used to know well—a friend I can't believe hasn't contacted me since Gregory disappeared with the girls. Vangelis owns a chic hair salon in Anchorage and is as close to a mutual friend as Gregory and I ever had. It was Vangelis who chided Gregory for his maltreatment of me early on in our marriage. We enjoyed double dates with him. He celebrated our daughters' births with us. Even after our separation and eventual divorce, Vangelis and I maintained infrequent but pleasant contact.

But today, I feel an unexpected chill from him. Vangelis walks away from his client to greet me. He tells me how sorry he is to hear about the girls, but when I share updates I've heard from the parishioners at the church about Gregory's gambling and cocaine dealing, his demeanor hardens.

"Who told you this?" His tone turns accusatory as he removes his apron and slips on his wool coat. Before I can answer, Vangelis excuses himself from both me and his client and leaves. I lock eyes with the woman left sitting in the salon chair. I wonder how long it will take before her color becomes officially overprocessed, and then I wonder when I lost my self-consciousness about spilling my guts in front of strangers.

❋ ❋ ❋

"Guess who's been dating Greg's friend Vangelis?" My too-busy-to-call friend Carol is gracing me with a phone call.

"How do you know Vangelis?" I ask.

"It only came up because he dumped her last week," she tells me, her speech more rapid than usual. "I knew she was dating someone, but she's never told me his name before. When she mentioned him today and said he wanted to marry another Greek, I asked her if he knew Gregory, and guess what?" Carol is barely able to contain herself.

"What?" *What! Get to the point.*

"Vangelis knows where he is. He's got his new address in Greece."

Here it comes: what I've been waiting for, and from a friend I'd have never thought to enlist for help.

"Where is he? What did she say?"

Carol tells me that her hairdresser is getting the address from home and will give it to her when they have coffee tomorrow morning. "She didn't want to talk at the shop, where other people could have overheard her, but she said that Vangelis sent them a box of clothes and toys in Greece, and that the address is definitely Greg's. We've got it!"

I love that Carol's joy mirrors mine. Soon I will have Gregory's address in Greece. And even if the attorneys' strike goes on longer, I will definitely have a starting point once it's over—a place where a private investigator can begin the search.

"Can I call you tomorrow afternoon?" I ask Carol. She tells me she'll call me as soon as it's over.

I can't wait. I will finally have some good news. I write down our conversation on some blank typing paper. I've been trying to keep copious notes about the recovery process to keep the details fresh so it'll be easier to retell the stories to the girls one day.

Though it's been only five months since they went missing, I imagine that the girls now probably look and sound completely different: sprouting adult teeth in place of their baby teeth and speaking a new language I don't know. If much more time goes by, will they know me when they see me? Will they forget me?

It takes all the restraint I have to wait until two o'clock the next day to call Carol. I'm a little dismayed that she hasn't called me yet.

Carol answers the phone with a flat tone, and I can tell she's dreading talking to me. "It's not good," she says. Vangelis and Carol's hairdresser have reunited. The coffee date was subsequently canceled.

My thirtieth birthday is on August 11. I've dreaded celebrating it without the girls. Birthdays for single mothers aren't much, in my experience. I don't have a mom or a dad to make a fuss, to send money, or to bake a cake, but at least I've had my daughters. Now they're gone, too. I wish there was some sort of fast-forward button I could push that would speed me right through my birthday and through the holidays.

When I arrive at work, there are gifts and flowers awaiting me from my coworkers. I get calls and e-mails all day long wishing me a happy birthday. When I return home, my next-door neighbor comes over promptly. "Can I take you to dinner on the Harley?" he asks. "It's not a date—just neighbor to neighbor."

I agree. What else have I got going? He's a great guy, and he isn't trying to date me. Old enough to be my father, he belonged to a biker gang in his youth. He feels sorry for me. So do I—at least we've got that in common.

After some Mexican food and light conversation, it hits me like a lightning bolt. I bet Gregory will have the girls call me on my birthday to lord their kidnapping over me. Nothing would make him happier than to hear my anguish on my birthday. The idea that I'm missing hearing my daughters' voices is all I can think about now, and after I tell my neighbor, we're back on the road in no time.

I have fifteen voice mails to wade through. "Hey, it's Ken. Happy birthday . . ." "It's your sister. Call me!" "It's Julie. Happy thirtieth!"

None of the messages are from my little girls. I'm the receiver of much birthday love, but my daughters remain mute.

I have to get out of the house. It's 8:00 P.M., still early enough to be light and sunny out in Alaska. I get in my car and go for a drive. When I see the neighborhood nail salon is still open, I quickly pull in.

I've thought about getting acrylic nails put on for a while now. My lifelong habit of nail biting has only worsened recently, making writing and phone dialing very painful. It hurts to affix acrylic nails to my swollen fingertips, but I hope it will help me stop biting altogether.

"Do you have an appointment, hon?" the receptionist asks. When I tell her I don't, she asks my name so she can write it in her appointment book.

"Lizbeth Meredith," I tell her, and we both notice when the only other nail client, a pleasant-looking woman in her midfifties, with short blonde hair, whips her head up to look at me.

"I'm Sid Jewell," she says. "I'd shake your hand, but I'm soaking mine. I'm a detective in the Crimes Against Children Unit. I know about you."

Unbelievable, the timing. She explains that she's just returned from a conference on missing children and hoped to meet me one day. "I don't dare say anything to Karen," she says, referencing my assigned detective. "She gets pretty protective about your case."

Detective Jewell says that she's very close to retiring and doesn't have anything to lose by letting me know what's going on with my case. I open my mouth to tell her about the chubby-beaver detective but close it before I sideline the conversation.

"She knows your ex-husband," she tells me, referring to Detective Rose. Detective Jewell says that months prior to the abduction, Greg called Detective Rose directly to introduce himself. He'd gotten her name and number from a mutual friend. He told Rose that his children were at risk of being abducted by their mother, and that he wanted to know what he could do to protect himself. She advised him of his rights over a number of phone calls, and they developed a rapport.

"She likes him," Detective Jewell says. "He set up the abduction with the information she gave him, and she didn't want to block his way when he took the kids. He's a smart guy, that one."

He *is* a smart guy, but I'm not too bad myself. I feel vindicated. I knew something more was at play besides my detective not liking me. My mind races with possibilities. *What can I do with this information?* Detective Rose's supervisor was pleasant but dismissive when I spoke with him about my issues with her, and I'm at a place finally where I don't need Detective Rose to move forward. But I'm angry, and that anger seems to be gaining momentum.

To the outside world, I look like I'm doing all right, since I refuse public demonstrations of raw emotion. Friends and coworkers alike shower me with feedback: "You're doing so well," and "I don't think I could manage as well as you if it were me." Sometimes the words feel like an accusation. And then, every once in a while, usually when I'm alone, I snap.

One sunny September night around bedtime, I'm driving home after dinner at a friend's house. As I hum along in my old Ford Taurus, I see a man dragging a woman down the sidewalk by her hair. At first glance, I think it's a stranger assault. Only when I roll down my windows and hear her screaming his name do I realize the woman's partner is assaulting her. I point my car straight at them and slowly drive onto the sidewalk. The man releases his grip, leaving the woman to fall in the grass. I continue following him in my car as he runs from me. *I have nothing to stop me. I could run him down, and it wouldn't make a difference to anyone.* The man begins to yell as he runs. The woman cries out, "Don't hurt him, please. I love him!"

I would be lying if I said that scaring this man spitless is less than wonderful, but it's also crazy, illegal, and completely pointless. I must be losing my mind. I roll the window down and give them the crisis line number at my work, then drive off, leaving them clinging to each other.

When I get home, I call my therapist's office and leave a message to schedule an appointment.

It's early October now, one of my favorite times of year. The leaves are gold, the sun sets at a reasonable hour, and the temperature hasn't become unbearably cold yet.

After work, I rent the movie *Eleni*. Inspired by the nonfiction book written by Nicholas Gage, the film illuminates the strength of his Greek mother, who ultimately sacrificed her life to the communists during World War II to give her five children the opportunity to live in America. The story follows Nicholas Gage's adult journey back to Greece to find and kill his mother's murderer. I so love the story that I gave my second daughter the middle name Eleni.

Maybe Mr. Gage will have some ideas. I do an Internet search from home, and twenty minutes after the movie ends, we're talking on the phone. He is an older man now and is not pleased that I've bothered him at home. I tell him that I named my youngest daughter after his mother and then stammer out my saga, realizing in the middle of it what a bad choice this was.

"I'm so sorry," I tell him. "I had no business looking you up. I just feel somehow that if I keep trying to move forward, I'll stumble on the one thing no one's thought of that will open the door to bringing the girls home. This was a dumb idea."

I'm dying to hang up. I'll bet he's dying for me to hang up. Mr. Gage hasn't any tips to share, but he is kind. "Good luck to you in finding your daughters. And it's much later here than in Alaska, just so you know."

Talk about overstepping my boundaries. I've invaded the space of a sweet stranger and amazing author late at night, as though my crisis has given me the right. It was plain rude.

"Do you know why you're so angry, Liz?" my therapist, Paula, asks me. She has on a tie-dyed jumper and wears her long gray hair loose around her shoulders. I wonder if she was at Woodstock.

Of course I know. My daughters have been abducted as payback for my leaving my violent marriage four years ago. Instead of getting to enjoy the fact that I'm working in a meaningful career after graduating from college and getting off public assistance, I'm having to turn the earth upside down to find my girls, who are innocent victims of their father. After years of fighting to find funding to get an education, fighting to stay alive on a meager budget, fighting to stay awake around the clock to study, fighting to keep us safe while we lived in low-income housing, and fighting to create a sense of normalcy for my kids when I should have had family to help, I'm living in an empty home. And instead of having government officials and local law enforcement work together handily to resolve this crime and, at the very least, be an asset to me in bringing the girls back in one piece, I'm fighting the corruption and deficits of our criminal justice system while the Greek lawyers are on strike.

I am so tired of fighting.

Paula understands but cautions me against complicating things further with my dysfunctional responses. "Of course you're angry, and that's okay. You'll have to accept that in yourself, but this isn't a license to go off on others or bleed all over them with your open wound."

I know she's right. I've been creating more problems for myself with my rage at a time when I cannot afford to alienate anyone.

Paula assures me that she doesn't want me to shut down or pretend everything's all right when it isn't.

"What you'll never hear from me are 'at least' comments," she says.

I don't understand.

"Let me give you some examples. 'At least your kids were snatched by their dad, not a stranger,' or 'At least you're young and can have more kids.'"

How does she know what people have been saying? I'm impressed.

"What I want you to do is to be in this moment. Be authentic. You can look at your situation and feel your feelings and stop fighting them. Notice your feelings and accept them, and remember to breathe. Breathe deeply."

Paula asks me if there are any spiritual practices or beliefs that help me.

Ever since I was a girl, I've had unshakeable faith. Maybe my mom helped cultivate it in me through her interest in religions and the occult, but I've never doubted the presence of God. In college, I threw myself earnestly into a fundamentalist-based college fellowship. I became part of a tight-knit community, a pseudo family, that taught me much about compassion and sacrifice—until I broke one of their many rules by marrying Gregory and then broke another one by divorcing him. Then, I *fell away*. This pseudo family that had replicated my real family seemed to disappear almost entirely. I think they worried that my sin was contagious.

The loss of that community never negated my feelings about God, but I have been more distant in my day-to-day practice, and I know better. People are fallible. People create religions and rules to serve their needs. God is not responsible for human shortcomings, and I need to find some comfort.

"No matter what you're going through, there are things to be grateful for in the process," Paula says. "I'm not saying you have to be religious, but I want you to be conscious. There are good things that are happening in the midst of this crisis, and you don't need to wait until the girls are successfully back to take stock of them. Between now and our next appointment, I want you to spend some quiet time thinking of what you're grateful for right now that's helping. Can you do this?"

I agree to and tell her I'll schedule another appointment as needed.

Before I go to sleep that night, I kneel by my bed, close my eyes, and give thanks.

Dear Lord, thank you for allowing me to be tested as a girl so that I have the backbone for this fight. Thank you for allowing me to be free of close, dependent connections that would blur my focus. Thank you for giving me my daughters and helping me know real love. Thank you for teaching me through my own abduction and alienation from my dad how damning it is for a child, because it's multiplied my energy to recover my daughters. Thank you for giving me the gift of discernment so that I am now quicker to figure out whom to trust and whom not to, who is toxic and who is healthy. Thank you for giving me the gift of oral and written communication, which will help me in sifting through this steaming pile of poo. Thank you for the fact that I'm no stranger to missing meals and having financial hardships so that I can withstand the tough road ahead. I have much to be grateful for. Amen.

Chapter 13

A YEAR GOES BY

Nine months. My daughters have now been missing for nine long months.

In nine months' time, I could have completed half of my graduate degree. I could have trained for a triathlon. I could have had a baby.

But since my life is on hold while I wait to hear from my lawyers that it is time to go to Greece, it is impossible to do anything of substance. And then finally, on December 28, 1994, more than ten months after the abduction and three days after the loneliest Christmas of my life, the Greek courts rule to recognize and enforce the American custody order.

I am ready to pack my bags, but the Greek attorneys set me straight. "We have no idea where the girls are at this time," Mr. Pappas tells me by phone. "And there's no reason to get the investigator on it just yet. Maybe around Easter here we'll have him look, but my brother and I are not ready to focus on your case as much as we would like to. We'll need to wrap up another case we're working on, and if the investigator finds the girls now but then they move to another area, what good will that do us?"

So, in order for me to get my children back, the moon will need to be in the Seventh House and Jupiter will need to align with Mars. Then the legal systems in America and in Greece will have to be simpatico precisely when my Greek attorneys have room in their busy schedules and when the private investigator has located the girls.

The odds don't sound too good. Plus, even if there is a trip to plan a few months out, I will need more money than I can possibly squirrel away at my job. Much more. Already, the costs of translating legal documents into Greek, plus the retainer for the Greek lawyers, are in the thousands. Add to that the price of a round-trip plane ticket to Greece, hotels, and more legal fees, and bringing the girls home looks even less likely. It's just as well that the lawyers aren't ready for me; I'm not ready for me, either.

I'm a thirty-year-old college graduate, yet I am needier than ever.

Do I mind asking for help? Memories from my recent past come flooding back. In one, I am standing in line at the supermarket with my sleepy daughters in the cart, both still in diapers. I'm so embarrassed to be using food stamps that I keep the girls up well past their bedtime for our weekly shopping trip to avoid public scrutiny, but on this particular night, it does not help. When I reach the front of the line, the checker seems to make a point of spreading my food stamps out in view of all, before she slowly counts them. A grubby man in a baseball cap and sweatpants leans close to me. "I wish I could pay for *my* food using food stamps." He grins, looking behind him for approval from his friend. My cheeks burn. I look down at my feet as my groceries are bagged. I say nothing, but I, too, wish that he could pay for his food using food stamps just once.

Some people feel entitled to say anything on their minds to someone down on her luck, and here I am, about to invite that kind of feedback all over again. It cannot be avoided. Getting the girls back home is a campaign, I tell myself, and I need to raise money if it is to be a successful one.

Ever since the *We Alaskans* story hit the paper, a steadfast group of people have asked how they can help. Some I know, some I do not. I've taken their names and phone numbers down, and after the New Year's holiday, AWAIC's development director volunteers to mobilize them for a variety of moneymaking opportunities.

"Sure, I'd love it," I hear myself saying insincerely. "Thanks so much. I really appreciate your help." *And I do appreciate the help, just not all of the commentary that comes with it. God, please keep me from snapping at the next do-gooder who says something stupid. Like the woman who asked if I should have enrolled the girls in tae kwon do to prevent their abduction, or the guy who wondered aloud whether I was inadvertently the cause of their disappearance.*

Then, as though they can hear my thoughts, I am racked with guilt. It's not my intention to be ungrateful, but I am not an extrovert by nature. Being the center of attention and sharing the intimate details of my crappy life in a group setting leaves me feeling naked. And then asking for money on top of it all makes me feel completely powerless. Naked and powerless.

But I've been the recipient of extraordinary giving before, and if I've learned anything, it's that the people who look like they have nothing to give are the ones who offer everything.

❊ ❊ ❊

I never believed in Santa Claus as a child, and the only Christmas tradition I stuck to as an adult was to fall into an annual fog of depression, around the end of October, which lifted just after New Year's. So when my landlord, Victor, told me in December 1991 that my new next-door neighbor called himself Santa Claus, I wasn't especially interested.

I was studying around the clock so I could finish my bachelor's degree in journalism and get a job before Marianthi got old enough to realize we were on food stamps. The girls were two and four, and we had been living on our own for more than a year. Nearing graduation should have been cause for celebration, but I was filled with dread. Gregory could not handle my independence, and the stronger and more independent I became, the more frightening his efforts were to keep me down. When I didn't respond to his liking, he extended his tactics to include our daughters during his visitation. Marianthi would give me a full report:

"Daddy says you're going to die and you're going to hell."

"Daddy says you're going to meet someone else and leave Meredith and me."

And finally, "Daddy says he hired someone to kill you."

I worked with the girls' counselor to do damage control as best I could and stayed focused on my classes. *Time-limited stress*, I told myself. Soon, I would put this mess behind me. Finish college. Get off assistance. Rent a nice home with a yard for the girls and me.

An unexpected ring of the doorbell broke my concentration one evening after classes. My new neighbor brought over a plate of warm sugar cookies. The girls were thrilled.

He really did look like Santa Claus. He stood about six

feet tall and had a long white beard, rosy cheeks, and a large, round belly. He looked to be in his sixties and wore a red-and-black-checked flannel shirt and faded jeans. I looked down and saw that he was barefoot, despite the freezing Alaskan temperatures outside. His toes were red and swollen, and he had long, yellowed toenails. He put his cigarette out when I invited him inside for a cup of coffee.

His name was Chuck Emplit. Medically retired, he had worked as a cook. Cooking and baking were still his passion. He said he had never married, had no children, and had no living relatives. "I'm not lonely, though," he said, probably noticing my concern. "I play cards with Victor and the guys on Saturday nights. Great group around here." Chuck would be moving from his two-bedroom apartment next door to a studio apartment in the same complex as soon as one became available in order to save money. But until then, he assured me, he was available if we ever needed anything. "Don't forget, girls," he said before leaving, "I'd like for you to call me Santa."

Every day when I returned home from classes, I had to pass by Santa's living room window to get to my own apartment. And every day afterward, approximately five minutes later, he was at my door—holding some special dish he'd cooked for the girls and me—waiting expectantly for me to invite him in for coffee. I always obliged, silently stewing at times, but coaching myself to be thankful for the company and the food. The girls were always delighted to see him, and by our second cup of coffee, I was too. We certainly ate better meals with him than we had since I had become my family's primary cook; they were a welcome diversion from my meals in a can. And it was obvious by his smiles and laughter that the visits meant a lot to him.

When Christmas came, less than a month after we'd met, Santa brought me a wrapped present. I felt horrible. I had nothing to give him, but he didn't care.

"Me and the guys were talking at cards the other night," he explained. "We were wondering why you haven't remarried yet. 'She's not ugly,' one of them said. 'She doesn't seem too unpleasant. Anybody would love those girls of hers.'"

He thrust a package into my hands. "We all pitched in," he said. I unwrapped the gift: *Better Homes and Gardens New Cook Book.*

"I think it'll really help," he said, grinning.

If only it were that simple. I committed myself to learning to cook after my college graduation that May and having Santa over for dinner, for a change.

The next month, I began a killer schedule in school, taking seven classes and one lab. I tuned out everything around me except my studies. Sleep became nonexistent on weeknights. The children received little attention.

I had grown almost nonchalant about Gregory's unexpected appearances around my apartment complex in the late evenings. I had even learned to sleep through some of the ruckus he created as he attempted to look through the curtains of our apartment. Victor was not so oblivious. "Your ex has been creeping around here again," he informed me over the phone. "I saw him on the balcony. Young lady, you've got to do something about this. I would hate to have to evict you, but I'll do it before I'll find you and the girls dead in the apartment." I dismissed his threat as an over-the-top response to watching too many episodes of *Cops.*

Close to Valentine's Day, Gregory must have decided to verify whether I had a new sweetheart. As the girls and I slept peacefully inside the apartment one night, he crept by Santa's apartment on his hands and knees until he reached my living room window, where he stood up slowly and began to pry the window open.

"You should have seen your ex when I threw open the door

and ran at him with my shotgun," Santa laughed the next morning. "He just scurried away into the night. I don't think he'll be giving you trouble again anytime soon, Liz," he said proudly.

After classes that night, Victor called me. I braced myself for another eviction threat, preparing an argument against it when he began. "Santa's decided to stay put in his apartment, instead of taking the smaller one. He told me he believes he's needed right where he is—with you and your girls. I told him he's nuts—'On your fixed income, you could use the savings'—but he would have none of it."

I went next door to confront Santa immediately, but he downplayed his role as our guardian angel, saying his extra bedroom came in handy. He wouldn't budge.

Santa and I continued our regular visits until around Easter time of 1992, when he was diagnosed with lung cancer. He shut his blinds, shut off his phone, and shut everyone out of his life. I stopped by to visit him, but he didn't invite me inside. He was smoking and listening to the radio. I was clearly interrupting his day, and he did not want to talk. From that day forward, I saw only the image of Santa through the blinds, his limp, overmedicated fingers holding a cigarette, the tip glowing. Two nights in a row, his lit cigarette fell and burned a hole in his carpet, Victor told me.

Now it was my turn to bake. I left a plate of chocolate chip cookies on his front step and darted away, praying Santa would not open his door and actually want to talk. I simply did not know what I would say to him.

In truth, his accidental fire setting was beginning to scare me. I worried something would happen to the girls and me just as our lives were about to improve. All that work to put our lives back together, just so we could burn to death in our sleep? My imagination ran wild.

But we did not burn up in a fire. Santa continued to grow

thinner and more remote. I continued to bury myself in my studies. And the girls continued to ask when Santa was going to bring cookies again.

And then my mother called. I had not seen her in years, since she'd left the state for a volunteer position at Oral Roberts University, abandoning her house and her business to languish in foreclosure.

"I'm coming to see you graduate," she announced. She ignored my less-than-enthusiastic response.

"We don't have room for you, Mother," I replied coolly. We really didn't, and our tiny apartment was filled with what Mother loathed most: children.

"Oh, don't worry about me," she said. "I'm going to stay with my friends Betty and Andy. Remember them?"

"But I already have plans graduation night with Laura and Sue."

It had taken me more than a year to rebuild relationships with some of my childhood friends. My husband didn't like me having friends, just like my mother never liked me having friends. "They're not a good influence on you," Gregory would tell me. I went along with it to keep the peace and had just now earned my way back into my friends' lives. I didn't want Mother's need to be in command of the day to interfere with my well-earned evening off. Gregory had even agreed to take the children the Friday night of graduation so I didn't have to pay a babysitter.

"I won't interfere," she insisted. "I promise. I just want to see my baby graduate and take you to lunch the next day."

It was no use arguing. Mother was coming. I would simply have to make the best of it. It would not diminish my joy about graduating.

I got a 3.45 grade point average that semester, a higher GPA than I'd earned in any of the previous semesters when I'd had fewer classes. Just two days before graduation, Mother called to tell me her plans to stay with Betty and Andy had fallen apart. "I'll just stay at your place, but you won't even know I'm there. I swear."

Two days later, I knew she was there. I knew by the way Mother lay in the middle of the living room floor and watched television all afternoon, eating and then growling at the girls when their play interfered with her shows. I knew by the way she grew quiet when I received a telephone call, and then became snappish after the call ended. And mostly I knew from that familiar queasiness I felt when old fears gnawed away at my stomach.

At least the girls will be with their dad and away from Mother for a while, I told myself as I readied for my graduation ceremony. While part of me would have loved for them to be there, it was scheduled to last four hours, much longer than their young attention spans could tolerate. I just wanted to get it over with without incident.

The night of graduation, Mother groused at my friends as they formed a receiving line after the ceremony. Gregory unexpectedly appeared with the girls in tow and lurked in the background, wearing a navy pin-striped suit and carrying a bouquet of flowers. The girls, pressed into his knees to avoid being trampled by the hundreds of other graduates, looked tired and miserable in their long taffeta dresses. Feeling guilty for being the cause of everyone's discomfort, I cut short my plans with my friends at the jazz lounge, returning grudgingly to my Mother-filled apartment.

We got ready for bed in silence, until I heard whimpering coming from the apartment directly below mine. It was the unmistakable sound of a hurt child. I ran downstairs and banged on the door. It opened, and out ran the nine-year-old neighbor child with a small trickle of blood coming from his nose. "What are you doing?" I shouted at the adult male standing in the door, surprising us both. "He's not your property! You could be arrested for hitting him!" I knew the chances of this happening were slim, but I wanted to make the point. After we exchanged a few more words, I left. Mother, who had put on a robe over her pajamas, watched us from the stairs.

She said nothing to me as I passed her on my way back home. Finally, standing outside the bathroom door as I brushed my teeth, she said, "You think you're better than me, don't you?"

In truth, I did. Mother had beaten her own children until she left them or until they were old enough to get away, and no one had challenged her. That I had challenged the father downstairs felt like a personal affront to her.

Years of unsaid words spilled out. My hands trembled so badly that I shoved them in my pajama pockets for safekeeping and told Mother what I thought of her parenting, of her grandparenting, and of her attempts to regain control of me during her trip. I was terrified by my own actions but had passed the point of no return. "I'm so sick of living my life in fear. If you want to have a relationship with me, it will need to be built on mutual respect," I told her. "Otherwise, this is it."

She never spoke another word and left the very next afternoon after making me pay for my congratulatory graduation lunch. And that was that.

I counted my blessings. Mother was gone. The girls were healthy and safe. And I had graduated from college. Now it was time to find a job.

❊ ❊ ❊

As the children and I rushed past Santa's apartment in early August, Marianthi began to whine.

"Let's go see Santa, Mommy."

"Later, honey," I said, tugging on her arm while holding Meredith.

"But I need to see him. *Now*, Mommy!"

"Not now, Marianthi. Later." I felt bad for being so harsh with her. *We'll see him later*, I told myself.

By the time we returned home three hours later, emergency medical technicians were carrying Santa's lifeless body out of his apartment.

Somehow, Marianthi had known.

Marianthi and I cried every day for a week as we passed by Santa's apartment. I was sickened by my reaction to his illness and sorry that I hadn't given in to my daughter's pleas to visit him.

Ten days after Santa died, I received a surprise visitor. One of Santa's card-playing buddies was at the door with two large boxes for me. He handed me an envelope. Inside the envelope was the handwritten last will and testament of Chuck Emplit.

To Amy Leigh Baker, I give all my sewing and embroidery supplies, Sony portable cassette player, and Ruger 10/22 semiautomatic rifle.

To Terry Russell, I give my video games, clock radio, and Americana radio.

To Janice Baker, I give my collection plates.

To my next-door neighbor Elizabeth (sp.?), I give all of my cookbooks.

❖ ❖ ❖

Yes, I despise feeling like a charity case all over again, but I will need to embrace humility and open myself up to any and everything people are kind enough to share. So let the fundraising begin.

First, there is a fundraiser at Round Table Pizza. Weeks

later, friends from work sponsor a garage sale and donate all of the proceeds to the girls' recovery. Next, the beauty school where the girls and I get our hair cut donates a day's worth of profits. A chapter of the Anchorage Fire Department collects more than $1,000, and the Petroleum Wives Club donates another $1,000. And as the one-year anniversary of the girls' abduction looms, a friend I met through AWAIC offers to throw a fundraiser at a starter mansion on the south side of town, Anchorage's financial capitol. This one is be a big deal. Invitations are sent to a database of known generous donors and to friends and family members of each of the planners. A popular caterer donates food and services, and I am invited to give a talk just before items donated by artists and merchants will be auctioned off.

It isn't often in my small life that I have a chance to rub shoulders with a bunch of rich people. What shall I wear? What shall I emphasize during my talk? Will they relate at all to my story or look at me with fascination? This event gives me something fresh to gnaw on.

In the end, I buy myself a brand-new blue floral A-line dress with a matching earrings-and-necklace set. It costs only $50, but I feel transformed when I put it on. It gives me just enough of a lift to get through the evening as I shake one hand after another, easily forgetting my germ phobia and lack of social confidence. I am among friends, and it is with this assurance that I tell my story of rags to $10 per hour to rags again, as I've coped with Gregory's ongoing control, until, four years after our relationship ended, he stole our little girls in a final act of retaliation. Then I take some questions from the audience.

"Do you believe you will get your daughters back?"

Not too sure about that.

Without missing a beat, I answer with a smile: "Definitely."

Within two hours, the fundraiser nets more than $10,000. Perhaps more important, it expands the network of supporters I am accountable to—more people whom I don't want to disappoint.

Some of the new supporters cosign a loan for $5,000 to cushion me from emergency, since I have yet to build my own credit. It soon will be time to go to Greece, and I am committed to pinching my pennies hard so that the money will last.

It has been nearly a year since the girls were kidnapped. A year in the life of a child is huge. Meredith was four when she was taken. A year added to that means that she has already spent 20 percent of her life without me. Marianthi is already seven now. The longer they are gone, the less likely they are to return.

Reassurance from my Greek lawyers about the girls' returning does not come. While they've been hoping I will wait until summer to go to Greece, the Anchorage lawyers want me to go immediately.

"Lizzie, at the risk of being crude, possession is nine-tenths of the law," Michael Kreider tells me. "You need to get there soon."

March 13 comes, the one-year anniversary of the girls' disappearance. A Monday. My friend Julie calls me as I get ready for work. It was her birthday lunch we were enjoying while Gregory executed his stealthy plans a year earlier. I should have called her, but I'm not feeling festive. "Happy birthday," I say weakly, feeling bad for the trauma she might now associate with her birthday for the rest of her life.

"I'm sorry, Liz," she says, choking up.

I'm sorry, too. I give no pretense of being upbeat. My daughters have been kidnapped. What could possibly happen now that would be any worse? I give up focusing on work and let my mind go wild.

My plane could crash on the way to Greece.

I might accumulate so much debt that I can't afford to raise the girls successfully once they return.

One or both of the girls could be injured or become ill, and I won't be there for them.

They could die.

By the end of the day, I am ready to finalize my travel plans, with or without my Greek attorneys' blessing.

With the help of Lynn, Gregory's ex-girlfriend turned travel agent, I buy a round-trip ticket to Greece for $600 for the first week in May, half the usual cost. I locate some youth hostels listed in my *Let's Go Greece* book, in both Athens and Thessaloniki, for less than $15 a day. I intend to keep my expenses under $1,000 for the two weeks I plan to be there. One meal a day at restaurants, and pocket change for snacks at kiosks if my hunger becomes unbearable, will leave the bulk of the remaining money for legal and investigative expenses.

My coworkers surprise me at our staff meeting with some good-luck wishes and presents before I leave: a pocketknife, a book to read, money, and a gift certificate to get my legs and face waxed. The last gift is from a dear Southern woman who says she wants me to have one less thing to worry about as I focus on finding my children. I feel loved.

Shortly before leaving for Greece, I receive a letter post-marked from Rhode Island. I can't think of anyone I know in Rhode Island, but the letter is clearly addressed to me. I open it slowly. It's a newspaper clipping, and underneath it is a well-penned letter of explanation from my paternal aunt:

Dear Lizbeth,
Your father passed away weeks ago of end-stage
lung disease. I know he always loved you. Here is
his obituary. I thought you would like to have it.
Feel free to write or call me if you need anything.
Love,
Your Aunt Jonell

My friend Ira will be sad when he finds out. This is my only thought: Ira will be sorry for me.

Ira is a lawyer friend of mine I met in college in Bellingham. We attended the same church and college fellowship, and Ira was one of the first people I told about my missing father. I also shared with him my mother's stories about how my father tried to kill her and her later reversal of opinion and insistence that I find him before he died. Ira located my father by calling directory assistance in Kentucky and getting a phone number that had been in service for less than an hour. Ira proudly replayed the taped phone call he had with my father.

"Hello, sir. My name is Ira Uhrig. I am an attorney representing your daughter Lizbeth. She has been looking for you."

After a pregnant pause, my father broke his silence.

"Well, I wundered whar she wuz!"

One week later, I found myself in Kentucky, meeting my dad. Just before I left, Ira helped me to regain my birth name: Lizbeth Meredith.

I haven't actually spoken to my father since I left Gregory, five years ago. My stepmother thought it would be too stressful for Dad to know about the turn my life had taken, so she intercepted my phone calls and letters to him, and my father never initiated contact with me. Given that I didn't meet him until I turned twenty and saw him on only a handful of occasions, all of which I initiated, I've had too little time with him to grieve him now. I have exactly one shred of evidence to confirm his joy at my existence: a letter he wrote me just after I located him. I keep it in a Ziploc in my file cabinet in my bedroom. I pull the letter out. The ink is fading, and the handwriting is unmistakably the work of an old, shaky hand.

Elizabeth, 5-28-85, 1:34 A.M.
Saturday I went to Stafford airport to pay for your
ticket. Reservations did not tell me there would be
a $10 charge for mailing a ticket. So you will find
ticket enclosed.
    I haven't seen your picture yet, and I can't
wait. You are getting a tremendous response from
brothers to sister, uncles, aunts, and cousins. The
whole family, all the way back. I think it's so nice.
    Again, I thank you so much for making it
all possible. We are all looking to June 8 for your
arrival. Call me if you need anything. Collect. That
means next week, next year, and years after again.
I am so thankful and proud of you.
Good night.
Daddy

I remember at the time feeling crushed that my father mis-spelled my name yet delighted that he offered the promise of an extended family and a future together—a future that never quite panned out. But I can't wallow in this new loss now. There is no time to grieve my dead father.

The truth is, his death comes as a relief of sorts. One less loss to think about. Now when friends ask about my father, I can legitimately say that he's passed away, rather than say that he's intentionally or unintentionally frozen me out. Still, I am both surprised and delighted to be included in his obituary, listed as one of his seven children. I am the daughter of Kova Meredith. Now I have proof. It's only after I reread the obit-uary a few times that I see I'm listed as being from Arkansas. Close enough. At least my first name is spelled correctly.

My father's death gives me incentive to redouble my efforts. I also have incentive. I have to find my girls. Time is passing. I will never get this lost year back, but I can keep the rest of our lives from slipping between my fingers. I didn't know my father, but my daughters will know their mother. The worst thing I can think of is not that I will be permanently impoverished after finding my children, or even that they will die without me. The worst thing would be if the bond between us were forever broken.

I put the letter back in the envelope and begin rummaging through my closet for my carry-on.

Chapter 14

ALMOST DOESN'T COUNT

Three days later, I hop a ride to the airport to catch the red-eye, toting only my journal and carry-on bag. No sense in packing heavy when I don't know how long I will stay at any one location. The less I bring, the less I have to lose. Once seated, I take one last look around me and record the image in my brain before closing my eyes, just in case it's the last thing I ever see. Flying scares me senseless.

It's the first week in May, more than fourteen months after the girls' kidnapping, and days after the Greek lawyers have told Michael and Jim in Anchorage that they're ready to focus on my case. "Tell her to come to Athens," Michael Pappas says, "and from there, my brother in Thessaloniki will help her find her kids. We'll execute the court order the Hellenic courts have accepted, and Liz will return with her girls."

Most of the lawyer-speak occurs between my Alaskan lawyers and the Greek attorney in Chicago, who then downloads it to the attorneys in Greece. I've been updated when necessary, and I've participated in some teleconferences, but I'm careful not to call the Greek lawyers out of turn. I'll fax my questions or concerns to them—anything to save time and money.

My flight connects through New York and Germany. Nearly a full day after leaving Anchorage, I arrive in Athens early in the afternoon. Safe. Alive.

Athens has more than three million people, easily five times the population of the entire state of Alaska. The city is loud and smoggy, but I can't help notice that even from my view in the taxi, the magnificent sites of the Acropolis and the Olympic stadium are breathtaking. I am in another world.

I have been to Greece one other time, in the spring of 1988, with Gregory and ten-month-old Marianthi. I was twenty-three, and we were losing our home then, but Gregory insisted we could afford the trip and the opulent baptismal reception at a local taverna. I spent much of the three-week trip alone while Gregory played poker in men's-only coffee shops in Thessaloniki. When I wasn't alone, I was being followed by his four-year-old niece or being watched closely by his mother and other relatives as they motioned to me and smiled, speaking Greek to one another. But whenever Marianthi napped and Gregory's mother was there to watch her, I seized the opportunity to walk around the streets of Thessaloniki alone, peering in bakery windows and breathing in the smells of spanakopita, *tiropita* (puff pastry filled with several types of cheese), and other types of breads and cookies. I tried to memorize the sights and smells and sounds of Greece, not knowing whether I would ever have the chance to return.

Yet seven years later, here I am. I walk the streets around the hostel, inhaling the familiar smells of this country: oregano, garlic, and cigarettes. I feel instantly at home. These are the smells my children smell. They are hearing the language I hear, watching the same channels I watch. I am close to them again, on their side of the world. I don't know their exact residence in Greece just yet, but I will find them.

Back at my hostel, I shower and change into a long denim skirt and a short-sleeved shirt and vest. I had asked Dina what would be easy yet respectful wear in Greece: I need clothes I can wash in the sink of the hotel or hostel bathroom and that will help me fit in. "You don't want to show your knees or go sleeveless. No open-toed shoes," she said.

After dressing, I call attorney Michael Pappas, who gives me directions to his office, located in the heart of Athens.

I set off on foot. It's less than two miles from my place. Almost immediately, a man on a motorbike starts following me. He whistles and makes kissing noises.

"*Eme kherea,*" I say, hoping I've spoken the right words. *I am a lady.*

I am the only one who thinks so. Soon, he is joined by another man, on foot, who speaks Greek too quickly for me to understand. He, too, is gesturing and making crude noises. And then there's a third.

By the time I reach the law office, I feel like the pied piper of creepy Greek men, who look disappointed when I reach my destination.

The law office is smart and modern. Art, professionally framed family photos, and large plants are all around.

Michael Pappas himself looks smart and modern as he extends his hand and greets me in perfect English. His broad shoulders and handsome smile belie the fact that he must be in his late fifties or early sixties. His suit is obviously expensive, and I note how his younger employees regard him with absolute deference. He is the epitome of elegance, and I am impressed with his confident style.

Mr. Pappas directs me to see about getting passports issued

for the children at the American embassy. Gregory quietly received the children's passports three years earlier, just before the divorce was final, before the heavy restrictions on his ability to travel with the girls became part of the court's order. I will need to get passports issued to me so that once the girls are located, I can leave the country immediately. After I secure the passports, Mr. Pappas wants me to fly to Thessaloniki, where his brother, Panayiotis, has his own law practice. "My older brother is happy to be a liaison to you in Thessaloniki, should you need one, and has already enlisted the help of an investigator. You'll need to keep a low profile in Thessaloniki so your ex-husband doesn't take your daughters and run again. We'll be in touch."

I have one more question: "What can I do to blend in better with the Greek women? I think I'm wearing the same kind of clothes as the women I'm seeing but seem to still be attracting a lot of stray men."

Mr. Pappas only laughs. "You can't help it," he says. "They know you're an American, not by your clothes or by your coloring. It's your gait. These men know you're an American by how you walk, and to them, that means you are . . . how do you say? Promiscuous." He smiles and shakes my hand. "We'll be in touch."

I have been dismissed.

Hailing a taxi, I go to the American embassy and meet with a Greek staff member named Ionna. She is a careful listener and seems sympathetic to my cause. She encourages me to contact the Central Authority and have them get the Ministry of Education to conduct an investigation. They alone will have the record of my daughters' enrollment in school. Perhaps I won't need a private investigator for long after all. She tells me that contacting the media could be useful but discourages any attempts to pressure those in authority to publicly air dirty laundry. "Last year, a foreign woman came to Greece and picketed outside her children's school. The schoolteachers blocked access to her children. She got a lot of media attention and made a lot of enemies. She left alone, without her kids."

Ionna's story gives me goose bumps.

Ionna reminds me that aside from replacing my daughters' passports once I have regained custody of them, there is not much the embassy can help with.

"The American embassy, like any embassy, is a guest of the country in which it resides. We cannot control the Greek government and have no authority over how it follows the Hague Convention. However, if you as an American citizen violate the Greek laws, like by trying to re-abduct your children, we must work with the Greek authorities to see that you're prosecuted to the fullest extent of the law. Do you understand?"

I nod my agreement and ask if Ionna has the name of any local women's group I could contact. I need some sort of social support. Ionna gives me the phone number of a woman named Karla who is a member of the International Women's Group. She says Karla married a Greek national and moved from her home in Canada to reside in Thessaloniki, where she writes for a tourist newspaper.

I thank Ionna and decline the taxi she's offered to call for me. It's an unnecessary expense, and besides, I love walking.

"Be careful on the streets, Liz," she tells me. "There are men who flock to American women all over the place, and we've got a lot of gypsies who will try to surround you and take your money, too."

Wouldn't they be disappointed in my cash supply? I muse, and take the long walk, unmolested, back to my hostel, where I sleep like the dead.

The next morning, I fly to Thessaloniki.

Thessaloniki is the second largest city in Greece between East Europe and the Mediterranean. With just a fraction of Athen's population, Thessaloniki is warm and lightly windy, and it feels familiar to me. The prospect of finding the girls here is far less daunting than it is in Athens, and I find my youth hostel with ease, happy to find my room unoccupied by other guests.

First thing in the morning, I map out my path to the law office of Michael's brother, Panayiotis, and just a few wrong turns and a lot of catcalling men later, I find it.

The law office is small and undecorated, as though the space was rented only a few days before and there hasn't been any time to hang pictures or art on the walls.

Panayiotis looks nothing like his brother. He stands close to five feet ten and has a shock of short-cropped white hair. His skin looks freshly sunburned, and his smile is broad. He is bombastic where his brother is calm.

Panayiotis speaks caveman English ("Me Panayiotis, you Lizbeth") and relies on his daughter, Zeta, a petite, thirtysomething woman with a layered bob, expensive shoes, and a prominent nose, who is a lawyer in his firm, to interpret for him. Her best friend, Poppy, is the third lawyer in the office. Poppy is taller than Zeta and has long brown ringlets, fair skin, dimples, and a Lauren Hutton gap between her two front teeth. She looks as though she's constantly suppressing a giggle.

Panayiotis's name troubles me. It doesn't sound like it's spelled. Panayiotis. He laughs when I try. "You say *Pan*, as in Peter Pan," he tells me, "and *yoitis* sounds like *yotus*, rhymes with *lotus*."

He's funny. I like him already. Normally, I would never call an older man by his first name, but I'll call him Panayiotis to keep him separate. I have four lawyers, including two Michaels and two Mr. Pappases, so this will have to be the way I keep them all straight. So Michael is Mr. Pappas in Athens and Panayiotis is Mr. Pappas in Thessaloniki.

While copying my custody documents for Panayiotis, Poppy and Zeta pepper me with questions about my children. How old are they? How much time did they spend with their father before the abduction? Did they know much of the Greek language before the kidnapping?

Panayiotis shoots them a warning glance, so they invite me to lunch to get their questions answered. Suddenly, things are looking up for me.

Lunch in Greece is not the hour-long scramble I'm accustomed to as an American. It is an event to relish.

We sit outdoors in the sun at a small restaurant, and I watch in awe as Poppy and Zeta order dish after dish, along with retsina, Greek wine that tastes like white zinfandel mixed with pine tar. I ask for a small salad. *Must save money. This is not a luxury vacation*, I remind myself, and we agree to go Dutch, rather than split the final bill evenly.

Our waitress places our food in the middle of the table. Each of us receives silverware, and it's time for combat eating. I lunge across the table and spear my salad with my fork. Poppy and Zeta help themselves to my salad, and I in turn enjoy some of their chicken and potatoes swimming in olive oil and lemon; meatballs; and *horta*, a spinach-like dish popular in Greece. The retsina flows freely, and when we run out, the waitress appears with more. It's strange for me, drinking alcohol in the middle of the day without worrying about breaking the law or violating work protocols, but I'm in Greece now. We've traveled on foot, and all the businesses close for three hours at lunchtime here to accommodate the postfeast nap.

I like watching Poppy and Zeta, and I enjoy talking about something besides my missing children. Their voices grow increasingly loud and their hands gesture dramatically as they speak. Zeta lives with her parents, as most Greek adults do until they marry. Poppy lives alone in an apartment her family owns. They both belong to a theatrical group with several of their other young attorney friends. They are both single, both close to their families.

I sit back in my chair, fully relaxed, happy to watch my new friends. Poppy asks me, "Where are you staying, Liz?" When I tell her about the hostel, she wrinkles her nose. "Come stay in my spare bedroom. I have plenty of room, and my parents help me with expenses. It's settled, then! You will be my guest."

"No, I really couldn't." I can't believe how generous Poppy is. Zeta is smiling.

"It is settled, then," she says firmly, "and I won't take no for an answer. You will stay with me. I only need time to prepare the spare room."

And in the blink of an eye, my life in Greece has changed. I will no longer be living among the Greeks as the bereaved mother at the mercy of this foreign culture. I will live with them and become a small part of their community. I must be a good houseguest for Poppy. Moping, fuming, and gnashing of teeth will be done out of her earshot.

"Well, I would love to, but it will be for only a short time. I promise." I add, "Mr. Pappas expects this whole process of finding the girls will take a week, ten days at most."

Ten days later, my daughters' whereabouts are unknown. I am living with Poppy, and we've settled into a comfortable routine. I join her for breakfast in the morning and do the dishes after she leaves for work. Before lunchtime, I walk to the law office, a nice, brisk jaunt along the ocean, while Greek leches trail me. Once in the law office, I wait for Panayiotis to give me an update. He's hired a private investigator, and every day the three of us speak over coffees delivered to his office. Our conversations are brief, ten minutes at most, and then I take the oceanside walk back to Poppy's, stopping along the way to have a chicken gyro and an Amstel Light for the equivalent of two American dollars. When I reach her place, I settle in to read and reread one of the few books I've brought and write in my journal while sunning on her balcony. Poppy returns home from work and fixes dinner, usually some variation of rice and tomatoes and garlic that I love. She lets me make dinner for her once; from that point on, she is firm about being our chef.

Poppy has sticky notes on every surface of her apartment with words written in Japanese, the fourth language she's taught herself, and because she is so adept at foreign languages, she gives private language lessons sometimes after work. She gives me Greek language lessons, too, so that I will be able to speak with my girls when we're reunited.

Yasou. (Hello.)

Kalimera. (Good morning.)

S'agapo. (I love you.)

Trapeza. (Bank.)

I am not an enthusiastic student, but Poppy is patient and optimistic about my skills. "Great! You're quick," she says. And before I know it, I'm reading and speaking basic Greek.

Poppy invites me into her social circle as well, allowing me to accompany her to her theatrical group, where I meet Thanasis, a budding composer and attorney; Christina and Maria, two more lawyers, around thirty years old; and Christos, a lawyer and active communist. They are warm and welcoming and assume that I am simply an American tourist who has befriended Poppy, and Poppy and I do nothing to correct their impression, since Mr. Pappas expressly warned us about sharing too much with outsiders.

My new friends invite me occasionally to take part in their activities—plays, concerts, and group dinners. They speak English, and they love to laugh. I appreciate the departure from my current crisis, yet it feels wrong. My daughters have been kidnapped, and I'm out having fun.

Still, it helps me pass the time and avoid some of the sadness.

Each night before bed, though, it's impossible to avoid sadness. I think about the girls and how long they've been missing. Over a year and counting. I wonder if they think I have forgotten them, or if they think about me at all. And despite the fact that I'm closer in proximity to them and have a wonderful team of people helping me with their recovery, it feels like we are making no progress.

"You will find your children and return," Poppy yells out from her room, as if she hears my ponderings. "Of this, I am sure. My mother tells me each obstacle is for good, and I believe that."

❋ ❋ ❋

In time, I begin to piece together how I fit into the Pappas brothers' world. I assumed Panayiotis and Michael Pappas are law partners; they are not. Michael Pappas, the younger, richer brother in Athens, is only contracting with his older brother, Panayiotis, on my case. Panayiotis isn't making much money on it—a fact he reminds me of from time to time—but is forced to do all of the grunt work, since Gregory and his family are suspected to be living in or just outside Thessaloniki. The court filings, possible future hearings, all of the details, will have to be handled by Panayiotis. And since Zeta and Poppy are focusing their attention on me, Panayiotis's whole work world has been rocked by a case that will give him little benefit. I am a great inconvenience to Panayiotis.

❊ ❊ ❊

It's not until my third week that my impatience takes over. This stay, this situation, could go on forever: Out of the 10,080 minutes each week offers, I am spending only fifty minutes hearing about my daughters. Out of those fifty minutes, only about ten of them appear to have any substance. I still don't know where my girls are. I'm not sure what the plan to find them is. And I don't have the plan B I need to feel more in control when the unknown plan A doesn't work.

I don't have Internet access in Greece. It's not widely available to the public here, so I can't fill my unspent time looking at databases or reading articles that might help, or that would at least burn some time. I call Karla, the woman Ionna told me about. It's an awkward conversation at first, but she warms up to me when I tell her how I came to get her contact information.

"Come to our women's group," she says. "I can pick you up. I'm going to promote my writing at the next meeting, and I know the members would be interested in your story."

I decline the invitation. Mr. Pappas would kill me, and I don't know what of value I would accomplish for my children. Karla understands. "Let me know if you want me to write a story for the newspaper I work for," she says. "I think people, particularly the ones who read my column for tourists and expats, would really relate to it."

I am energized when I hang up the phone. A new friend. I call Poppy at work to tell her about Karla and instantly regret it. "Liz, does Mr. Pappas know what you're doing? I don't think he'd approve at all," she whispers sternly. "He's not in a good mood anyway. He and his brother have been fighting on the phone about your case. They're all talking on the phone now."

The "all" Poppy refers to is Panayiotis and Michael and

the private investigator. The private investigator Panayiotis hired found the girls once, in the small village of Tyrnavos in central Greece, where Gregory took them to visit relatives, but after all this time, he still has no clue where they live in Thessaloniki. Now, amid the passage of time, Michael Pappas is not happy.

"Bug the phones," I tell the investigator through Mr. Pappas in Athens, who translates.

"It is against Greek law," he reminds me.

Against the law. My children have been kidnapped. Isn't that against the law? Why should I care what is against Greek law?

"We live here, Liz," he reminds me before I get the chance to voice my objections. "Long after you go home, we will still live here."

I know he's right, but it doesn't make it any easier to hear.

Poppy takes the phone again. "I think they've got something they want you to do. Come to the office. I'll see you here soon."

"I'll be there," I tell her. I worry that she sounds worried. "Just please don't say anything about the call." I feel like a bad child. I'm thirty years old, and I'm still being told whom I can and can't talk to.

I slip into a sweater and my long denim skirt. It's become a uniform for me in Greece, but I don't mind. It's quick and low maintenance and doesn't appear to ruffle any feathers.

Is it my imagination, or have the gypsies and the leches multiplied today? During my first trip to Greece with Gregory, I was fascinated by gypsies, but now, as I walk along the ocean, I am accosted at every turn. By the time I reach the law office, I'm completely frazzled.

"Liz," Mr. Pappas says, "today we visit."

"Visit who?"

"My brother to explain." He dials Michael Pappas in Athens, putting him on speakerphone.

"Greetings, Liz," he says, in the same take-charge voice that Bosley from *Charlie's Angels* uses. "I trust you are doing well. We are all getting impatient with the lack of progress, so today my brother will take you to the district attorney's office and let you visit the American consulate alone to enlist their help in finding your daughters."

I'm all in. Until Michael Pappas continues.

"I do not want you to tell the consulate staff that we are helping you. So please do not tell them anything we've discussed about the girls being located briefly at Greg's family's home. If the staff knows of our involvement, they will be reluctant to help. You must go by yourself so they will take pity on you. Make them think you act alone."

I stink at lying. I don't like doing it. But if my attorneys think this is necessary to our success at moving forward, then it will be done.

The district attorney visit is quick. We find him in court—a short, sweaty man sucking a cigarette like a pacifier. He grunts his responses to Panayiotis without looking up, waving away the cloud of smoke to get a clear glimpse of us, before directing us to make an appointment if we want his time.

Consulate staff can see me in a few days, so on Friday I put on the only dress I have with me—a forest-green polyester garment that is slightly too large and falls just above my ankles—along with a touch of lipstick, and walk to the consulate. I'm looking more pale and tragic than usual.

Inside, I meet staff member Penelope Dimos, a short Greek woman with round cheeks and dancing eyes, and Robin Thomas, a Jane Goodall–look-alike American I can imagine roaming the Sahara in a dune buggy, camera hanging around her neck.

"We heard about your children from our embassy staff," Ms. Thomas begins. "I want you to know how sorry we both are."

This is the first time government staff has said something so kind to me, and I feel a lump forming in my throat.

"But I've placed a few calls," Ms. Dimos adds.

From her call to the Ministry of Education, Ms. Dimos has learned that the girls attend grade school in Oreokastro, an upscale suburb of Thessaloniki.

Oreokastro. We have a location name. Finally.

"They're in kindergarten and second grade," she continues, "and they're in good health." This, she tells me proudly, she has learned from the call she placed to the girls' school. *Uh-oh.*

My heartbeat quickens.

"Thank you so much," I tell her, as I catch my breath. "Is there anything else I should know?"

Ms. Thomas and Ms. Dimos exchange a worried glance.

"Nothing," Ms. Dimos adds, "because at this point, the staff member told me she would have to tell the children's father about my call."

"So what did you say in response?" I hear a small tremor in my voice. *Please let this be good.*

"Don't worry. I didn't say anything," she says. "I hung up."

"You what?" I cannot believe what I'm hearing. *Am I a moron magnet, or are government workers the dumbest creatures ever?*

"Well, I didn't want to tell them everything," Ms. Dimos says, shifting in her chair and looking to Ms. Thomas for help.

"These aren't easy circumstances for us to deal with," Ms. Thomas explains. "We don't handle a lot of child abductions. I'm sure it will be just fine."

My head is spinning. I knew it was a mistake not to level with them from the beginning. My lawyers are going to flip. I'm going to flip.

"I think hanging up may have sent all the wrong signals to them," I say. "I just hope Gregory doesn't take the girls out of school now."

Taking a deep breath, I rise from my chair. I could strangle Ms. Dimos. I could reach forward and wrap my hands around her chubby neck and squeeze with all my might. But it would not bring my girls back. Maybe nothing will bring my girls back now.

I choose not to choke her, but Ms. Dimos still looks like she might cry. There is no question that she is trying to help. Ms. Thomas squeezes my hand firmly. "We wish you the very best. Let us know if we can help you again."

You've done plenty, I want to say, but the words don't come.

There is no time for a meltdown. I can't make enemies of the consulate staff. I will need their help one day. I can't tell the Pappas brothers how absurd I thought it was to begin with to withhold information from the consulate staff. It would injure the Pappases' pride. As it is, Panayiotis will be very embarrassed to tell his brother about this catastrophe. My Greek support system might implode if I don't react carefully. I have to hold it together.

I walk back to Panayiotis's office, dreading his reaction to the news. This trip to Greece was for nothing.

The sun burns my eyes as it reflects off the sea, so I pull my sunglasses out of my purse and put them on. I usually avoid wearing sunglasses. They seem to mess up my depth perception.

A gypsy boy approaches me as I walk. *"Drachmas, parakalo?"* (Money, please?)

"Get out of here!" I shout, surprised by my own ferocity. He disappears.

While I replay the appointment with consulate staff, I am oblivious to the fact that I am being followed. Behind me, a man on a scooter revs his engine. Another lech. His kissing and sucking noises are loud. Too loud. I spin on my heels. "*Eme kherea*," I say. He laughs and continues with his kissing noises. I move closer to make my point in English. "If you continue to bother me, I will slap you!" I demonstrate what I mean by simulating a slap in the air, close to his face. But the combination of my compromised depth perception and the fact that rage exaggerates my gestures results in my right hand connecting hard with his right cheek.

I just hit a man. In a foreign country. In public.

We both stare at each other for a split second. "*Signome*," I say. (Excuse me.) I can think of nothing else. My children are missing. My lawyers have failed me. My consulate has failed me. My support system might leave me. And I am in a country where men think I am a whore and the gypsies think I am rich. Nothing is as it should be. So I slapped a man. Didn't he deserve it somehow?

A giggle escapes, more out of shock than amusement. My victim is not laughing. He spits right at me.

Off I run, as fast as my feet can carry me. My dress is too long and my shoes are uncomfortable, so I'm not fast. The scooter is even slower. I look back to see my harasser turned victim's angry face yelling something I don't understand. A few minutes later, I reach my dreaded destination.

"She did *what*?" Panayiotis's already red face turns redder. "This is not good news." He calls Michael Pappas in Athens and puts him on speakerphone, telling him the news.

"They did what?" Michael repeats. "Why would they do this? Whose side are they on, anyway?"

As the two brothers speak in Greek, I stare ahead in my chair. What a day. My faith has been trampled, and I have subsequently terrified a child and assaulted a lech.

I can't understand a fourth of what they say, but the tension between the brothers is palpable.

Poppy and Zeta appear to have temporarily ducked out. I don't blame them.

After he hangs up the phone, Panayiotis exhales deeply and phones Ouzounis, the private investigator. Ouzounis promises to go by the girls' school the following Monday, but he is not hopeful, Poppy tells me later.

"You'll get your children," Panayiotis soothes when he sees my despair. "Just be patient, okay?"

I nod and try to smile.

"Now, don't worry today. I have a plan. You come with me. My wife. Zeta. We go to beach. Beach house. Halkidiki. Two days. You feel better."

This time, my smile is easy. It is a generous offer, and I need something to look forward to. I accept his invitation. Poppy will probably be relieved to have a break from mopey me for a weekend. And I need the distraction.

Five hours later, Panayiotis picks me up at Poppy's. His lovely wife, an auburn-haired woman who is inexplicably comforting to look at, like a human quilt, is in the passenger seat. I sit in the back next to Zeta, who fumes at her father as he sings along loudly with his Three Tenors cassette.

Over the next two days, I enjoy feeling like a part of this family's life, and they care for me well. Mr. Pappas's wife cooks, Zeta and I suntan, and Panayiotis by his very nature entertains. Together, we eat meals, go for walks, and visit the ancient ruins in Halkidiki. I feel badly for my negative thoughts about the lawyers' efforts, and for enjoying my time in the most brilliant-looking beach location I have ever been to in my life, while my children are probably suffering. Has their father taken them further into hiding? What is his state of mind?

I take long walks on the beach. I'm so preoccupied thinking about my daughters that I barely notice a stinging sensation in my left foot.

When I return to Poppy Sunday night, she looks refreshed and sincerely glad to see me. I must have been wearing hard on her. We go to dinner at a local diner, and as she speaks, I feel surprisingly woozy. Poppy looks out of focus to me, and suddenly I feel hot.

"Are you okay, Liz?" she asks, midway through an update about her theatrical group.

I ache like I have the flu, but I know what a worrywart Poppy can be.

"I'm fine," I lie. "I'm tired is all."

I barely notice that the pain is increasing two days later, just after the investigator confirms that the girls have not returned to their school in Oreokastro. I call my Alaskan attorneys from Panayiotis's office. Jim Swanson doesn't mask his devastation. Michael Kreider, ever the pragmatist, tells me to come home. "Look, kiddo, it's like when I go bear hunting. If I surprise the bear or back him into a corner, he'll come out on the offensive. It's far more dangerous to keep up the fight at that point. Sometimes you have to realize when it's time to retreat. You'll try again, but it's not meant to be just yet."

Tears roll down my cheeks. I can't believe the feisty lawyer is telling me to give up.

"But the passage of time works against us. You've said it yourself," I argue, not ready to admit defeat. "Can't I see whether we can get the local media to help with finding him?"

"Trust me," Michael says firmly, "this just isn't the right time."

My trip is over. Mission not accomplished. After I hang up the phone, I begin the walk back to Poppy's. My left foot feels heavy. Each step becomes excruciating, and I take off my left shoe. My foot is red and slightly swollen. I stuff it back in the shoe and limp back. Poppy is just behind me, and we take a bus to dinner. I don't mention my foot pain because I see no need to worry Poppy unnecessarily. I play with my french fries while she gives me a snapshot of her day: Zeta went home early. Panayiotis was in a bad mood. Poppy wonders aloud whether she's doing a secretary's job, despite having a law degree.

My head begins to throb. *Am I having an asthma attack? Why is it so hard to breathe?* Poppy stops talking and looks intently at me, feeling my forehead with her palm. "Liz, you're burning up! Why didn't you say something?" Poppy pulls me up by my arm and leads me outside. My breathing becomes labored as we wait for a bus, which seems to arrive in slow motion. All of the seats are occupied, so we stand at the front of the bus in the aisle and grip the rails tightly as it weaves through traffic in the narrow streets. I hold on until I have no energy left. Then I collapse.

When I awake, I am in Poppy's apartment. Dr. Cassavas, Poppy's childhood friend, is now leaning over my swollen foot.

"It looks like a bee sting," I hear him tell Poppy while he prepares my steroid injection. "An allergy to a bee sting." My poor circulation only compounds my delayed reaction to the sting. Now, as I drift off to sleep, I hear the doctor tell Poppy that he might have to amputate my foot. I can hardly believe my ears. *My kids have vanished again, and I'm going to be an amputee.*

The next morning, I awake and pull off the blanket to view the damage. My left foot looks like a blackened pork loin, but it's still attached to my leg.

"Are you really going to cut it off?" I ask the doctor when he comes in to check on me. He only laughs. "I would not have said it in English if I was serious," he says. "I was making a joke."

Dr. Cassavas tells me that my foot is filled with staph infection. I won't be returning to Alaska anytime soon.

My problem quickly becomes Poppy's burden. Like a dutiful mother, she wakes several times a night for the next three days to check my fever and refresh the damp washcloth on my head. I can see the fatigue and worry reflected in her eyes, and her brown curls seem to be wound more tightly than usual.

I am nine years old, walking outside in the Alaskan summer in our big yard in Chugiak. I am with my two older sisters and my mother when I feel the assault. Something is pelting my face. I cover my face with my hands and start to cry.

Crying is risky business around my mother. She hates the sound of it and lashes out reflexively. But this time, when she sees my eyes begin to swell shut, she becomes a tireless nurturer.

"You're allergic to yellow jackets," she explains. I see the worry etched on her face. Mother keeps a damp washcloth on my head and caters to my every need. I revel in her attention. It's too bad I don't get sick more often.

I am on top of the world for the first day, slipping in and out of a peaceful, medicated slumber. Two days later, when Mother's compassion shrinks in direct proportion with my healing, I miss her, this gentle, loving woman I've only just met.

After a week of lying about Poppy's apartment, I hobble to a nearby kiosk for an American magazine. Two old grandmothers walk by, wearing black dresses and stockings to honor their dead husbands. Though I smile at them, I am jealous. I wish my husband had died. They both stop and stare at my black, swollen foot.

"Have you tried olive oil and garlic?" one asks.

I thank her for the tip and hop home.

When my fat foot heals enough, I resume my walks to Panayiotis's law office. As the days go by, I can't help but notice that his mood swings are becoming as expansive as mine. One moment, he treats me like a second daughter; the next, I am the elephant in the room that he speaks about and around.

"I have plan," he tells me one morning. "My brother tell you." He calls Michael in Athens and puts him on speakerphone.

"Good morning, Liz," Michael says. I marvel at his perfect enunciation. "I have decided that you should accompany my brother to meet with the consulate staff."

I try to imagine meeting with Ms. Dimos and Ms. Thomas after their fatal error. It sounds like a miserable idea. "The staff will accompany you and my brother to meet with the district attorney to find out the options you have to get your daughters back. Please know that this isn't the time to rehash what happened before. We're looking to the future. I trust you will do your best to cooperate."

Panayiotis and I look at each other with matching dread. This won't be fun.

I assume the consulate staff will fear this visit as much as I do, but Ms. Dimos and Ms. Thomas appear genuinely pleased to see us. We drive with them to the courthouse to meet with the district attorney, the same man who shooed us away before.

Panayiotis rambles, interrupting the consulate staff anytime they attempt to interject. He turns redder when Ms. Thomas or the district attorney speaks, and I hear him use the same phrases over and over again.

"He says he is not your lawyer, and anything he's done for you, he's done out of the goodness of his heart," Ms. Thomas explains, looking annoyed. "He says he's given you a place to stay, since you had nowhere to wash your clothes."

I am aghast. So is she.

"Where did you find him?" Ms. Thomas asks.

I look at Panayiotis, hoping he does not understand the question. Ms. Thomas speaks to the district attorney in Greek and warns me that Mr. Pappas sounds confused about the legal maneuver he is planning. She outlines three possible courses of action to address the children's abduction:

The consulate staff can contact Gregory and invite him to join us all in a discussion about the children's possible return home.

She can serve Gregory with a court order by mail. If he does not appear before the court within three business days to hand the girls over, he will be considered a fugitive.

I can press charges with the local police in the suburb where Gregory resides. A warrant for his arrest will be generated, but it will be good for only twenty-four hours before it dissolves, and will not be a priority for police.

"Will they at least look for my daughters that day?" I ask.

"No. Sorry," she says. And when the twenty-four hours passes, the police's fake quest for my daughters will be over.

Three hollow options. In the first, I can hope Gregory will meet us and work out a gentleman's agreement. In the second, we can give him time to beat a path out of town by serving him with documents through the mail. I favor the third option, but I have to consult with my lawyer before proceeding. And Panayiotis's words continue to replay as I leave. I am a burden, and he wants to wash his hands of the situation. How humiliating.

That night, I tell Poppy about my day. Zeta has already approached Poppy at work about placing me elsewhere, but Poppy won't have it.

"I have you here because I want you here. I love you being here. They just want to control all the details."

This is a brave woman. My presence threatens the peace in her work life and in her personal life, yet she refuses to be swayed.

"It's okay, Liz," she says. "My mother tells me each obstacle is for good. And I believe that."

I love Poppy's platitudes. I love that she repeats them, and I love that she believes them. I will miss living with her when I return to the States.

I call Michael and Jim in Anchorage; they have teleconferenced with the Greek lawyers. All four of the attorneys, from Athens to Chicago to Anchorage, agree that each of the three options the district attorney has provided would only damage the case further.

"Your visit is over," Panayiotis announces.

My children are now even deeper in hiding. My relationship with my Greek lawyers is fractured. Poppy will not be able to keep me in her home, since Mr. Pappas has told her I have to return to the States. I cannot afford to defy Mr. Kreider and Mr. Swanson without pissing away my Alaskan support network. And my left foot is still swollen and infected. Not at all the image I have created in my mind so many times before when I have pictured getting off the plane in Anchorage.

❖ ❖ ❖

It's June now, six weeks since I arrived in Greece. Poppy takes me on the city bus to see Zeta one last time before I leave on the red-eye tonight. I catch the eye of a little girl who looks to be around six or seven years old. Next to her is a little boy around the same age, and their mother is sitting next to him.

"I will bring two children home from Greece," I tell Poppy, only half joking. "They may not be *my* children, but I refuse to return alone."

Our laughter simultaneously fades when we watch the little girl snuggle into her mother's arms.

For now, my girls will have to remain in hiding with their father in Greece.

I try to talk myself into some perspective. Somewhere in the world at this exact moment, a mother's child is killed. Somewhere else, an elderly couple boards a plane for a dream vacation. Somewhere, a young couple stands at the altar, about to be married. Somewhere else, a baby is born. The world contains billions of people all caught up in their own important reality.

This brings no comfort.

Screw them all, I think. *My children will not be returning home with me.*

Chapter 15

REGROUP

The long flight home gives me a chance to regroup. I have a whole aisle to myself on the plane, so I stretch and elevate my left foot, still swollen from the bee sting. Returning alone stinks, and not just for me. I have failed my daughters, and who knows what kind of damage I've done to the life they had grown accustomed to at their Greek school? I've also failed my growing support network, who will expect good news when I get home. They will need to know that I'm unfazed and that this first trip was a critical part of the children's recovery process, not a waste of their resources. I've forged some lasting friendships in Greece that will be invaluable to the process later. So what if my children didn't come home the very first time I went to get them? I'll get them next time.

It's a hard sell, even for me. When the plane touches down in Anchorage, I'm glad to take a taxi to my empty house.

I have a night to rest before I tell the story of how my near-successful trip turned on a dime.

"Why don't you just join something?" my mother asks me.

I'm thirteen. This is my mother's solution for every problem that moving place to place creates for me. I roll my eyes at her as soon as I'm out of her line of sight.

You'd think I'd get the hang of it, moving around and making new friends. Other kids seem to, but I'm increasingly self-conscious. Almost overnight, my long straight hair has turned into a long Afro that I pick, instead of brush. My glasses are thick. My clothes are vintage, and my skin is pasty. My weight fluctuates dramatically in proportion with my binge-purge eating habits.

Like what? What shall I join? I've never played sports. I'm not clever enough for the honor society or the chess club. So where does that leave me?

It leaves me trying volleyball in the seventh grade in Chugiak. It leaves me running track in the ninth grade in Tacoma, a lap behind everyone else but still running. It leaves me playing junior varsity basketball in the tenth grade in Anchorage, traveling down the court unguarded, shooting the ball without impediment, only to realize that it's after halftime and we've switched sides.

These efforts leave me with a collection of Most Inspirational Player awards by the time I'm an adult, because that's what happens when you fail miserably and keep showing up. You become *inspirational*. That, and you learn the value of joining. You realize that when you're part of a team, no matter what your weaknesses are, the strengths of others can dilute them. And you learn that no matter how bad you feel about yourself, someone in the group can help identify the hidden strengths you didn't know you've had all along.

My mother never attends a game or a meet, but I remain undeterred. I will keep showing up. I am not a quitter.

The day after my flight home from Greece, I return to work wearing a brave face. Then I pass by the volunteer who covers the front desk in the morning. Lindsey, a married woman in her thirties who has mentioned before that she's desperately trying to have a baby, has attended the fundraisers for my girls in the past and always asks for updates on them when we're alone. Now she looks up from her phone call with a bright smile and questioning eyes. I try to smile back and shrug. Instantly she breaks eye contact and continues with the caller. Am I imagining it, or is she blinking away tears?

But I can push past this. Of course I can. I grab the stack of messages in my mailbox. Nearly all of them are requests from private companies and government agencies for a presentation on domestic violence. We're still riding the wave created by the Simpson and Goldman murders, and public interest in this epidemic for women is still strong. It seems everyone wants to know how. How to recognize the signs of domestic violence. How to protect employees when an estranged partner arrives at the workplace. How to encourage a sister or friend who is acting differently after meeting her new beau.

My workload has multiplied. An increase in public interest means opportunities for speaking, educational grants, and program development have increased—new outlets for my experience. And this work may be the one place that personal disclosure for the purpose of educating the public is completely appropriate, so the work often provides new interest in my own children's disappearance. The national spotlight on family violence helps me keep local interest in my missing daughters alive.

Working in the trenches of domestic violence feels good to me. It's familiar. Intuitive, even. It's not always good for those around me.

"Can I see you when you have a minute?" I know who it is without looking up from my desk. Hazel is my most senior employee, and as reliable as they come. Twenty or more years older than I am, she is an empty nester, who fills her leisure time with square dancing, quilting, and taking care of her coworkers.

"Sure." I say. "What's up?"

Hazel clears her throat and looks down. This can't be good.

"I just want to let you know I'm in therapy now."

"Oh," I say, not sure whether a supervisor is supposed to know this about her employee.

"That's okay," I say. "You don't need to tell me." *Please don't tell me.*

"It's about your kids," she says. "It's not your fault, but it's brought up some old family issues for me." Hazel dissolves in tears. "I've got a lot of abandonment issues that can't be buried anymore."

I'm not sure what to say. Shall I hug her? Send her home? I guess I can apologize for having my kids abducted, or for continuing to work afterward, but it won't help her. My mess of a life has upturned her orderly one.

"I understand," I tell her. "Let me know if there's anything I can do to help."

It's not as though I speak much about my missing daughters to my coworkers. Work is my escape, and I plan to keep it that way. Plus, clients considering leaving their own cruel relationships will be frightened into staying forever if they catch wind about my girls' disappearance.

The one constant reminder of my girls at work is the missing-children's poster from the National Center for Missing & Exploited Children hanging prominently on the bulletin board in AWAIC's lobby. Since the girls' last names are different than mine, no one will know they're my daughters—or at least that's my theory.

After Hazel's tearful confession, I meet with a client named Debbie, a forty-five-year-old Alaskan transplanted from the Denver area. She moved here with her second husband, a slightly younger intellectual type who works in forestry. Debbie is beautiful and aloof, and I get the impression she thinks the experience of being physically assaulted repeatedly by her husband is more embarrassing than traumatic. In groups, she sits far from the other women, like she's worried she'll catch a cold. Meeting with her individually is never pleasant, either. Debbie is prickly and defensive.

Following our appointment on Monday, I escort Debbie to the lobby. Group begins in thirty minutes, so she decides to wait and thumb through magazines. She looks up at the poster of my daughters. They look more like me than I realize. "Is this yours?" she asks angrily, pointing at the girls. *That's poor grammar.* "Are these your daughters?" she asks, her eyes moistening.

I could lie. I should lie. But the intensity of her reaction catches me off guard.

"Yes. Yes, they are," I say, trying to sound neutral. Professional. Anything but emotional.

Debbie pulls on her jacket and zips it, giving me one last, hard look before she leaves. I doubt I'll see her again.

If there are protocols about having one's children stolen, I don't know them. Given that my job isn't to tell women to leave or to stay in their relationships, I don't want to sway their decision by demonstrating all that they could lose if they left.

✻ ✻ ✻

Outside work, I do my best to function as a normal human with a whole life, rather than as a single mother who has lost her reason for being. Through work, I take classes in grant writing and sign language that fill my evening and weekend hours. I pound out my frustrations with the legal system at the gym. I go to counseling. And at night before bed, I create mental images of the girls getting off the airplane in Alaska, greeted by a host of our closest friends, who are, naturally, joyful. I can't imagine how the girls may have changed physically, so in my images they look pretty much the same as they did last year, just with longer hair and broader smiles.

I also stay in contact with some of the other left-behind parents from the Washington DC focus group through e-mail. Two of the members have been in contact with their missing children, and three others have made failed attempts to bring their children home. It's good to know I'm not the only one. Most of the parents have had contact with the abductors, and a few have gotten to talk to their kids, but I have yet to hear from Gregory.

Out of the blue, I get a message from him at work. He gives careful instructions to my coworker to have me by the phone on August 1 at 11:30 A.M. I've been back from Greece for a month already. Why is he calling now? And why should I take orders from him? I hate letting him be in the driver's seat, but maybe he's sick of living on the run. Maybe this will begin the dialogue we need to coordinate the girls' return. Or maybe I will simply get to speak to them.

I've heard that most abductors contact the victim-parent soon after the abduction. It gives them an opportunity to gloat and increase the misery of the victim-parent, and to feel out what the consequence for their crime will be. Have the police been called? Are lawyers involved?

Michael Kreider agrees to join me at AWAIC on the designated day. If anyone can keep me calm, it is he. He joins me in my office a few minutes early, and the call comes in at the precise moment Gregory specified. I put him on speakerphone so Michael can listen in.

"This is Greg. I want you to listen and listen good. I heard that you were in Greece recently. Not even the electric chair or a lifetime in jail would keep me from blowing your brains out if you ever come close to the girls again. That's a promise."

Click.

And there it goes. I hoped for dialogue. I got a monologue.

Are the girls healthy? I don't know. Do they even live with him? I don't know. All I got was another death threat.

There is no way I will follow Gregory's orders. It's not possible. I'm not sure how I will find them or how I will afford to keep looking, but I'll try anything.

Over the next few weeks, I reread Betty Mahmoody's *Not Without My Daughter*. I wonder whether I could do what she did and move to Greece semipermanently. Learn the language. Get a job. Hire an investigator. Find my kids. Stealthily re-create a relationship with them and then sneak out of the country and back to America.

A lawyer I know from work suggests I hire mercenaries to abduct the children and bring them home. For a mere $50,000, I can get a team of big, scary men to grab the girls from their father's clutches and deliver them to me, though maybe not all in one piece, and perhaps not during their first effort. Subsequent efforts will cost another $50,000 apiece. Nothing is guaranteed.

Or I can continue on as planned, doing things the safe, legal way. I haven't lost my case through the Hague Convention. My Greek lawyers have assured me from the start that they have successfully handled similar cases.

The problem is, I still have very limited funds. So I choose to save money for a second trip, rather than paying my Greek legal bills, which of course reduces my lawyers' incentive to work the case to my liking. They speak directly to Jim Swanson or Michael Kreider. On at least one occasion, I learn that Michael has paid them with his own money to keep us plugging along.

It's autumn now. I feel, with more anxiety than usual, the sunlight lessen and the temperature drop. Time is passing. I need to plan my return to Greece. The attorneys in Greece serve Gregory with the court ruling by publishing it in Greek newspaper ads, since we can't find him after the foiled recovery effort.

I call the attorneys in Chicago. They sound as frustrated with me as I am with them. "We're not ready to have you go to Greece just yet. We don't know where Gregory is. And we don't have a new investigator." The first one quit after the fiasco with the consulate staff, so a new investigator has to be hired. At their encouragement, I call Michael Pappas in Athens.

He sounds exhausted by me. "Please be patient," he says, before he gives me a quick update and says good-bye.

I *am* being patient. At least I feel like I am. The girls have been gone for almost a year and a half. How can I be more patient?

I need more time. More money. More patience. Everything I don't have.

I decide to write more. It's cheap, and it doesn't require patience. I write to my senators. My congressman. Television shows and magazines. I write in my journal. But it is my letters to Poppy that give me the greatest comfort.

10/95
My Dearest Poppy,
Greetings from Alaska, and best wishes to you and
your family.
I thank you so much for your help. I am
trying to keep my hopes up, but it is getting
harder. I don't know where my girls are or when I
might see them again.
How is Zeta? Are you dating someone? Is
there anything new to speak of in my case?
I send you my love,
Liz

Not long after, I get a reply:

11/95
My Dearest Liz,
I salute you and look forward to your return to
Greece.
Nothing has changed in Thessaloniki. I
continue my job at the law office and continue
teaching language lessons in the nights. Zeta sends
her love.
I do have some news: I have come into
contact with a private investigator who I think can
help you. His name is Manolis. He has promised
that for $12,000 he will find your girls and help
you safely reunite with them. He has worked as a
bodyguard in Athens and Thessaloniki, and, Liz, I
believe he can do the job.
Mr. Pappas has no idea that I have been
contacting the investigator. If he knew I worked

on your case, I would lose my job. This is for sure.
I ask you to please keep this a secret. Call me.
      I do look forward to meeting your girls.
Kisses,
Poppy

Poppy ends every phone call and letter with the same sentiment: *I look forward to meeting your girls.*

When Thanksgiving arrives, so does my seasonal depression, dimming my energy and confusing what bit of clarity I have left.

My Dearest Poppy,
Please forgive me in advance for my tone, but I feel
sometimes as though I am losing my mind. There
is still no progress with the lawyers in getting my
girls home. Mr. Pappas says to be patient and
wait. Mr. Kreider says that waiting will only make
things worse, and that time works against us.
      I am most interested in your investigator
contact, Manolis. Please give him my address so
that he can give me some quotes about the scope
and cost of his work. I will not tell anyone of this.
I do not want to cause you any harm. I just want
my daughters home safely.
      I send my regards to your family.
Yours,
Liz

Poppy isn't the only person I write. I write to my Greek lawyers, in Chicago and in Athens. I learn that faxing my attorneys in Chicago is much wiser than calling. It allows for the time difference and spares me the humiliation of asking them to do something for nothing. They can glimpse the fax at their leisure, instead of returning a phone call and billing me for it later. I want them to keep the girls in their thoughts. I fire off a fax requesting that a private investigator tap Gregory's brother's phone lines over an upcoming Greek national holiday. No response. I send a similar letter to Mr. Pappas in Greece. Again, no response. I call Jim and Michael, who confirm my fears: the passage of time weakens my case. "Possession is nine-tenths of the law," Michael Kreider tells me again. "And you ain't got it."

It's a call to action.

Manolis, Poppy's private investigator, gives me his quote by phone: for $12,000, he not only will find my daughters but will guarantee their safe return to me. He intends to whisk us out of the country by helicopter and says that he has a bulletproof vest for me to keep me safe from Gregory. Flamboyant, sure, but I admire his confidence.

Twelve thousand dollars is a lot of money that I don't have. The Pappas brothers have warned me against hiring my own investigator. "There are too many con artists out there who have no idea what they're doing, Liz," Michael Pappas said. "Trust me. In time we'll have a new investigator to work with. But we must pick someone we trust."

But they haven't picked someone. And I don't trust them enough to wait around for them. I wire Manolis a down payment but don't tell the Pappas brothers. Manolis calls to confirm that he has received the money and he has good news. "I've seen your girls," he says. It's almost too good to be true and too quick to be believable. Still, I am cautiously optimistic. There is a trip to plan, and everything else will fall into place in due time.

Heather contacts Congressman Young's and Senator Stevens's offices to inform them of my upcoming trip. She's been acting as my political liaison all along, and I'm grateful to have her in my corner. Senator Stevens's office contacts the State Department to ask for its support. In January, Senator Stevens's office forwards me a telegram it received from Richard Le Doux, consul general at the American embassy in Athens, in response to the senator's communication.

In that document, the consul expresses his concern that my intended actions would place my children at risk.

> *Greek government authorities have cooperated fully with Ms. Meredith in her legal efforts, and a Greek court has validated her custody order of the US court, in accordance with the Hague Convention on International Child Abduction. However, her attempt to have the court order executed by a Greek bailiff in May 1995 was thwarted when her ex-husband apparently discovered what was going on and disappeared with the children. . . . She was encouraged to keep the consul general informed of the case but has not contacted our office again.*
>
> *After receiving your letter, we asked Ms. Thomas to check with the local police; she discovered that they have no record that Ms. Meredith ever filed charges against her ex-husband. It appears from your letter that Ms. Meredith has decided to act on her own. . . . Although we would like very much to help, we have no police function in this country and cannot assure the safety of private individuals in Greece; moreover, we could not act in violation of Greek law, should the father obtain an emergency court order to reverse Ms. Meredith's actions. She might also call the Office*

of Children's Issues at the State Department,
which has wide experience in dealing in custody
cases and stands ready to advise parents in Ms.
Meredith's situation.

❖ ❖ ❖

The hair on my neck stands up. *Ex-husband apparently discov-*
ered what was going on. I do not appreciate the lack of account-
ability for my ex-husband's having *apparently* discovered what
was going on.

And I am faulted for not pressing charges. The State
Department's Office of Children's Issues earlier sent me a booklet that warned against pressing charges against an abducting
parent while attempting to invoke the Hague Convention,
since it could be "counterproductive and should be considered
as a last resort. You should also realize that the extradition of
the abductor to the United States is unlikely, and that neither
extradition nor prosecution of the abductor guarantees the
return of your child and may in some cases complicate, delay,
or ultimately jeopardize return."

Does the government really not know what the government has advised on this issue? And why have I sustained any
faith in them?

My fingers fly across my keyboard.

Dear Mr. Le Doux,
Rest assured I have no interest in handling this
case—my custody problems, as you referred to
them—illegally.

I summarize my efforts to legally seek my daughters' return, pointing out the dismal outcome of the consulate staff's assistance and the fact that I've been rebuffed by the Ministry of Justice and the district attorney's office.

I would like to add that my experiences to date with the Office of Children's Issues have been less than illuminating as well. Initially, I was told to cooperate with the local police in Alaska after I submitted the application for the Hague Convention. When I did and a felony warrant was issued, a staff member at the State Department reacted in horror, saying that now the chances of the children's being returned were slim and I should ask the police to drop the warrant. The same woman said that she looked for months on a map of Greece to find a town that did not exist, in an attempt to locate my ex-husband's family. She said she got the name of the town from my attorney in Alaska (which he wholeheartedly denies.) Perhaps. But Greece is a small country, and a lunch-hour break spent looking on a map should correct such a problem. My complaints have been handled in general as "it's not my fault; it's someone else's."

Surely, we can do better.

I look forward to your input and assistance. I have every faith that this issue can be handled in an organized and intelligent manner, paving the way for the next similar case. I participate in the American Bar Association's International Child Abduction Project and am hoping that Greece will

one day be an example of how these cases can be
resolved efficiently.
        It can happen.
Sincerely,
Liz Meredith

I'm tired of having to apologize to different government agencies for the mess I'm in. I am sorry that I don't have any money to pay the bills, and I'm sorrier still that I don't have a rich family to rely on. I am sorry that my government officials don't have the balls to stand up for me. But with my sorrow comes gladness. The intentional gladness I've learned in therapy. I can sleep on the streets if I have to. I can adapt like no one else I know. I'm glad that I don't have hovering parents or a trust fund to weaken my character, or a new husband to divide my interests or weaken my resolve. I'm even glad that I'm a kidnapped daughter whose father forgot to keep looking for her. All I have is my love for my daughters and a belief that love is enough. And I have an amazing support network, a crisis-response team that will do whatever they can to help, so long as I keep the faith.

I complete the arrangements for my second trip to Greece, and this time I tell my friends and coworkers that I will not return to Alaska until my girls are with me. Enough time has passed. It is time to bring my daughters home.

Chapter 16

GOODBYE MARTYDOM

Keep your head, I tell myself as I board the plane on a cold February night. *It will all work out. Just don't step on any more toes in Greece.*

The Pappas brothers are so incensed at my decision to hire an investigator on my own that they've quit the case altogether—a fact that they relayed to the Chicago lawyers, who called just before my taxi to the airport arrived.

I get it. I've second-guessed them. I've gone around them to work independently. I've hurt their pride. I've been a headstrong, pain-in-the-ass American woman. But everything I've done has been with the intention to bring my daughters home. That has to be worth something.

Greek men of their generation are used to calling the shots. I don't know if it's the same for my private investigator, who's at least twenty years younger than the lawyers, but I know I can't afford to ruin any more relationships.

By the time I reach New York to change planes, the Chicago attorneys have talked the Pappas brothers off the ledge, and I now have legal representation and a private investigator. "Mr. Pappas wants to meet with you and Manolis immediately when you arrive in Athens," one of the Chicago attorneys tells me when I call him from a pay phone at the airport.

Whew. Crisis narrowly averted.

* * *

My private investigator, Manolis, and his entourage, complete with a driver and an interpreter, meet me at the airport in Athens. I can tell by the way he's scrutinizing me that I'm not at my best. After two days of travel, I'm tired, hungry, and unshowered. I probably look homeless.

Manolis looks like a portly Keanu Reeves, with dark, spiky hair and almond eyes. He gestures for me to follow him. "We take you to bank to make payment," the interpreter tells me. "Soon you will owe more."

This isn't the start I was hoping for.

A quick ride after the money exchange takes us to Michael Pappas's office. I'm surprisingly relieved to see his familiar face.

"Liz," Mr. Pappas says, as he extends his hand to shake mine, "you look lovely, as always." I admire his efforts at pretense, however disingenuous. I sign the document he's prepared, which holds him unaccountable for Manolis's actions.

"Manolis wants you to know that he's picked a hotel for you," Mr. Pappas says, smirking. "He'll be staying in the room beside yours."

"For security," Manolis adds. Now he speaks English.

It is six more hours before I can finally settle into the small hotel room in Thessaloniki that Manolis and his crew take me to. Manolis, true to his promise, is in the very next room, and he knocks on our common wall to let me know that he's there for me.

❖ ❖ ❖

The sound of someone knocking at the door interrupts my sleep.

"Liz, it's me. I Manolis," he yells loudly, "Get dressed, yes?"

After I throw on my robe, I open the door. Manolis outlines the rules of our working relationship: I am not to leave my hotel room without him. I am to eat all meals in his presence, since I am not allowed to go anywhere alone. I am not to make telephone calls to any of the Greek friends I made last year. I cannot call any of my Alaskan friends without his permission. I must not speak with my lawyers without his knowledge. I must report every move I make to him. And I will most certainly owe him more money, which he will need soon.

I'm suspicious about how much Manolis's English has improved overnight. And I feel claustrophobic, like when I was married. In the six years since I left my husband, I have never allowed anyone else to control me. But Manolis assures me he has my interests at heart and does not want Gregory to be tipped off again. Besides, I've already spent the family farm and jeopardized my relationships with my lawyers and Poppy. Now, in this male-dominated country that has swallowed my daughters, it is not the time to assert my independence. I will have to stifle my feelings for a little while longer.

I agree to his rules. I've hired him anyhow, so I guess it doesn't make sense to fight him. It's not like I can find someone new this late in the game.

"So, tell me about your week," Poppy says, after she releases me from her embrace. She's invited Manolis and me to her place for dinner. I notice immediately that her dark-brown ringlets have grown much longer and the circles under her eyes are more pronounced.

I've missed her. Poppy is family to me. I'm sorry that this is the first time I've seen her on this trip. I wish so badly that I could ditch Manolis and just enjoy the night with my friend. I've been with him 24/7 since I arrived in Greece. We've made two long car trips to Katerini—the village where some of Gregory's relatives live and where Manolis says he once saw the girls. We've visited the district attorney, who told us to find Gregory and serve him with the Greek court's decision to recognize and enforce my custody rights, and then wait for three days for Gregory to kindly hand over my daughters voluntarily. (What abducting parent would wait around after he's been notified that the left-behind parent is nearby, ready to assume custody of his kidnapped children?) We've consulted with a judge, who agreed with the district attorney about the process of recovering the girls, and who added that she believed it would be a crime for me to rip the girls away from their home in Greece. And we've visited the office of the bailiff, whom I paid to serve the custody order to Gregory's brother in Thessaloniki.

I tell Poppy about my long, stressful week while I watch her cook in the kitchen, and Manolis occupies himself watching television in her living room. He opens the retsina I've brought and pours himself some in a shot glass he finds in Poppy's cabinets. Poppy is making some version of her specialty—garlic, tomatoes, rice, and some variety of herbs—and it reminds me of our time together last year. I feel relaxed and happy for the first time all week as she updates me on her job and on her developing relationship with an older Italian man she's met through friends. And then Manolis comes into the kitchen.

I've never asked Poppy where she met Manolis, but as I watch the two interact, it's clear to me that they are not friends. She stiffens when Manolis reaches around her to get wineglasses for the retsina. It seems pompous of him to make himself at home like this without asking her permission. Manolis pours some retsina and gives Poppy and me each a glass before raising his in a toast. "To the girls," he says, and we clink our glasses together.

To the girls. Where *are* the girls?

"Dinner is ready," Poppy announces. We serve ourselves and relocate to the living room, making a picnic on the floor. I haven't eaten anything but a small chocolate earlier in the day—I'm famished. I would normally be self-conscious eating and drinking so fast, but now I'm happy to refill my plate and glass. It feels great to have familiar food in a familiar home.

As I clear the dishes and load Poppy's dishwasher, she and Manolis begin speaking in Greek at a pace I can't possibly keep up with. Poppy shoos me out of the room, telling me to use her phone to call Heather Flynn in Anchorage. I feel like a child being sent to her room, but I'm overdue to talk to Heather so I oblige. It takes a while to dial all the numbers to call out of the country and to reverse the charges. I don't reach Heather, not at home and not at work, and when I return to the kitchen, Poppy and Manolis are speaking in raised voices. Poppy has tears in her eyes. They stop speaking when they see me.

"Manolis tells me you'll be moving hotels soon," Poppy tells me. "I wish you could stay with me, but Mr. Pappas won't have it."

I know this already. Poppy's told me before. I wonder what's really upsetting her. Manolis stands up and gets my jacket. "We leave," he says firmly. I can tell by the crushed look on Poppy's face that this might be the last time I get to see her, and Manolis's clenched jaw indicates he doesn't want to talk about it with me. I've been so glad to see Poppy again that this sudden plunge in the evening's mood is especially sad.

Manolis still seems angry when we walk to the bus stop. "Tomorrow, we move hotels. Less monies," he tells me, and I don't disagree. I'm worried that my money won't hold out. We don't know where my daughters are yet. I need to assess my budget to see where I have wiggle room.

We walk in silence from the bus stop to the hotel. "Next week, I go alone sometimes," Manolis tells me.

I don't mind the idea of Manolis working without me. I'll welcome the break from him. He grunts his good night, and I am alone in my room, finally.

I take stock of my expenses, making a balance sheet in my journal. I have paid my Greek attorneys $3,000. I still owe them $9,000. I paid $700 for my plane ticket. I've paid Manolis $5,000 and will give him an estimated $10,000 more. I've borrowed $15,000, I have $4,000 worth of credit on my Visa, and an additional $2,000 cashier's check, which will help with food and hotel expenses, long-distance charges, bailiffs, and other miscellaneous costs. Since coworkers have kindly donated their leave to me, I will still draw a paycheck every two weeks. If I can find the girls and depart quickly, I can keep my expenses to a minimum of $30,000. But if it takes a long time, my expenses will multiply. The only line items that I can definitely control are the food and hotel, and so far I'm skipping meals when I can. The less expensive hotel room will be good.

With any luck, I will have all the debt paid off by the time the girls reach their thirties.

The next morning, I move to my new digs with Manolis's help. He's wearing a sport coat and has put mousse in his spiky hair, but he offers no details of his day ahead, and I don't ask him anything.

The Vergina Hotel is more in my price range. My room is the size of a college dorm room, and the sparse white walls are decorated with one mirror and a large clock. The room has a small refrigerator, a television, a shower and toilet, and a complimentary village of black bugs. It costs me the equivalent of $30 a night, made less by the fact that Manolis will not be staying on the other side of the wall. "Too much," he says, rubbing his fingers over his thumb to symbolize money. *So much for security*, I think, but I'm relieved. I don't need him sleeping in the next room.

"You are here," he tells me, pointing to the room. "I pick you up for dinner," he adds, before he leaves for the day. "No phone, no walk outside. Just you. Safe." Cracking a smile, Manolis hands me a book a friend gave him for me that is written in English. "For you. It's love." I have to laugh. Manolis has given me a Barbara Cartland novel. I don't read romance novels anymore. I gave them up after I left Gregory, when I no longer needed a reason to numb my pain. But my pain has returned, and what else do I have to do?

When Manolis closes my door, I feel like I can exhale. I'm sure in time I will get lonely and bored, but for now, I've got the television, I've got a book written in English, and I've got my journal, something I rarely use unless I'm in dire straits. Life is good.

I flip to a blank page and start writing.

March 5, 1996
Today it is six years to the day since I left my
husband. Since then, I've been on welfare, raised
two children through diaperhood, got my head

screwed on straight, earned my degree, found a niche in my job, got a promotion, bought a fixer-upper home, fixed it up, and made incredible and interesting friends. And had my children abducted.

❋ ❋ ❋

I've now been living on the down-low in my hotel room for two weeks. Two weeks where my only company has been TV and my journal since I finished the romance novel days ago.

To keep madness at bay, I've created a little routine for myself in my tiny hotel room. First, I wake up and take a shower. I watch two soap operas in English while walking in place to get some exercise. If I'm lucky, Manolis remembers to call me and take me to lunch. If I'm unlucky, I take a nap to pass some time until dinner. Then I put on some makeup and comb my hair in preparation for Manolis's arrival. It doesn't feel like a date, per se, but he is my only form of human contact, so I give it more weight than it deserves.

Before and after dinner, I have plenty of time to read, reread, and triple-read my book. When I get tired, I lie on the bed and watch the teeny black bugs march in a circle, and I'm careful to keep my feet up and the blankets tucked in so they can't crawl up onto my bed.

I'm in my third week before my hunger and loneliness reach a critical pitch. Manolis calls less often, showing up late or not at all for mealtimes. The only food I have in my hotel room is an occasional Kinder egg (a chocolate candy with a toy on the inside) Manolis brings me. I have no food and an infinite amount of time to think about it. When I look in the mirror, I can see I'm more pale and drawn than a just-over-thirty-year-old woman should look.

You look like your mother.

"You look *just like* your mother." Gregory loved telling me this throughout our marriage. He knew I would rather resemble a troll. In actuality, there are many worse people to look like than my mother. I've inherited her clear skin, her high cheekbones and upturned nose, her medium-full lips. But it's hard for me to separate how my mother looks from how she is. Cunning. Self-centered. Moody. Explosive.

Last year's conversation with my mom over coffee was so revealing. "I'm so glad I didn't go to a psychiatrist, like people suggested," she told me proudly. The comment seemed random. I hadn't ever told her to go to a psychiatrist. We hadn't been talking about her mental well-being or her violent mood swings. So where did that come from?

"Because I've been able to pray through my problems, and I don't believe in taking medications. The Lord has seen me through it just fine."

Just fine. Absolutely. No relationship with your six devastated adult children. Several failed marriages. No friends. No career. Perfect.

Note to self: see psychiatrist when back in America to rule out genetic predisposition for batshit craziness.

"I hope you don't get fat like your mother," Gregory taunted not long after our wedding. I hoped not as well. I hoped it so much that I succumbed to strange techniques to prevent further chub, like eating just once a day and drinking rock salt with water for its laxative effects. I would purge my potential likeness to my mother if it killed me.

This is ridiculous. Reliving the most painful memories associated with the most toxic people in your life. It's over! You're free. Don't let them speak through you anymore.

I open my hotel window to watch life on the streets of downtown Thessaloniki. I'm so hungry it's ridiculous. I'm cold, too. There's a damp kind of cold in the air in Greece in March that reaches my bones and that I can never seem to shake, and my room has no heat adjustment.

When I poke my head out, I don't notice the chill any longer. I smell food. Meat and garlic and baked goods. There is a bakery close by. There are kiosks brimming with candy. There is a street vendor serving meatballs, souvlaki, and chicken. Even the chestnuts smell good, and I don't even like chestnuts. There's a local fast-food restaurant, Goody's, not far away. So why am I waiting for Manolis? If he's so concerned about my security, he would stay closer to me. I've hired him, not the other way around.

I change from my leggings and pajama top into my blue Dockers and a sweater and apply some nude lipstick. I'm going out. By myself. And I'm going to eat.

I feel like such a rebel as I take the stairway exit to avoid being seen by front-desk staff. I feel liberated.

I buy candy for my room and small bottles of retsina (it's cheaper than water, and I figure I can keep drinking the hotel's tap water). Then I get some meatballs and potatoes from the street vendor and wolf them down. The meatballs have a wonderful fatty texture to them, and I can taste the lamb, oregano, and cinnamon clearly. I've arrived in heaven. In a matter of minutes, I feel full.

Like a raisin that's turning back into a grape, I'm hydrating. And I'm thinking. I did promise not to ruffle feathers unnecessarily on this trip. I've so offended the Pappas brothers. I don't want to alienate Manolis, too. But I can't keep up this submissive-client routine, either. I promised myself years ago that I wouldn't continue to be a doormat. I will try to be patient, but I'm going to have to set some limits. I have contacts in Greece whom I can rely on. I'll make a gentle threat to Manolis. He must find my daughters quickly, and I know just how I can help light a fire underneath him to do it.

I call Karla, the journalist I met last year through the embassy. She writes for a tourism magazine and has offered to help. What if I threaten Manolis with going to the press? What would happen if he thought I'd expose his deficits? But I don't ask Karla if I can write an exposé. I tell her that I'm looking to use publicity as leverage with the private investigator.

"I have a friend that I think you need to talk to," Karla says. "My friend Rhoda is a journalist for the *Greek Times* also. Her husband is a professor of law here. They're parents. They will care. I'll call Rhoda and let her know about you. Stay in touch."

And not more than thirty minutes later, I am on the phone with Rhoda. She's friendly and compassionate and also interested in helping me.

"Write me your story," she tells me after we talk for a few minutes. "Write me something prescriptive. What do you want other foreign parents to know about how to get their kidnapped kids back? Something that tells your story without limiting it to just your story. Like, what would you tell other parents in your shoes? You write it, and I'll give it my byline. My editor won't care."

I thank Rhoda and put this tip in my back pocket. I feel better already. After I hang up, I almost immediately get a call. I assume it is Rhoda with a final tip on writing the article.

"You have a box at the front desk," the hotel clerk announces happily. He must know how small my life is. Immediately, I go downstairs to pick it up.

"Maybe it's from your mother," he says hopefully, and I can't help but laugh. What a sweet sentiment. The box is huge. The return address is AWAIC. It's my coworkers. I don't correct him. Why burst his bubble? As I go back upstairs with it, I try to remember the last time I got a box of anything from my mom. In college in Washington, she would send me some clothes every once in a while in too-small sizes to remind me that I needed to lose weight. When I married, I got a box of her old dishes as my wedding present. And when my second daughter was born, she sent me used baby clothes with stains all over them—punishment, I assumed, for my naming the baby after my father's side of the family. But on Christmas, birthdays, or other special events, she's consistently done nothing to honor the girls and me. I'd be lying if I said that it doesn't bother me, especially when I see some of my other friends go on trips with their moms, or see the way their kids love time with their grandmothers.

Sometimes I blame my mom for this mess I'm going through, as if my life has turned into the consequences of her actions. She was in violent relationships. So was I. She married a guy who skirted his child support, just like she ditched child support for her left-behind sons. I married a guy who did the same when I left him. She kidnapped some of her kids. My children were kidnapped. I don't think I'm being superstitious. It feels like there's a psychic connection somehow between my life and hers, no matter how hard I've tried to be different. I can only hope the solution to repeating these cycles is to do my best to change course, and the most important way I can do that now is to rescue my girls.

The box is filled with candy bars, books, and notes of encouragement. It feels like Christmas in March, and as I open my first Snickers bar in ages, I know I'm not alone.

A few days later, after I've had a chance to pen my article on paper and make several other day trips out of my room, Manolis stops by to make plans. He's eating *koulouri*, a circular, sesame seed-covered roll he likely picked up from a street vendor. He offers me a piece, which I accept, tearing off the stale end.

"You. Me. Giorgios," Manolis says between bites. "We go to Gregory's sister's village, soon, okay? Tomorrow."

"Fine," I say. Anything will beat another day alone in my room.

We leave early in the morning, Giorgios, Manolis, and I. I sit in the backseat of the old sedan and say nothing as we drive for what feels like hours. The cool air warms as we make our way through winding fields and dirt roads. I nod off for a nap, waking when Giorgios honks the horn at a herd of sheep blocking our path. *At least the girls aren't in Antarctica or some other place even colder than Alaska*, I remind myself. Most tourists in Greece don't get to see this back-roads beauty. I feel like I've entered an earlier time as I watch an old man with a long white beard and a staff trailing a herd of sheep.

The long dirt road finally takes us to a school. Inside, we find the principal's office and Manolis speaks quickly with him. The principal shakes his head and gives me a sideways grin. I feel like he is supportive. He gives Manolis a map to another school to check. We get back in the car. Manolis says nothing. We drive to the next school. Same result. Finally we head to Tyrnavos, where Gregory's sister, Despina, lives with her husband and their three children.

I remember Tyrnavos better than I thought I would. It's cloudy and dirty, just as it was when I first visited. As we near Despina's home, a modest house surrounded by parched grass, I see her outside, beating the rug on the clothesline. I slink down as far as I can in the back of the sedan. Despina's hair has turned from gray to white, but otherwise she looks the same as she did when I met her seven years ago at Marianthi's baptism.

Aspa, Despina's oldest daughter, emerges from the home and walks dangerously close to our car. She is a young woman now. Aspa doesn't look directly at me, but I see a faint smile on her lips, and she looks in my direction as she enters a neighbor's home. She has seen me.

Why did she smile? Aspa and I got along well when I visited nearly a decade earlier. Is she glad to see me, or does she know something that I don't?

I slowly return to an upright position to watch. Manolis has a brief exchange with Despina. I don't know what they're saying, but their tone is tense. Despina's cheeks are red; she and Manolis gesture dramatically. Aspa appears outside again and stands at her mother's side and pats her shoulder. Manolis turns on his heel and gets back in the car, slamming the door.

"Gregory's sister said he left Greece," he says, "but then she said she didn't know where he was." Manolis assures me he has interrogated her sufficiently, and now she is too intimidated to protect her brother any longer. He has shaken the bushes enough that we can sit back and wait awhile. "Be patient," Manolis says. There's that phrase I despise. *Be patient.*

I feel sick. The very idea that Gregory has left the country with the girls is unbearable. I've been in Greece for three weeks now. How long will it take for him to get sloppy and resurface? Or is Despina simply lying?

Perhaps staying in my hotel room all day long isn't so bad after all. I can't take too many more emotional highs and lows like this. I miss my bug colony.

On the way back to Thessaloniki, we stop for a late lunch at a small restaurant, where we're seated outdoors. We eat in silence. Despite my upset, the food is amazing. I order chicken and roasted lemon-garlic potatoes and *horta*. I nearly forget that Giorgios is with us until he and Manolis begin to banter after dinner. Their conversation turns into a laugh fest, and I can only imagine, judging from their inflection, that they're talking about wine, women, and song.

I wonder what would happen if I lunge forward and stab

Manolis in the neck with my fork. Would the Greek court system hold me accountable, or would it consider that I've been driven to madness by the sum total of the circumstances—my missing daughters, my forced isolation while he bilks me for more and more money? Would my crime garner enough attention that my daughters would see me on the TV news and know that I'd come to Greece for them?

I know I'm just projecting my frustrations. I have a quick temper at times, but I'm not the assaultive type. I've simply grown exhausted of lying in wait.

In the car on the way home, I close my eyes and try to squeeze out the men's voices. The images of Greece haven't changed since my first and second trips, and I don't need to open my eyes to see what is there: stooped, old Greek grandmothers with slight mustaches wearing black housedresses, shopping the open markets. Groups of Greek men with prominent mustaches sitting in the windows of coffee shops, playing cards and smoking cigarettes. Schoolchildren playing on the streets and in parks with their mothers and grandmothers. And in the country, old, bearded goat shepherds walking slowly behind their animals, carrying their staffs. Nothing ever changes.

It isn't until I get back to my room and take a hot shower that I feel the impact of the day's disappointment. I miss my little girls, and I don't feel any closer to finding them now than I did when I first got to Greece. What if I fail and can never bring them back? And what if all this time without them has made me too self-centered to be a good mother to them? How much of this do I do out of my love for them, and how much is so I won't disappoint others? Does it even matter?

March 20, Wednesday
I spent most of the weekend alone. Manolis
promised Friday that we could go to the movies.

He showed up at 11:00 P.M., and I sent him away.
I had a quiet weekend, with only meager funds
to cover meals. I faxed Karla a list of things one
does when seeking the return of one's abducted
children, to be published in the Greek Times.
Rhoda told Karla the paper would use her byline
so as not to create trouble for either her or me.
Karla, at my request, called friends who are
affiliated with the TV station. They said they were
interested in helping get the girls! But as of today,
I've not heard back from them.

By Monday, I'd completely run out of
money and my credit cards wouldn't advance
any more cash. I knew I'd be paid again soon
when payday at AWAIC came, but for now, I
had nothing left in my bank account. I was cold,
hungry, and feeling vulnerable.

Manolis called tonight and said he'd be
over at five. He showed up at nine. We had a
nice dinner. When we went back to the hotel, the
evening clerk excitedly told Manolis that I had
received a telephone call from a Greek woman,
who had left no message. I could tell by their
familiar interactions that Manolis had instructed
the clerk to monitor my calls, and I was horrified.
I was paying the investigator, who was successfully
tracking me, not my kids. I stormed off into the
elevator and said good-bye. Manolis pushed his
way into the elevator, against my wishes and
objections, and followed me to my room. He told
me to call my female caller. I told him I didn't
know who it was and I wouldn't make any calls
at eleven at night. He kept on, and I told him to

leave. He called me strykla, a derogatory term for
woman, equivalent to witch, and slammed the
door. I was so enraged I couldn't sleep.

My feuds with Manolis, the lack of progress on the case, and my dwindling resources all lead me to call the American embassy the next morning to touch base. And while I'm on hold, Manolis begins banging on the door to my hotel room. "Liz! Liz! Open the door! Please!"

Somehow, he manages to make the word *please* an offensive command. I can hardly hear the person who picks up on the other end of the line, the pounding and yelling are so loud.

"I'm sorry; could you repeat that last word?" I ask through gritted teeth. Manolis punches the hotel door harder now.

"I'm on the phone! Come back later!" My nightgown is too short to let him in anyhow, even if I did hang up the phone.

But the knocking continues. After I hang up, I put on a robe and knot the sash tightly, purposefully. I am about to embark on a real-life boxing match. I open the door to find Manolis standing there with a woman friend of his I recognize. She agrees to translate. The two come into the room. It's on.

I throw the first punch. "Your behavior is unacceptable to me. I am tired of being called names, tired of your temperament, and unimpressed with your investigative tactics." I watch Manolis's face as he listens to the interpreter.

Before he can return the punch, I continue. "I want us to sign a contract, and I'm going to the media, as I'd—"

"Liz, listen to me," he interrupts. Then he speaks through the interpreter.

"*Wait!*" I hold up my hand in front of his face. "When my lips are moving, yours should be in the resting position!"

Manolis looks like he's been slapped. I give myself a mental pat on the back for that one.

"Okay," I say, satisfied that I've made my point. "What do you have to say?"

Manolis looks helplessly at the interpreter and then begins to speak.

"He says he's nearly found your husband, but he worries Gregory may have left the country first," she says.

I glare at Manolis. "Then I'll blame you for it," I say. "I hold you responsible. Find my children. Immediately!"

Manolis grasps my hand and gives it a squeeze. Seeing that I am unmoved by the gesture, he backs out of the room, followed by the interpreter. With a good slam of the door for dramatic flair, I raise both fists in the air and celebrate my first victory. I have imitated his explosive behavior perfectly, and it's worked.

Manolis scrambles to tap Gregory's brother's phone. Is it an illegal maneuver in Greece? Sure. I knew that after my first failed trip to retrieve my girls. Tapping phones is illegal in most countries.

Do I care about any of that?

Not in the least.

My days of being a long-suffering rule follower are safely behind me now.

Chapter 17

FOUND

It takes just a few days for the phone tap to work. Gregory calls his brother. I never understand exactly how the rest of the information is revealed, but I do know that Manolis receives Gregory's phone number, and from there, his address. That is all that matters.

Gregory is now living in a suburb of Thessaloniki called Perea. It's a fishing village less than an hour away by car.

Manolis calls Gregory to negotiate a visit between the girls and me. I just want him to find Gregory, grab the girls, and fly us away in the helicopter he promised so long ago. Is this too much to ask? Manolis reminds me of the process: we'll need to get the updated court order to be served to Gregory through local law enforcement, and then he'll have three days to hand the girls over to me so we can fly home to America.

The phone call between Manolis and Gregory goes on at length; Gregory is friendly at intervals and rageful at others,

Manolis tells me over dinner Sunday night. "He threatened to kill me. Now I'll need $10,000 more to keep up the investigation," Manolis says. "We're at a critical point. I can't work on any other cases, and I need the money."

Not this again. What a bastard. When he knows I can't possibly walk away, when I'm feeling hopeful and vulnerable, he dives in for whatever's left. I promise Manolis $5,100, all the money in the world I have immediate access to. He asks for more. He's got me between a rock and a hard place. "Screw off," I shoot back.

He only blinks at me. "You will have your children soon," he says. "Gregory said you can visit the children soon. But he wants to talk to you about it tomorrow by phone. He has conditions."

Conditions? The man who stole my daughters and who may face criminal charges has conditions? He's got a lot of nerve.

The next day, Monday, I walk to the bank and get a cashier's check. I take it to Manolis's office before my appointment to speak with Gregory. And as soon as I hand the money over, the phone rings. Cue the telephone call. It's Gregory. I wonder for a second whether Gregory watched me walk into the investigator's office. My stomach churns when I hear his voice.

"Are you there? Listen, Liz. I've changed my mind. You can't see the girls after all. I asked them if they wanted to see you, and they said no."

"Really?" I say, trying to sound bored, because there's no way I'll give him the satisfaction of knowing how deeply this cuts me. "Okay, then—I guess there's nothing to talk about. Bye."

I hang up, furious at Gregory, furious at Manolis. I am tired of being at the mercy of domineering Greek men.

The next day, I get an early phone call from Mr. Pappas in Athens letting me know that today Manolis plans to serve Gregory with the court order and have the judgment executed. "Can you find a friend to be a witness to this in the next ten minutes? And are you prepared to pay the bailiff the $1,000 fee?"

No to both, but away we go with the money I do have— the driver, Manolis, and me, off to Perea. Manolis is even more animated than usual on the drive and keeps looking back at me from the front passenger seat. "Liz. Today. You. Children. Go." He points his left hand and makes a flying motion. Manolis truly believes the girls and I are going to fly out of Greece today. I do not. It sounds too easy to be trusted. I give him a nod of acknowledgment.

I obsess over my wardrobe. I didn't have time to fix up. I'm wearing a long-sleeved, plum-colored T-shirt and my navy Dockers. I probably look a mess.

Inside the police station, we find a young officer slumped at his desk. He looks as though we've just interrupted his nap. He wipes his mouth, and his eyes dart from me to Manolis to Manolis's driver. Then he calls for the chief of police, a sharp-looking man with graying brown hair and big brown eyes. He reaches Gregory by phone after Manolis gives him the number.

The three of us wait quietly as they speak. Manolis's eyes get bigger and his face turns red. I know the news can't be good. When the police chief hangs up, he turns to Manolis to speak.

Manolis clears his throat. "The officer has learned that your ex-husband has filed paperwork with the court to keep you from the girls. A court date is scheduled for a month from now."

My heart has been stomped into the ground. How can this be happening?

I call Michael Pappas in Athens with Manolis's phone, and he confirms Manolis's story. "Liz, there is good news, though. You can go see your beautiful daughters. Now! In the school. Go visit your girls and call me later. We'll discuss the other matters at length then."

The ride to the grade school takes but a minute. I see Gregory, already there, waiting for the girls to leave class. As soon as he sees me, he runs into a phone booth. He has aged by a decade in the past two years. Life on the lam has taken its toll. I follow him into the phone booth. I am not afraid. I should be, because Manolis is sitting across the street, watching me from inside a building. So much for his being my fierce protector. I don't need him anyhow.

Gregory is calling staff inside the girls' school to keep them in the building, away from me. I step in behind him. "You look old," I say. It's unnecessarily mean but true, and I feel good saying it. I pull my disposable camera from my purse and snap a picture of him. If he disappears with the girls again, I'll need an updated image.

I walk away from Gregory and into the school. It looks like any American grade school and smells musty. As a foreign woman in a Greek school, I suspect I'll be stopped in my tracks. But I'm welcomed by English-speaking teachers and a principal who, I can't help but notice, is a tall, attractive man, wearing a button-down shirt, jeans, and fancy eyeglasses.

"It is a pleasure to meet you," he says, and the teachers huddle around him. *Really?* I want to ask. "You must come back tomorrow during school hours to see your daughters. They've left the building with their father just now."

I can't believe how kind they're being to me. No one has been this nice to me lately. Now I want to cry.

"Are you sure?" is all I can think to say. I use my sleeve to wipe my nose.

"Of course I'm sure," he says gently. "They're your kids."

After all the horror stories I've heard about Greek schools blocking foreign parents, I am not prepared for this. It's my first Hallmark moment of this trip. It's a miracle. It's a real-life miracle. I can see my daughters, so long as Gregory doesn't disappear with them again and withdraw them from school. I practically float outside and scan the school yard for signs of Manolis.

"My job with you is finished," he tells me.

It's a hard landing. So much for his original promise to helicopter me and the girls out of Greece. And why doesn't Manolis want to get a beat on where the kids are living with their dad, in case Gregory runs off with the girls again? I guess it's just as well, though. I will be fine without his help.

All night long, I sit up in bed, ruminating over what tomorrow might hold. Maybe the girls will run to me, crying with joy. Maybe they won't even recognize me. Or maybe their father will take them and go further into hiding.

I remember this feeling. It's the same one I had a decade ago, just before I met my own father for the first time, when I obsessed on the plane ride over whether or not he would hug me and break down. Would he be glad that I had finally found him? Would he be pleased that I had restored my birth name already? I remember getting off the plane, scanning the lobby for my father, only to be pawed by a group of welcoming aunts, uncles, and siblings I'd only just learned of.

In the end, my father was the slim, white-haired man in jeans and a white T-shirt slowly working his way toward me. His skin was tan and leathery, and his cheeks were hollow. He stopped a distance ahead and simply stared at me, unsmiling. Finally, he extended his right hand to shake mine. Not exactly a made-for-TV reunion, but it still ended my prereunion anxiety.

I remember the long ride out to my father's farm in Bee Spring, which spanned more than a hundred acres. I remember my great-aunt Cynthie, then in her nineties, flying out of her trailer parked on my dad's land, wearing a housedress, knee socks, slippers, and horn-rimmed glasses, her waist-length white hair flowing in the wind as she ran with her spindly arms outstretched. "Wee-ell," she sang out, pinching my love handles after she gave me a bony hug, "ain't you a fleshy thing?" So my freshman fifteen had a new name, and I had family straight out of *Deliverance*. "I always told Kovie, I says, 'Kovie, one day that little girl will look you up, just like them shows on TV.' And here you are! Just like on TV." She poked her finger into my protruding stomach and smiled triumphantly.

I remember the days following, the few conversations with my dad, the easy rapport with my new brothers and sisters. And I distinctly remember telling myself that I would never subject my kids to a divorce. My children would have two parents and would know their heritage. There would be no need for lawyers. No missing parent. I remember vowing that my future children, above all else, would not inherit my freaky family history.

My eyes finally get heavy just before my alarm rings.

I take a quick shower and put on my long forest-green dress. Makeup can't compensate for my pallor. The dress is too large now and hangs on me like a sack. I look pitiful, and I look old for a thirty-one-year-old. Hopefully, the girls won't notice this.

I hop a bus from Thessaloniki to Perea. It's a forty-five-minute ride, and it gives me plenty of time to rehearse what I will say to my daughters. It shouldn't be too hard, since my Greek language skills are limited.

Hi. I love you. I've been looking for you for a long time.

That's it. Maybe I'll repeat it once or twice, but nothing else seems appropriate. Anything more might cause stress or anxiety or promise something I may not be able to deliver.

Chapter 18

REUNION AND ARREST

I need to call my attorney. As the bus nears Perea, I feel my composure go out the window. My anxiety is at a fever pitch. The bus slows to a stop. Perea really is a sweet-looking seaside town. I didn't notice it before. I was too clenched, wondering if I'd actually see my daughters. But now, as near as I can tell from peering out the window, I'm glad that my children are living in a peaceful place. I stand up and sit right back down. My feet have frozen beneath me. The bus driver clears his throat and looks back at me impatiently. When I ask his help in finding the school, he chuckles before pointing and nodding to the street in the direction just the right of the bus.

A few minutes later, I am there. I dart into the phone booth outside the school yard to call Mr. Pappas. He always keeps his cool. Again, he reiterates the importance of not disrupting the school day. "Make your visit short. Respect the school's routine, and they'll invite you back. Go on in, Liz. Be brave," Mr. Pappas says. "It won't make things any worse than they already are." I agree and hang up.

How can things get any worse?

There is an excellent chance that my daughters will not even be at the school. Maybe Gregory has taken them into hiding again. Or maybe he won't let them attend school until he thinks I've left. Or maybe the school staff will block my access to the children. I know the warm reception I received yesterday from them should make that an unlikely prospect, but it's still a possibility.

Perhaps the scariest thought is that the girls *will* be at the school. Will they remember me? Will they be scared of me? Or will they be happy to see me? Will they run to me or run from me?

I walk inside. A few of the teachers are huddled in the hall, waiting for me to arrive. The first teacher says to me in English, "I'm so happy to meet you. I really admire your courage." She is a tall fortysomething-year-old who I imagine has daughters of her own. Her eyes shine brightly.

All my worries are for nothing.

I thank her, and she leads me to the hallway outside Meredith's class. I take a deep breath. This is the moment I have been waiting for, yet I'm frozen. How curious I must be to the teachers. No wailing or gnashing of teeth. I am wooden. The teacher opens the door and urges me in. There, inside the classroom, I am the center of all attention as the children crane their necks to look at me and whisper to one another.

"Eleni, is this your mother?" the teacher asks excitedly in Greek.

My little girl is sitting within spitting distance of me at her desk. Meredith is astonishingly scrawny and pale. She's wearing an oversized gray sweat suit, and her hair is pulled back in a headband. She's six now, and the rosy cheeks and stocky build she had at four are long gone. She smiles at me, her eyes glistening. "Come outside to see your mother," the teacher urges.

Meredith stands up from her chair and runs as fast as her skinny little legs will carry her, with her arms outstretched. I reach down and scoop her up and carry her to the hall. She is practically weightless and immediately nestles her head into my shoulder. Tears spill down her cheeks, and I feel her shoulders trembling. I sniff her hair and inhale. She smells just the same. She smells exactly the same. My baby.

This is my fantasy.

In reality, my youngest daughter looks petrified and clings to her desk as though she is preparing to be violently ripped from it.

"Eleni? Eleni!" Meredith's teacher says in a loud, scolding whisper. She leads my daughter out of the classroom and turns custody over to me in the hallway. "This way you can have privacy and class will go on for the others," the teacher explains.

I lean down slowly and tell Meredith that I love her in Greek. "S'agapo, Eleni."

"S'agapo," Meredith responds obediently.

While we visit in the hallway, two teachers stand nearby, wiping away their tears. I have no tears to dry. After I've waited so long for this moment, it doesn't seem real. I tell Meredith I love her and that I've been looking for her for a long time. The second part I say in English, and I don't think she understands me. Meredith begins to cry and says a phrase I cannot understand. Feeling helpless, I try to quiet her. Her teacher intervenes. "She says she's afraid of her father." Meredith repeats the phrase, and her teacher soothes her while another teacher pulls Marianthi out of her class by the arm.

I have to do a double take when Marianthi is led to me, dragging her feet and avoiding eye contact. My formerly delicate, meticulously groomed daughter now has dark-brown hair hanging in her face, covering much of her yellowed skin. There are deep circles under her eyes. She is considerably rounder and taller, which makes sense, since she will be nine on her next birthday. She is swallowed by a wool sweater that, like a dress, hangs over her sweatpants, which are dragging on the floor. "Marianthi, don't you love your mother?" her teacher asks. "Tell your mother you love her, Marianthi."

I know that her teacher means well, but I feel sorry for Marianthi. It is awkward enough. She doesn't need to be put on the spot. Marianthi struggles to comfort her crying sister, to no avail. Meredith's cries grow louder, and now her shoulders are trembling. Her teacher ushers her back to class, and Marianthi looks at me accusingly.

I stick to my plan, which isn't hard, since I know so little Greek. "I love you, and I've been looking for you for a long time."

Finally, the dam breaks.

"I am afraid to go to America!" Marianthi says in Greek. She raises her fisted right hand as she says it and waves it in the air while her teacher interprets. Then she repeats it again and again. It seems scripted, and it scares me.

What has her father said to scare her into compliance?

I end the visit soon after that, trying to assure her I am here only to visit. Marianthi returns to class, and I sit in the hallway with a few of the teachers and debrief.

"You must take the children and leave Greece," one of them tells me. "These girls don't come to school much. They don't do well here. They aren't cared for properly. They are dirty, and they wear the same clothes every day. There's nothing for them here."

I ask if I can come back tomorrow. The teachers unanimously agree that I can. That I must.

My girls. I have seen my girls. Two years and almost one month after they disappeared, I have seen my daughters.

On the bus ride back, I map out the next few days. As soon as I reach the hotel, I will call Poppy. And Manolis. The lawyers. Heather. Karla and Rhoda. And I will visit the girls at every opportunity—unless they go missing again.

Will Manolis even care? I wonder as I dial his number. He doesn't deserve an update, but I have to know for myself that it matters to him. Instantly, I hear the emotion in his voice as I share the news. "See? You will get your children back, Liz. I told you."

My anger evaporates. He cares. Manolis has led me to my daughters, and despite his Neanderthal behaviors, he does care.

Everyone I call is happy. Heather urges me to take the girls and come home as soon as possible. And Poppy wants to celebrate.

An hour later, I join her and Zeta at a taverna for lunch. They give me crushing hugs before we sit down at the table to celebrate, and they listen intently as I tell the story of our reunification. "We must celebrate with all of our friends this Friday night," Poppy says. "Thanasis. Christina. Nikos. Maria and Christos. Friday night for dinner, the old theatrical group." I look forward to seeing them all again, but I can't help but wonder if they will be angry when they realize I lied to them last year about who I am and why I had come to Greece.

Michael Kreider calls from Alaska just after I return to the hotel. The Pappas brothers have updated him. The district attorney's office in Thessaloniki will soon reconsider Gregory's objections to my custody and possibly throw them out. This is welcome news. "But you're in Greece. They might not, and if they don't, the girls are going to possibly be placed in the Greek foster care system. Just until April. To prevent their father from taking them further into hiding."

Foster care? What a hideous thought. How much more can my girls take? But it's just a maybe. Maybe the court will throw out Gregory's motion and I can go home with them soon.

My hopes are reinforced by a call from the law professor who is married to Rhoda. I can't believe he's calling me. I've never met him or his wife. He tells me that he contacted the Ministry of Justice on my behalf, hoping pressure from a former coworker of theirs would help my case. "They've got to do the right thing, Liz. I've been reading up on cases like yours, and I'm sure the Greek government will be compelled to return your children to you."

I'm blown away. In one day, I have had more support from Greeks than Gregory probably has had over his lifetime. Someday I'll write about this experience and I'll remember to tell how gracious the Greeks have been to me, an outsider, despite all the stories I've heard about their protecting their own above all else. Tomorrow, I can visit my daughters at their school. And if what I'm hearing rings true, our reunion might even be permanent soon. For the first time in two years, I go to sleep, looking forward to waking up again.

In the morning, I take the bus to Perea. My worries have been for naught. The girls are in school! This time, they look happy to see me, and we exchange hugs and kisses. Marianthi turns to her teacher and whispers in her ear. "She says she wants you to buy her a doll," her teacher says, and laughs. Meredith runs to me and greets me in English. A few of her friends come over to meet me. I sit outside on a bench and watch the girls jump rope and play dodgeball during recess. Every couple of minutes, they look back at me to make sure I'm watching. I wonder if they told their father about my visit yesterday. I can't imagine that they did, or they probably wouldn't have been able to return today.

As soon as the recess bell rings, it's my signal to leave. I make my way back to Thessaloniki to face another long evening without progress in the courts.

The next day, a Friday, I stop by the bakery before I get

on the bus to Perea and buy an assortment of Greek cookies for the girls' classrooms. Soon, I am surrounded by smiling, grateful children at the girls' school. My daughters look proud to have me feed their friends. Marianthi takes her place by my side on the bench at recess, staring straight ahead. I urge her to go and play, but she shakes her head and holds her ground. Meredith watches from her spot on the playground and waves. Our relationships are warming. Still, I have a growing sense of unease. Why hasn't Gregory taken the girls into hiding again? What's up his sleeve now? And will the girls really have to live with foster parents while we hammer out the legal proceedings?

Just hours later, I am in celebration mode with Poppy, Zeta, and our other friends in a fancy taverna. It's wonderful to see them all again. No one scrutinizes me for lying about why I was in Greece in the first place. They simply raise their glasses to toast the fact that I have found my children—children they didn't even know existed until today.

I feel young again, and set free somehow. I fill and refill my glass with retsina. As the drinks flow and bouzouki music plays in the background, my tongue loosens. I tell my friends more about my life with the girls. Having them. Losing them. Finding them. And meeting them again. They're drunk, too, and easily laugh with me and cry with me. They toast to me. "*Stin iyasus!*" and "*Opa!*" they say, as they clink their glasses against mine. "To your children!"

"You can stay with me if you need a place," Maria offers. I thank her, letting her know I plan to leave as soon as possible.

"I'm sure my parents would let you stay with us. I'll ask, just in case you'll be here longer," Thanasis says.

I am speechless. No anger or resentment from any of them. My Greek friends are lovers, not fighters. They work hard, and have plenty of time and money at their disposal. And they are generous with everything that they do have. We close the taverna down and make a commitment to stay in more regular contact, which is something I can do, now that I'm no longer in hiding and Manolis has left my employ.

Saturday comes. Still nothing from the district attorney's office. Mr. Pappas calls from Athens. "Gregory's decided to allow you to visit the girls over the weekend. Sunday afternoon at a restaurant called El Greco. Don't get excited, because it's probably just a way for him to look good for the courts."

"That's great," I say. "I don't care about the reason. I'll take it."

"He says you can see the girls at the restaurant, and he says he'll leave you alone while you and the kids visit there for an hour or two around noon."

I thank him. I can't believe this sudden stroke of luck. My weekend has a point to it now. I can't believe Gregory's really going to let me visit the girls alone. Maybe it's time to go shopping and get my daughters presents.

I hate shopping—anytime and in every country. It combines so many of my least favorite activities: walking among lots of people, inventorying, negotiating, spending hard-earned money. But Marianthi has asked for a doll. A *koukla*, she said in Greek. Her sister will want one, too.

Shopping today is a privilege. It's been years since I've had the pleasure of buying the girls toys. Today is sunny, and the sidewalks are inexplicably free of other Saturday shoppers.

I wander the streets of Thessaloniki. The shops are jam-packed with leathers, trinkets, jewelry, and loud makeup. As soon as I see a toy store, I duck inside. Two porcelain dolls stand out on a top shelf, both with strawberry-blond hair and velvet dresses. They look alike. Sister dolls. The girls will love them. I have them wrapped in tissue paper and placed in separate boxes. Mission accomplished.

❀ ❀ ❀

On Sunday, I'm jolted from sleep by the ringing phone. It is Mr. Pappas from Athens. He skips the morning greetings.

"Brace yourself. Gregory has now rethought his decision to let you see the girls. He wants you to bring a supervisor. He's moved up the time to ten this morning, instead of noon. Can you agree to this?"

My cheeks burn with anger. Of course Gregory wouldn't make things easy. What choice do I have?

If I say no, Gregory will tell the children I canceled my time with them.

If I say yes, I will need to ask one of my Greek friends to come along on short notice to supervise the visit. But there is no way I will cancel my time with the girls.

"I'll be there. I just need to make some calls," I tell him.

My first call is to Christina, who agrees to help as long as Thanasis can go with us to the visit. She calls him, and he quickly rearranges his schedule to accommodate the request. The three of us meet up at the bus stop, and they hug me excitedly, as though I've invited them to a birthday party. Never mind that it is rainy out and I have effectively obliterated their Sunday afternoon plans. "We're so excited to meet your daughters," Thanasis says, and Christina agrees.

I look at them through the girls' lens.

Christina is gorgeous, with clear, fair skin set off by her brown lipstick, and dark-brown hair styled in a smooth, shoulder-length bob. She is medium height and slim, and wears a solid-black pantsuit.

Thanasis is only slightly taller than she, with brown hair and glasses and a wide, dimpled grin. He is adorable and has dressed like a Mormon missionary for the task ahead.

The bus ride takes forever today. Every five seconds a passenger rings the bell to stop, and the traffic leaving Thessaloniki is especially dense. Finally, we stop close to the restaurant. I grab a mirror out of my purse and apply brown lip gloss. My skin is a half shade warmer than albino, and my eyes have deep circles under them. The lip gloss perfects my accidental Gothic look, and I wipe it off quickly. No need to scare the poor girls. I grab the boxes with the dolls inside them, and we exit the bus.

Gregory, the girls, and Gregory's sister, Despina—the only people inside the restaurant—are sitting at a booth. The girls look frozen and stare ahead.

"I'm staying," Gregory says. "You want to see the kids? Then you'll see me, too." He laughs.

I wish him dead but don't want to let any emotion register. He isn't worth it.

Despina whispers in his ear and giggles, and Gregory comments back in Greek.

"She said you were looking thin and pale, and he told her it was likely due to the trauma of missing the girls," Christina explains.

Nice.

"Would you girls like something to eat or drink?" I ask Marianthi and Meredith.

Both shake their heads no vigorously.

"Look! I brought you dolls. See, Marianthi, it's the doll you asked for." I place the dolls, still in their boxes, in front of them.

Marianthi stares ahead, and her chin begins to quiver. Meredith looks down. Neither makes any effort to look at her doll. It feels like they've been conditioned to reject me.

Gregory abruptly moves tables to sit with his sister. Marianthi says something to Christina I can't decipher.

"She says her appendix hurts her, but she doesn't want you to know about it," Christina says.

The girls relax just a little and talk to Christina and Thanasis. Through them, I learn that Marianthi loves geography and Meredith enjoys math. They don't get to have their friends over to visit them, and they watch a lot of television, according to Marianthi. I sit and watch them. I feel Gregory and Despina watching me. This is a very awkward visit. It takes a half hour before the girls are comfortable enough to pay attention to their dolls. Just then, Gregory pipes up. "It's time for us to leave, girls. Get your jackets and tell your mom good-bye."

"Can I have a kiss?" I ask.

Meredith leans forward and kisses me. Marianthi turns her head away at the last moment so that I end up kissing her hair.

The visit is over in less than forty minutes. *No matter*, I think. *I can see them tomorrow during school recess.*

We're all quiet on the bus ride back. I can't thank Christina and Thanasis enough for giving me the chance to see my daughters, but I actually feel worse after the visit than before. To see the girls scared, and to hear about their life with their father, is so dismal. I hope the court rules, and fast.

On Monday when I go to the school, the girls aren't there. Meredith's teacher explains that Gregory took them away early in the morning.

Where have they gone? Has Gregory punished them for enjoying their dolls? What if he has run with the girls again? How far can I go, and how much longer can it take to bring the girls back home to Alaska?

But not long after I return to my hotel room, I get a call from Manolis.

"Liz, I speak to district attorney," he says excitedly. "Tomorrow. You. The girls. To Alaska."

I know better than to bite that apple. I'm grateful for the

call, though, and I'm half glad Manolis is still on the case. I call Mr. Pappas in Athens; he sounds cool and indifferent. "Manolis will handle this," he says. At any other time, I might worry about what happened between him and Manolis to cause him to distance himself from me, but this news, if true, is too exciting for me to get bogged down with another conflict.

I call Michael Kreider in Alaska. He sounds more positive. "Well, kiddo, apparently the district attorney in Thessaloniki paved the way for you to leave soon. The wheels are finally in motion. Cross your fingers."

I hang up the phone, overcome. More than disbelief, the sum total of emotions running high and low, day after day, month after month, year after year, has left me with a zero balance in my feelings account. I just hope the girls will be at school tomorrow.

I stay up all night long, staring at the television and waiting for the morning to come. My bag is already packed. I'm checking out of this hotel. Finally. I'm saying good-bye to my bug friends, and in doing so I'm pledging that this time is really it. I'm getting my girls and leaving Greece.

Manolis arrives just after eight in the morning, and together we go to the Children's Issues division of the police department in Thessaloniki, hoping they'll accompany us and coordinate the girls' legal return to me. It's a brightly lit room with a few workers at their desks.

Nine o'clock comes and goes, and then ten, and then eleven. I sit tapping my foot, my knees stiffening, my stomach rumbling. Manolis paces in the lobby. People chat in Greek all around me, but I can't focus well enough to translate any of it. Finally, Manolis comes back into the office, makes a call on his cell phone, and then hands it to me. It is Mr. Pappas from Athens. "Manolis would like you to understand that you will owe him $7,000 more dollars."

For what? I want to scream. I can barely utter a response, and I end the conversation abruptly. I wonder if this delights Mr. Pappas, who warned me about being scammed. I should have listened. I was wrong. But now is the time to find supporters, not to create a stir. I go to the pay phone and call the American consulate staff in Thessaloniki. I need an interpreter, and I need an advocate. And I need them right away. Manolis stands next to me, eavesdropping. "They will interrupt my work," he tells me after I hang up. "Remember what happened last year?"

How can I forget the catastrophe last year? I asked the consulate staff for help but gave them only some of the information I had, and the staff inadvertently tipped off Gregory.

This time will be different. The consulate staff will know everything that I know. I will be sure of that. We've all learned from past mistakes. I feel like Manolis's real concern is that staff will now interrupt his heist on a lone American woman who desperately wants her children back.

Within twenty minutes, a bailiff arrives and a female police officer arranges for us to go to Perea. The consulate staff show up in a limousine; Robin Thomas and Penelope Dimos wave from their tinted windows. "We'll follow you there," Ms. Thomas says, smiling.

I breathe a sigh of relief. I have advocates.

Manolis and I ride in silence. I turn my back to him and look out the window. It is a cloudy, ominous day, not what I pictured for the day when the girls and I would be reunited once and for all.

When we arrive in Perea, we pick up the police chief and head to El Greco, the restaurant where Manolis believes Gregory is working. None of us speaks. I'm so worried, my ears are whirring. I feel like I could faint. Gregory comes out of the restaurant. The police chief gets out of the limo. He is joined by more police officers, who confront Gregory. Something doesn't feel right about this. Gregory appears neither surprised nor worried. They all look too relaxed and open for my blood. They follow Gregory to his nearby apartment, disappearing from view.

We wait for them to return with the girls. And wait. And wait some more. A half hour later, the group emerges. An officer holds the girls, who look scared and confused but don't struggle against him. A young woman with frizzy red hair who looks to be in her twenties walks behind them. She doesn't resemble any of the relatives of Gregory's that I've ever seen. She looks plenty upset.

The officer holding the girls approaches me. He nods toward the redhead. "Babysitter," he explains, leaning in to me to transfer my daughters. The girls begin to cry, so he lowers them gently to stand on the ground.

"Take them. We'll distract the father," he says. The other officers are listening to Gregory and looking back at me. As I reach out to pick Meredith up, she pulls away. Marianthi screams and squirms. My grip on Meredith remains firm, and I pick her up. She begins to kick. I set her back down. The babysitter, who has been inching closer and closer to me, scratches me. I scratch her right back. I look around and see officers yelling at one another, divided in their opinions about the right course of action. Manolis disappears. Only the consulate staff stand by my side, and the conflict about who the girls should go with is looking more and more like a riot. We are all pushing, yelling, and screaming.

"Maybe you should wait to take the girls until after the April hearing," the police chief offers.

What April hearing? Has no one told him that the hearing scheduled for April will no longer be necessary?

Gregory will never wait around for me to take the girls at

a later date. My custody rights have been recognized in Greece. I will leave the country with my daughters and return home to Alaska as soon as is humanly possible.

Finally, we are all ushered into the police substation. Meredith clings to Gregory, winding her arms tightly around his neck. Marianthi sits without expression in a chair next to her father. He speaks to the girls quietly, and they begin to cry. The longer he speaks, the more loudly they cry. The police continue to banter.

After what feels like an eternity, the district attorney's office calls and confirms that I am to have custody of the children. "You can press charges of kidnapping against the children's father if you'd like," Ms. Dimos tells me. I've been so focused on what everyone else is doing around me that I've forgotten about Ms. Dimos and Ms. Thomas.

Using Ms. Thomas's phone, I call Mr. Pappas in Athens. He discourages me from pressing charges. "What do you have to gain?" he says. "You have the girls now. You can leave. Pressing charges will delay your exit, I'm afraid."

I agree. I need to keep my cool. And then I see Gregory.

"Just put the past behind you, Liz." He smiles.

I whip around to the police chief. "I'd like to press charges for kidnapping."

The process takes forever. After I have been questioned and the paperwork is complete, Gregory is placed in handcuffs and leaves with the officers. The girls and I leave with the consulate staff, careening down the street in the limousine like a getaway car in a bank robbery. The girls shriek, and not because of the driving. They are traumatized. I try to comfort them, but they pull away from me as though I am the Wicked Witch of the West. I try not to topple over them as the limo makes hairpin turns.

Ms. Dimos is much more successful at consoling the girls

than I am. She sings them a Greek nursery rhyme, and both girls are giggling by the time we reach the consulate headquarters. Large steel gates open, and we disappear underground, into a small tunnel that leads to the garage.

For two solid years, I have heard from every government official I have spoken with about what the American consulate and embassy cannot do. They can't protect me from legal consequences if I do something illegal to recover my children. They cannot provide legal assistance. They cannot provide financial assistance or any kind of resources.

What *can* they do? Plenty, it turns out. They have shown up on a moment's notice. They have helped me through the parking lot brawl so I can assume custody of my daughters. They have helped us get away safely and have helped comfort my crying daughters. And now, finally, the three of us are together again, contained safely inside the protective gate and cement walls, compliments of the American consulate.

It is a miracle I would love to celebrate, but I know better than to get complacent.

"The first thing I'd like to do is leave Greece as soon as possible," I tell Ms. Dimos and Ms. Thomas as we exit the garage. I stop in my tracks when we get inside. The interior of the consulate is amazing. Downstairs, there are large, homey offices. Upstairs, there are endless bedrooms and bathrooms. It's like a palace, or maybe it's just that my hotel was that crappy.

"Here's your room," Ms. Dimos tells me. "We'll get some clothes together for the girls. We have staff whose kids have outgrown theirs."

A few minutes later, she delivers a pile of clothes around the girls' sizes. Boy clothes. Patterned polyester pants and large sweatshirts.

"Thank you so much for all your help. Really. Thank you. But I still want to leave Greece tonight," I tell her.

"But there aren't any flights leaving later tonight. I already checked. There's a train leaving for Albania, but it isn't safe for women and children to go there alone. Tomorrow, you can leave from Athens first thing. There's a flight going to France from there. You can make your connections after you get there," she tells me.

"I really don't think staying in Greece a moment longer is a safe idea," I tell her. I'm trying not to be an ungrateful jerk, but I can't stand the idea of one more thing going wrong. "I'll take my chances in Albania. Really, it'll be okay."

"We can't risk your safety," Ms. Dimos says, just as determined as I am. "And the girls need the rest. Try to settle in for the night," she urges.

Every time I've gone against my instincts, I've regretted it. Yet I'm locked in the consulate building with my kids. I'm tired. They're beyond tired. And I can't imagine trying to force my way out. I'd have to be crazy to make enemies of the consulate staff now, after all they've done for me. It's with more than a little relief that I relent.

I draw a bubble bath for the girls in the bathroom nearest to our room. This, it turns out, is a hit. They act as though they haven't bathed in years, giggling, splashing, and cavorting.

I step out and call Heather in Alaska. She is over the moon to hear about the girls and me, tucked safely inside the consulate. Still, she can tell how jarred I am. "I just think I should be on my way," I tell her, "but they won't let me leave here, and I feel trapped."

Heather sympathizes and offers to do whatever she can. "I'll call Senator Stevens's office; you call Michael Kreider. I know it's impossible, but try to get some rest after that. I have a feeling you'll need it."

I call Michael and talk over my worries about possibly being blocked from leaving Greece tomorrow. He sympathizes but reminds me not to burn my bridges. "Be patient, kiddo. You're almost home." I'm sure he feels as helpless as Heather does, and no one, including me, knows for sure what key will unlock this puzzle of how to get us home.

I get towels for my daughters, now shriveled from their long bath, and get them into makeshift pajamas—sweatshirts from the pile of donated clothes.

Senator Stevens's office assistant calls me promptly to confirm that the girls and I are safe. "We hear you're being held hostage inside the consulate," the female caller said. "Are you okay?"

The consulate staff hover around me. I feel like I'm about to become a tattletale. "Thank you. We're fine. Really. Yes, I'm sure."

I don't feel fine, but the consulate staff has helped us so much. How can I possibly say anything to the contrary? I may not agree with their decision to make us stay overnight, but we're a far cry from hostages.

By the time I finish my phone calls, the girls are crying. I rush to them just in time for Marianthi to vomit in the toilet. Meredith quietly watches as I bathe Marianthi all over again. Ms. Dimos rounds up some toys, and we attempt to distract the girls. I can't help but mourn just a little for the lovely dolls I bought, left behind in the ruckus. By the time I get the girls tucked in bed, they are both trembling and whining. I have nothing to offer. My energy and my empathy are gone, and they don't seem to have much use for them anyhow. I sit on the floor and write in my journal.

Triumph is hollow when children suffer.
I believed I would likely give up today.
Please, God, make it work.
Many to thank.

❊ ❊ ❊

I sit awake and watch the girls. I haven't been near them while they sleep in twenty-five months. I listen to their rhythmic breathing with a new sense of wonder.

By the time 5:00 A.M. rolls around, I hear the consulate staff bustling downstairs. I tiptoe out of the room to see what's going on. "We've made arrangements for you and the girls to go to Athens this morning," Ms. Dimos tells me. "From there, you'll catch a flight to France with the children. We've got to get moving, though, in case we run into problems."

Thirty minutes later, my tired little girls are dressed and ready to go. They look disoriented, and once we load into the consulate limousine, they begin to cry.

"I've taken the liberty of using a different last name for you," Ms. Dimos says over the girls' cries. "It's Miller for today," she says, handing me the airline tickets.

The government is encouraging me to sneak out of Greece with my children. Weird. Shouldn't I be able to leave with my head held high after all we've been through? I don't want to slink away like a common criminal.

"Is that really necessary?"

"I don't want any harm to come to you, but we heard this morning that Gregory was released immediately after his arrest," she says breezily. "He's been making a disturbance at the airport."

I *knew* it. I desperately wanted to leave Greece by train last night to avoid this very thing.

"We'll drive you directly through a back way at the airport," Ms. Thomas says. "He won't see you, and you can get directly on the plane. Don't worry. You'll be safe."

We'll see. The word safe has been so overused during this

trip. By Manolis. By the lawyers. By the consulate staff. By me. But despite all the assistance, I don't feel safe at all. I feel the breath of Disaster on the back of my neck right now. If only I can make it out of Greece with my girls, then I will feel safe.

The limousine driver takes us to the back of the airport, where the planes are departing, and we get out and go through a side door into a private room.

"Ms. Barnes will meet you at the airport in Athens," Ms. Dimos says. "From the embassy. She'll help you with passports."

What would I do without her? She's thought of everything. I'd forgotten about the problem with the passports, and help from Ms. Barnes, from the American embassy, is the only answer to that problem.

"Good luck, girls!" Ms. Dimos kisses their tear-stained faces. "Don't cry. You're going home! You're going to Alaska, girls!"

But the girls are not easily comforted. They are tired. They've been ripped away from their routines in Greece and from their father. And they haven't eaten any real food in a day.

Nothing I can say will make it better. Tears roll down their cheeks. I try to be cheerful, but it must come off as fake as it feels, so I focus only on finding our seats in the plane. As we take off, I try to find something cheery to say.

"Girls, we're going to France," I tell them. "We can go to Euro Disney!"

They both look at me blankly. "Mickey Mouse, remember?"

Slight grins form on their faces. It's a cheap trick. I've always wanted to take them to Disneyland in America. Now we get to do something a little more exotic, and besides, they deserve some sort of reward just for making it through the ordeal. So do I. We need to bank a new, good memory together.

Our plane lands in Athens less than an hour later. We are halfway out of danger.

The girls are starving, and as soon as I find a vending

machine, I buy some stale sandwiches and soda pops and we settle on a bench, waiting for Ms. Barnes. I struggle to unwrap the vacuum-packed sandwiches without dropping them. I haven't met Ms. Barnes before, but I talked to her on the phone once or twice last year when I was in Greece.

"You must be Marianthi and Meredith," she says, and I look up to see a tall, handsome, blonde woman in a navy-blue suit looking down at the girls. "I'm Liz Barnes," she tells me, and before I can shake her hand, Mr. Michael Pappas joins us.

"So, these are your lovely daughters?" he says, bending down to get a closer look at the girls.

Two years of work, and he finally gets to meet my children and enjoy the fruits of his labor. The girls like him immediately. I feel myself relax just a little. All the planning, the waiting, the arguing over how to proceed, it's finally panning out. My girls will return home safely to America after all.

Mr. Pappas hands me some custody paperwork. Ms. Barnes takes the school pictures I brought her and uses a small machine to create passports. Mr. Pappas sits erect on the bench with us; his confidence is contagious. The girls squirm in their chairs after they finish their food, and Mr. Pappas speaks to them in Greek.

After Ms. Barnes hands me the passports, it's time. They walk us to the immigration office. The children, still sad but slightly more energized, fall in line behind me.

There are few people boarding the plane for France, and the children and I are in the back of the line. I turn back to wave to Mr. Pappas and Ms. Barnes, before handing our passports and paper tickets to the customs agent. He reads our names aloud once. Then a second time. A smile spreads across his face as he calls out to a second agent in Greek.

Terror pierces my heart. A sliding door shuts behind us. We are walled off from Mr. Pappas and Ms. Barnes.

"Is your name Lizbeth Meredith?"

"Yes," I say, instantly wishing I could take it back after he shoots the other agent a knowing look. "Yes, it is."

"You're under arrest for child kidnapping. Please come with me."

Chapter 19

LIMBO

It's easy for me to escape. I've had plenty of practice. So handcuffs and jails and big, scary men be damned. You can't scare me. I'm gone.

I don't return for a few hours, but I watch the mess play out like a bad docudrama. Woman is arrested in a foreign country, accused of stealing her stolen children. She sits in the airport security office, frozen, staring ahead, feeling guilty for signing the onslaught of paperwork the police officer pushes in front of her, all written in Greek, after her request for an interpreter is denied. She should know better. She is soon joined in the office by her daughters, who remain in the care of the lawyer and government official advocating on her behalf. Woman's former husband magically arrives on the scene just afterward, though he himself lives a four-hour drive away. He swoops up the woman's stolen children and easily reclaims them, letting the whole room know he's seen the airline manifests and knows that the woman is traveling under the last name Miller, inadvertently acknowledging that he is a police informant. Phone calls are made between police agencies in Athens and Thessaloniki, and the Athens police are furious when they learn that the kidnapping allegations by the woman's former husband are indeed false. Police release the woman. They escort all of the parties out and return her daughters, who withdraw from her touch as though they've been burned by fire and run back to their father. A pulling match between the parents ensues, and the fighting is contagious. The police officers argue with her former husband but then back slowly out of the melee. Former husband slaps the woman's face as the scramble for the lost daughters continues. The husband then enjoys a temporary win.

And with the slap, I'm back in the nick of time for a few police officers to re-engage just enough. There is help. From the police. From Mr. Pappas. From Liz Barnes. Enough to get my daughters back and to be whisked away in Ms. Barnes's car after Mr. Pappas tells me that I'll have to stay in Greece.

For how long? I want to know.

"At least for the next few weeks," he says. "I'm sorry to tell you that there'll be court hearings to sort this all out."

A few weeks? I'm flat out of cash. Flat out of energy. Flat out of hope. And where on earth will I go with these girls? They don't speak English, and they don't want to be with me after the turmoil of the last couple of days.

"You and the children are welcome to stay with me for a little while, until we know more about what's going on," Ms. Barnes says weakly as she stares ahead. "I live in a secure building, and there's plenty of room."

"We'd love it," I say without hesitation. I know it's an offer Ms. Barnes instantly regrets, but I have no other options.

I'm too tired to put up any arguments, anyhow. I'd like to be in a real home. I can save a little money while the girls and I regroup.

During the ride to her home, I look at Ms. Barnes as she makes pleasant conversation with the three of us. She has a pale, clear complexion and dresses modestly; I imagine her to be well-read, like maybe a lit or history major in college.

We drive up to her home, and the gates to her yard open like magic. I swear I can hear her thoughts leaking out her ears. *Don't let them in. It'll be anarchy. Run!*

I wonder if she's violated her professional boundaries as a government employee by letting us stay with her.

Her house is a two-story, marble-floored dwelling complete with a library and a maid.

"You're welcome to stay in this bedroom," she says, motioning to a spacious guest room. "We ought to all relax tonight, but tomorrow you should really get started on making those calls your attorney mentioned."

I've already forgotten. Mr. Pappas told me to get to work on getting the girls a forensic psychologist to evaluate them and later testify in court to the reasons why abducted children might later cling to their abductor. How will I do this, knowing so little Greek?

"Can't you do it?" I want to ask. But no one else knows my schedule, my whereabouts, and my finances as well as I do. It's time to put on my big-girl pants and be a mom.

I know I'll need to get a teacher to tutor the girls in English, on the off chance that a social worker or judge interviews them later. The Hague Convention's extradition treaty gives reasonable assurances that no one can put abducted children on the spot by asking them to "vote" on where they want to live, but if I've learned one thing during this process, it's to plan for the worst.

After I turn on some cartoons for the girls, I call my law-yer Jim Swanson in Alaska. His sister Ann is with him, and after I tell Jim about the whole mess, she gets on the line. "I've thought about it, and I'm coming to Greece," she announces.

Did I just hear what I thought I heard? Did Ann really say she would be joining me?

Ann's eight-year-old son, Matt, is the center of her world, and I can't imagine her leaving the state of Alaska without him, much less leaving the country.

"No way," I tell her. "You've got Michael and Matt to take care of." But Ann won't budge. "Nonsense. They'll do just fine. I just think you could use some support, since you don't have family to come to court on your behalf."

I definitely need the help. My father is dead. My siblings are scattered all over the United States, and I've kept them at arm's length throughout the process. And my mother, if she were anywhere in the vicinity, would manage to get us both ejected from Greece without the girls. Ann's help will be very much welcome.

"Besides, I can help the girls to remember their life in Alaska. I'm bringing some of their toys and old pictures," she says.

Ann is a godsend. Whatever I have done to deserve her and her family's support escapes me, but I am thankful for it nonetheless.

I call Poppy last. My arrest has demolished her faith in the abduction recovery process. "I was sure you and the girls were finally going home together. I am so sorry for you, but I have news. Christos from the theatrical group said he would repre-sent you as your defense attorney if you need one, no charge. Thanasis said you could stay with his mother and father in Thessaloniki with the girls if you need to, for as long as you'd like. Maria and Christina send their love and will support you in any way you need. You have friends here in Thessaloniki,

Liz. I won't be able to see you, very likely, because Mr. Pappas has told me to stay out of it, and I need to take care of the office while he works on your case. For this, I am sorry, but soon you'll have Ann here, too. You are not alone."

I'm not alone, but I sure feel like I am sometimes.

The kids and I spend the rest of the day trying to stay out of Ms. Barnes's way, and I try to repair the harm the forcible removal of my daughters has caused. When I comment to them about a show they're watching, a game they're playing, what they might like to eat—if I so much as speak a word—I get a reproachful stare. They are furious with me.

Bedtime can't come soon enough. The girls strip down to their underwear and crawl in bed together while I wash up in the bathroom, and when I come back, they are huddled together in solidarity.

I mix my languages together. "Good night. *Kalispera*. I love you," I tell them. They say nothing. I slip into bed, careful not to touch them and cause more angst.

If I let myself think about it too much, I'll get sick. My daughters were ripped away from me more than two years ago, and they lost their mom, their home, their friends, their routines, even their language. And now, by showing up and trying to correct these wrongs, I've done it to them all over again. The losses. The trauma. Two years apart.

We should be in France right now. We should be celebrating. Now, the future is as unclear as it ever was. Can I take this? The courts? The language barrier while lining up services? My stressed-out girls? The mounting debt? This is the first night in more than two years that I'm sleeping in the same home as my daughters, but as I drift off, there is no peace.

❖ ❖ ❖

I open my eyes. Gregory is standing over me, the girls tucked under each of his arms. "You think I can't find you?" he says with a sneer. "I told you years ago if you left me, you'd never see them again. Say good-bye now. Forever."

I shoot straight up. The girls shift in bed next to me.

It was only a nightmare. My heart is beating wildly now. After a few deep breaths, I sink back into the bed.

The next morning, I sneak out of bed, creep upstairs, and begin making calls to find a psychologist before the girls wake up. My attempts at Greek aren't sufficient to relay my needs effectively. How do you say in Greek, "Hello, I'm in Greece temporarily to bring my abducted daughters back home to America. They don't speak English, and I'll need you to prepare something for the Greek courts. Can you help me, please?" I have no idea. Instead, with the Greek-English dictionary in hand, I stammer "*Kalimera. Melahtah Engleekah?*" (Good morning. Do you speak English?)

Call after call turns up nothing. Maybe it is the noise I make with each call that wakes the girls. I hear the sound of rattling metal while I'm dialing another number, and I look out the window to find the girls, wearing their borrowed clothes, fumbling with Ms. Barnes's gate, trying to escape.

I slam the receiver down and run outside, reaching them just in time. "What are you doing? What are you *doing?*" I yell, despite the fact that it's clear. They are getting away. From me.

Marianthi's chin trembles. Meredith's gaze is steady, but her eyes pool with tears. I reach out to hug them, but they recoil. It takes everything I've got to soften my tone enough to speak gently and eventually coerce them back inside.

❉ ❉ ❉

A few days later, Ms. Barnes tells me that she is hosting a tea party for coworkers. "I'd invite you, but it's not a child-friendly function. But I called a friend I think you'd enjoy spending the day with. She's got a little daughter for the girls to play with."

Though we've known each other for only a few days, I've spent a lot of time talking to Ms. Barnes by now. Enough time through shared cups of coffee and tea to know that she's smart. She's compassionate. She's intuitive. Enough time to trust her judgment.

Mimi, she explains, was a young American tourist who met and married a Greek entrepreneur more than a decade earlier. She has now made Greece her home. She, her husband, George, and their four year-old daughter, Margot, live with George's mother in Chalandri, a nearby northern suburb of Athens.

This is fine, I tell her. In truth, I am relieved to be spared a social event. During the best of times, in my own hometown and in my own language, a tea party has never been my thing. Though I like people in small doses, I don't like group events. The idea of making stilted conversations with strangers in my current condition is entirely unappealing.

❉ ❉ ❉

I knock on the door ever so softly. I'm never inclined to knock on a stranger's door in real life, but here I am in Greece with my Greek-speaking daughters. This is unreal, so why not?

The door opens. Mimi is a dead ringer for Goldie Hawn in *Private Benjamin*. She holds the phone in one hand and a cigarette in the other. She smiles and waves us into the house without interrupting her conversation, which is in fluent Greek. I have found a friend.

Mimi lives in a two-story home—Spartan-styled with white walls—that her husband inherited from his family. It comes with all the amenities, including his mother and his childhood furnishings.

"Don't mind me," she says as she hangs up the phone. "My life's always a little crazy, trying to help George with the business and shuttle Margot to her lessons. And dealing with her," Mimi says, pointing her head in her mother-in-law's direction, rolling her eyes, and laughing. "So if I seem a little scattered, just bear with me."

Her mother-in-law looks like every other Greek widow. She wears a black housedress and scarf and keeps her smiles to a minimum to demonstrate her eternal grief about the death of her husband.

The girls' mouths fall open when they see Margot's room. She has shelves of dolls, a television and VCR, and a closet full of dress-up clothes. Margot shares her toys, pleased to have older visitors. For the first time, I see my daughters forget about their current stressors and play with abandon like any other children.

I'm pleased that the girls are happily occupied while I enjoy time with an adult, and Mimi isn't just any adult; she's someone I would be naturally drawn to under normal circumstances. Mimi lights another cigarette and pours me a cup of coffee. We sit on the patio and talk straight through the afternoon, until her husband comes home for dinner.

George is in his early forties, a round-bellied man, who stands around five foot nine and has dark-brown hair and smiling, brown eyes. He wears a button-down shirt and tie, which he covers immediately with an apron.

"What's for dinner, George?" Mimi asks, giving him a quick kiss. He smiles good-naturedly and opens the refrigerator.

The resemblance between Mimi's marriage and my own is nil. Her husband seems easygoing and fun. The household chores are done mostly by a maid or by George's mother, Mimi tells me, and the laundry is done by an Egyptian woman who comes by twice a week. Sign me up for Mimi's life. The children play together all afternoon and watch *Balto*, an animated movie based on a true story about a dog that intervened in the 1925 diphtheria epidemic by bringing a life-saving serum to Nome, Alaska. My daughters are mesmerized. I feel like a normal mom with normal kids under normal circumstances. I so needed this day, and so did the girls. Before it's time to leave, Mimi tells me that her family has a membership at the local athletic club and invites me and the girls to be her guest there soon.

"Do you girls swim at all?" Mimi asks my daughters. When they don't answer, Mimi asks it in Greek, and my daughters answer affirmatively, with giggles.

"We don't have swimsuits or anything," I tell her.

"Don't worry about a thing," Mimi says. "I've got extra everything around this place, I swear."

I hug Mimi good-bye. I have a skip in my step as the children and I walk back to Ms. Barnes's house. Now I have two friends in Athens.

Over the next few days, I add to the numbers. Through Mimi, I meet her best friend, Fern, an American woman who, like Mimi, met and married a Greek entrepreneur on a visit from Florida a decade earlier. Fern later divorced her husband and married a Greek physician. With him she has two children, a boy and a girl, who are around the age of my kids.

Then I meet Chris, a Scottish woman who teaches English at a private American school in Greece. Chris is in her late fifties and reinvented herself after her kids were grown by divorcing her husband and moving to Greece. With her short white hair and ruddy, round face, Chris reminds me of an older version of Mary Poppins, and I know my kids will love her. She's a natural choice to tutor the girls, which she agrees to do after meeting them.

Next I meet Sandy, a quiet British woman who married Lambros, the equally quiet Greek owner of a neighborhood bakery. They introduce me to Theodora, a Greek woman and diner owner, who tells proudly of her younger years living in New York City. "I love that place! I wonder to myself sometimes: Why did I even come back to Greece?"

Thanks to Ms. Barnes and to Mimi, I now have the beginnings of a whole new community. After a week at Ms. Barnes's house, I rent a room at the Acropole Hotel, about a mile from her home, which offers a free continental breakfast and a neighborhood setting. I'll miss having Ms. Barnes to talk to, but she needs her own life back, and I need to work on becoming a family unit with the girls again.

The Acropole is a three-star hotel with a large, welcoming lobby and a kitchen on the side that feels like home. The front desk staff are equally welcoming, and every worker, from the maids to the clerks, seems enamored with my daughters. This will be a perfect setting for reestablishing our relationships and routines, and for having English lessons with Chris in the hotel lobby.

Our days develop a certain rhythm. Every morning, we wake up in time to dash downstairs to the lobby for our complimentary continental breakfast. The headwaiter gingerly makes conversation with the children as we have our hard-boiled eggs, toast, and chamomile tea. "Don't waste your food, young ladies. Eat! Eat!" Once the girls finish breakfast, the hotel maid arrives to give them congratulatory hugs.

Next, it's time for Chris to give them English lessons in the hotel lobby. Afterward, we go to Sandy and Lambros's bakery, where the equivalent of three American dollars allows all three of us to eat spinach or cheese pies. Then we return to our room, watch *Sailor Moon*, doze off for a nap, and follow the nap with a long walk.

It is our daily walk that becomes the most restorative part of the day. The girls are forced to need me, whether it's to tie a shoe or to give them my hand to hold to cross the street. I am useful. I notice that the physical distance between the girls and me shrinks. Conversations flow easily as we scout for giant tortoises or navigate our way to the church playground for time on the swings and slide and in the sandbox.

"Push me, Mom," Meredith yells out in English as she sits on a swing. Marianthi watches as I help her sister sail in the air. After a few pushes, Marianthi tentatively sits on the swing next to her sister. "Push *me!*"

After an hour or so at the playground, we walk back to the hotel room. Then it is time for dinner, usually at the hotel's restaurant or across the street at Theodora's diner. Then bath time, then bedtime. Rinse and repeat. Once I hear the girls' breathing become rhythmic as they lie in bed beside me, I know they are asleep. Now I can obsess.

I obsess about Gregory. Where is he? What will his next move be? Does he know where we are? I also fret about money. But my worst ruminations are about the future court hearing.

It looks grim, not having any family from America by my side, particularly since Gregory has a large, close-knit family. Add to that the fact that the girls have already spent two years in Greece. A judge might ignore the promises of the Hague Convention to send the abducted children back to their place of habitual residence. Two years' time is nothing to an adult, but for the girls, who were four and six when they were abducted, it is significant.

After thirty minutes of indulging in my anxieties, I generate a corresponding to-do list in my head.

Call Heather about possible fundraiser.

Connect with Thessaloniki friends for court support.

Call all attorneys involved in case to gauge likelihood of success in court. (Weigh the favorable opinions most heavily.)

Gregory never makes my list. He is out of my control, and I know the effort spent anticipating his next move will only drain me of my limited energy.

In mid-April, Mimi's family includes us in two important holidays. The first is Orthodox Easter, where we dine with Mimi's family on lamb and potatoes and plenty of retsina at a seaside restaurant. The second is Meredith's seventh birthday, just four days later. I missed her fifth and sixth birthdays, so simply being with her and her sister is pretty spectacular. Mimi invites us to her home for a party. With Fern's children, Margot and some of her friends, and a few stray neighborhood invitees, Meredith has a respectable gathering around a cake. We sing her "Happy Birthday" in English and in Greek. There are gifts and balloons and cake, and my youngest daughter splits her time between looking delighted and looking scared of something I can't understand.

Occasionally, just after English lessons, Mimi will drive the girls and me to the athletic club she belongs to in Chalandri. There, we spend the afternoon relaxing on the patio while the girls splash in the pool with Margot. Little by little, as their language skills improve and as we embrace the predictabilities, my relationship with the girls gets stronger.

Which isn't to say it's going perfectly. Sometimes I'm shocked at their lack of civility.

"Mom, I have to pee!"

I throw a towel around Meredith, who is wet and trembling as I help her out of the pool. We make a beeline for the ladies' room. "Here you go, sweetie." I let go of Meredith's hand, and she stands in the bathroom stall, urinating through her swimsuit onto the floor. She smiles afterward.

"What are you doing, young lady?" I'm trying to make an impression as her mother, as her embarrassed and irritated mother.

Meredith is unapologetic. "I had to pee," she says.

"Meredith Eleni, you use the toilet. That was *disgusting*! Now your swimsuit is filthy."

She shrugs her shoulders and runs back to the pool, jumping in before I can stop her.

I complain to Mimi, who listens without judgment. "You really should talk to Chris," she says. "She's mentioned noticing some things with your girls. Nothing too bad, but unusual in Greece."

"What things?"

"It's nothing to worry about too much," Chris tells me the next day after the English lessons. "It's just that the girls are speaking a type of hillbilly Greek, and they're pretty crude with each other. They say things that aren't appropriate for any young kids to be saying, let alone little Greek girls. Honestly, Liz, you can tell from the things they say that they haven't been cared for by their relatives or any reasonable adults."

I think about this after Chris leaves. Initially when I asked the girls how their lives were in Greece with their father, Marianthi spoke up quickly.

"We're happy here. We live well with our father," she told me. "We have toys and friends and family. We have everything here."

I didn't want to argue, but the things I had witnessed already—their lack of schooling, their frighteningly pale complexions, their substandard command of the Greek language— told a far different tale.

After a week of English lessons, I tell Meredith that her language skills are progressing quickly.

"We don't go to school much here in Greece," she says. "Daddy thinks you will find us."

I try to be nonchalant. "What do you mean, baby? You just stay home?"

"Daddy choked my sister for having a friend over. He choked her neck because a friend came over and she gave her chocolate. Daddy said you came to Greece to find us once, so we couldn't go outside anymore."

My daughters' childhood has been hijacked. They are living out my intended life sentence. I will escape no more. There is a lot to face if I have any shot at bringing the girls home and reconnecting them with the childhood they deserve.

Chapter 20

THE COURT DRAMA

"Let's get down to brass tacks," Ann says, after she gets settled in her room downstairs from us at the Acropole. She's just arrived by taxi from the airport in Athens in time for us all to eat dinner together, and already my daughters are squirming with anticipation.

They remember her. The mother of their little friend Matt who had not one but two drawers filled with candy in the kitchen. The mother who never had a bad day. The mother who invited them over for the annual Easter egg hunt in her yard, where hundreds of eggs were hidden in the snow. They remember Ann. They love Ann. Plus, they've seen her carry-on, filled to the brim with toys.

She hands Meredith a small doll and gives Marianthi a sparkly unicorn.

"Thank you!" they both say, like perfect little angels. Ann tousles their hair and turns back to me.

"I've talked to Jim, and he agrees that we need to be prepared to buy the girls' affections if we have to."

Ouch. Her words feel like a hand slapping me hard across the face.

Seeing my reaction, she continues. "It's just that we've got only a few days to break through two years' worth of damage, Liz. Don't look at me like that."

Ann has also brought us pictures from America. "Here's the new house your Mom bought, girls. And do you remember these dolls? Do you see your Legos? And we've got a few presents wrapped up for you in your rooms, too."

"Do we both have rooms now?" Marianthi's eyes widen.

"You do. Look! I took pictures of them." The girls nearly crawl on top of each other to sit close to Ann on her bed and view the pictures. "And guess what else? My brother Jim will be coming here in a couple of days to see you girls! Do you remember Jim?"

The girls nod happily.

It's working. Ann knows exactly what she's doing.

Ann makes our everyday routine 33 percent more fun. When the children get bored watching *Sailor Moon* in the afternoon, Ann gets a large box from the hotel kitchen, along with some scissors and a set of Magic Markers. Within two hours, she and the children have made an elaborate dollhouse out of the box, complete with a yard and pets.

Jim arrives on Thursday, as planned. The girls are pleased to see him, too, remembering him as the heroic Uncle Jim of their pre-Greece childhoods, as well as his generous nature. He reserves two extravagant suites at the Athens Hilton Hotel, one for him and Ann and one for the girls and me. Jim delights in watching the girls' faces as they open the door to our room, and his credit cards burn a trail through the city of Athens that leads from the Acropolis to the famous Plaka.

The children relax into their new lifestyle of the rich and famous. Happy grins now replace their wary expressions. And as their comfort and happiness increase, so does my confidence level about the upcoming court hearing.

With Jim there to work with the Greek attorneys, Ann and I are free to make the rounds in Chalandri and get a read on opinion surrounding our case.

"There's no doubt you'll win," Sandy says, as she packs our lunch of spanakopita. "Lambros ran your case by his retired judge friend, and he was confident you'll return to America with your girls."

"How can you not win? This isn't the Ice Age," Theodora says at dinnertime. "This is Greece. Justice was invented here."

But Mimi is far less certain. She tells me the story of a non-Greek mother she knew who divorced her husband and lost custody of their small kids. "Now she is forever stuck here, working a crappy job to support herself so she can have her occasional visits with her kids. Greeks stick up for Greeks, Liz. It's a poor, small country, and no one here would voluntarily send Greek kids out of this place. It just won't happen."

Mimi's message sends a shiver down my spine. I don't want to argue with her, but Greece signed on to the Hague Convention regarding international child abduction three years ago. They wouldn't have become a signatory without intending to honor it, would they?

It's Jim who brings me back to earth. We meet for lunch to discuss the upcoming hearing while Ann and the girls go to the park.

"The girls have to go to Thessaloniki with us. The judge insists that he get a chance to interview them."

This is counter to everything I've been told up until now. "But that's exactly what the Hague Convention is supposed to prevent: asking two traumatized kids where they want to live. How is that even fair?"

"There's nothing I can do about it," Jim says. "We can't violate the court's order." He pats my shoulder. "Don't worry; I think we'll be just fine."

But I am less convinced than ever. I never did find a forensic psychologist for the hearing, and although the lawyers haven't asked about it recently, it makes me wonder what, exactly, the court will base its decision on. And how are we supposed to travel to Thessaloniki without causing another scene at the airport? And who will watch the girls while we're in court? How can I be sure that they won't disappear all over again?

The Ministry of Justice offers police protection. Before my arrest, I might've felt reassured by police presence. Now, I can't tell anymore who is safe or not.

Poppy's sister offers us complimentary accommodations in their luxurious hotel, the Philippion. Ann pays travel costs for Chris to accompany us to Thessaloniki and supervise them.

To avoid the airport scene, Ann, the girls, and I take the six-hour train ride to Thessaloniki. We meet Chris and Jim, who flew in earlier, and get settled in the hotel. Police escorts lurk outside our hotel rooms. I can barely speak, I'm so nervous. I half expect our police escorts to burst into our rooms and take the children themselves. The Philippion is likely the fanciest hotel I'll ever stay in, but I can't exhale and look around. I just want this all to be over.

Jim, Ann, Chris, and I do our best to create a normal atmosphere for the girls, but they, too, seem more quiet than usual. I don't know what to say to them. A court hearing is a lot of pressure for any child. I remember talking to the judge as a small child when my mom wanted to change my last name to match her final husband's. I felt guilty afterward when I found out how my words to the judge later prevented my father from finding me. My kids don't need any more emotional baggage.

On the Friday morning of the hearing, the police drive us to court, careening to a stop on the sidewalk and pulling us out of the patrol car.

Once inside, I have to squint to adjust my vision. The courthouse is filled with a layer of cigarette smoke thick enough to sting my eyes. After walking through long hallways filled with curious onlookers, we reach our courtroom. I say good-bye to the girls, whom Chris will watch in a nearby room during the proceedings.

Inside the courtroom are both Pappas brothers and an attorney representing the Ministry of Justice, Mr. Kamares. Thanasis from the theatrical group is seated on my side, as well as his law partner, Nikos, and a female friend.

"Don't you have to work today?" I ask.

"No problem," Thanasis says, shrugging and giving me his dimpled grin. "We wanted to be here with you."

Ms. Hughes from the American consulate arrives and takes her seat on the pew.

On Gregory's side of the room, I see his sister, Despina; his brother, Costas; and some of his aunts and uncles. I also see a Greek man named Ari from Alaska whom I vaguely remember socializing with at the beginning of my marriage to Gregory. I haven't seen him since Marianthi's birth, but he looks exactly the same: short, fat, and shifty. He looks away from my gaze.

In the center are Gregory and his female attorney, looking at me and whispering to each other. I can't get over the fact that he's hired a woman to represent him—not a young woman who really acts as a paralegal for a male attorney, not an assistant attorney, but a real, grown-up, sharp-looking woman lawyer. She is the female counterpart to Michael Pappas.

In America, courtrooms tend to be the picture of best behavior. The two sides litigating sit a respectful distance apart, each ideally represented by counsel. Dressed in their best clothes, people speak one at a time, avoiding curse words and slang.

This is different. The hearing begins with all of the parties crowding the judge, moving closer and closer to him, speaking loudly and all at the same time. It looks like a sports event.

Michael Pappas sees my reaction to the disorder and quietly explains, "Our courts here still operate under the Napoleonic system. The judge doesn't read long legal briefs before the hearing. Everyone speaks at the same time. The judge will ask most of the questions. You're not in America, Liz."

The judge begins speaking. I turn my attention to the interpreter.

"This is a hearing about child kidnapping. The father abducted the children from Alaska more than two years ago, and then the mother attempted to do the same here."

"Your Honor," Michael Pappas interrupts, "the mother did not know about the impediment made in Greece—that the court changed its mind about allowing her to exercise her American custody rights that we had acknowledged previously. This was *not* the same."

This leads to an eruption from both sides that not even my interpreter can follow. Fists are clenched and feet are stomped as each person loudly tries to drown out everyone else.

"I'll need to speak with the children," the judge continues, "and each party will have one character witness."

Gregory's character witness is Ari, short for Aristotle. An old friend of Gregory's from Alaska, Ari looks like a pudgy Vegas piano player. He wears flashy clothes and jewelry, and his brown hair is perfectly coiffed. He has a boyish grin, and I remember him to be easygoing.

"I have known Grigorios for many years," he tells the judge. "I met Liz in 1985, and knew the girls and Liz after their divorce. I spent time with the kids regularly when they lived in Alaska."

True, I did meet Ari in Alaska, but I have only ever seen him four, maybe five, times total. Nothing close to regularly.

Ari says, "Liz gave him permission to take the girls to go to Greece, Your Honor. She was always at nightclubs after their marriage ended. She never went to church, and she wouldn't let little Meredith get baptized in the Greek Church. She beat Meredith. Alaska is bad for those children."

"What do you mean, bad for the children?" The judge leans forward.

"Alaska is a cold place to live," Ari says. "And Liz's mother has been divorced three times."

Five if you add up the annulment and the two marriages to my father.

"Does she live with her mother?" the judge asks, looking at the interpreter.

"No," Ari says, "but it's not the Greek way that she should be divorced so many times."

The judge shrugs his shoulders. "Your family is your family." He smiles, looking my way. "You don't pick them. They just are."

"And Liz works for a lesbian organization," Ari continues. "It's no good for the kids."

A lesbian organization? So, working with victims of domestic violence equals a lesbian organization in the World According to Ari. The judge does not seem persuaded by his testimony.

Now it is time for the Pappas brothers to cross-examine Ari. I would feel better if Michael Pappas began, but it is his brother who takes the lead. Panayiotis stands straight as an arrow, his voice projecting loudly. Though I can't understand what he's saying except through the interpreter, his confidence is apparent.

"Sir," Panayiotis begins, "how long have you lived in Greece?"

"I was born here," Ari answers. "This is my home."

"What I mean," Panayiotis says, "is how long have you lived in Greece since you moved back here from Alaska?"

Ari pauses. "I don't know, exactly," he says. "It's been a while."

"Has it been a year? Two years? Five years?"

No response.

Panayiotis pulls out a photograph of the girls and several of their friends at Marianthi's sixth birthday party.

"Will you please point out Marianthi and Meredith in this photograph, then?"

Ari looks helplessly at Gregory and then back at the picture before him. Finally, he points to two little girls in the middle of the photograph.

"Your Honor," Panayiotis says, "I would like to point out that Marianthi and Meredith are right here." Panayiotis points to the girls, standing together at the far right side of the picture. "Not even close to where our witness has pointed."

The judge glares at Ari. "You may leave the court, sir," he says sternly. "And I will warn you to refrain from speaking about things you know nothing of."

Now it is time for a character witness to speak on my behalf. Jim Swanson agrees to testify instead of Ann, since his gender and status as a lawyer will likely carry more weight with the court. Gregory bumps against Jim as Jim makes his way to the judge.

"I'll see you in hell," Jim growls under his breath.

Jim briefly outlines the legal history between Gregory and me, from our divorce to the abduction of the girls.

"Your Honor, I have known Liz for only six years, but in that time, she has grown to be like a member of our family. I have seen her with the girls on many occasions, including Easters. And I have watched her struggle just to keep a roof over their heads, just to keep them safe."

After a few more minutes of questioning, Jim is finished. Gregory's attorney has no questions for him. The judge calls a five-minute recess.

Now Gregory testifies. He's wearing a navy pin-striped suit, and if I didn't know him better, I wouldn't guess that he's nervous. His exaggerated smile to the judge is a dead giveaway.

"Sir, where do you work?" the judge asks him.

"Your Honor, I have been working as a travel consultant for the past two years at the Hotel Kastoria." He smiles proudly.

"How have you managed to work there for the past two years when it has been closed for five years?" the judge asks. "It has only recently reopened."

For the first time, the room is silent while Gregory struggles to think of another hotel name. "Your Honor, with all due respect, I'm nervous. I meant to say the Hotel Argo. Anyway, Liz let me take the kids to Greece. I asked her if I could, and she said yes. I have been falsely accused here."

He can't scurry away fast enough. My lawyers don't have much to ask him, since the judge has already shredded Gregory's integrity.

Finally, it is my turn to speak. All eyes are on me as I move closer to the judge.

"Ma'am, is it true that social workers have been called in Alaska about your abusing the children?" the judge asks me.

"It is true, Your Honor," I say without hesitating. "Anytime I refused to reconcile with my husband, he would call a social worker or a welfare worker, and then my house would be full of strangers, undressing my children to search for bruises, looking through my closets for possible hidden money. It has been a way to punish me for leaving him. So yes, it is true that social workers have been called. It is *not* true that I abused the girls."

I feel a sense of peace as I speak. For so long, I have waited for a chance to set things right. A chance to be heard. And now that the time has come, my words have not failed me.

I testify about my marriage, my separation, and my divorce from Gregory. I divulge to the court about living with the fear that he would take the most important thing from me: my children. I speak of the efforts I've made to find the girls and bring them back once Gregory did take them, and the legion of friends and community members, both in Alaska and now in Greece, who've joined me to help bring the girls home.

"I know I can trust the Greek courts to do the right thing, or I would never have pursued these legal efforts to recover my daughters," I say in closing, making direct eye contact with the judge. "I trust the court will look at the Hague Convention on its merits, and in doing so not pressure my already-damaged daughters further by asking them to choose where they would like to live."

"Thank you, ma'am. You are correct," the judge tells me. "Thank you for your testimony. I have heard all that I need."

His expression softens as he looks at me.

After the judge leaves the room, I am hugged from all sides. "You won for sure," Thanasis tells me. Jim Swanson, and Michael and Panayiotis Pappas are visibly pleased with their own performances and how our side of the hearing went. I look at the bench behind me. Ann Kreider and the consulate staff are sitting close to my young attorney friends. I do wish Poppy could have come today.

Once the girls meet individually with the judge, it is over.

I resist the urge to ask my daughters how it went. It's done. I need to hold on to that. Relief washes over us all as we head back to the Philippion Hotel to celebrate our victory.

Now there is nothing left to do but await the judge's ruling.

Chapter 21

THE WAITING GAME

The waiting takes longer than I could ever have imagined. We return to Athens and to the Acropole Hotel the next day. Jim returns to Alaska on Monday. Seven days later, Ann follows.

"I know you guys will be right behind me, Lizzie," she says, as she gives me a hug good-bye. "I just *know* it!"

I want to believe her, but with each passing day, a little more doubt creeps in. We expected to hear the ruling within five to seven business days. What possibly could be taking so long?

Watching Ann leave in the taxi, the girls look deflated, and I feel puny and alone.

As if she can hear my troubles, Poppy calls with news from Thessaloniki. "I heard from a court secretary that the judge in your case told her after your hearing, 'No one would ever separate that mother from her children.'"

I wait for Poppy's translation.

"You will go home with your children. This is sure," Poppy promises.

Poppy gossips about other happenings in Thessaloniki with our theatrical friends, but my mind is stuck on her earlier words. *You will go home with your children.* And I want to believe them. Sometimes when I rewind the court-hearing highlights in my mind—Gregory's being confronted about his consistent untruths; his character witness's inability to pick out my kids in a photograph, despite claiming a certain closeness with them; Jim Swanson's testimony; even my own words—I know deep down to my core that the judge will rule in my favor and I will soon take the girls home to Alaska.

Now it's early May—two weeks out from the hearing. The girls and I remain even closer to the hotel, just in case the call about the ruling comes. The hotel staff comprises our social circle. The maid, a strawberry-blonde woman in her late forties, plays with the girls each morning as we breakfast in the lobby, singing nursery rhymes and playing peek-a-boo with them. *Does she think they're babies?* I wonder. Greeks seem to coddle their children more than I am used to, but the girls love it.

In the confined space of our hotel room, we have ample opportunity to get up close and personal, and now that the girls' command of the language has returned, they comment on the physical changes they've noticed in me since our years apart.

Meredith mentions a disturbing conversation with her father. "Daddy says he had to stab your tires in Alaska because you had a boyfriend," she tells me one day, her eyes boring into mine for a response.

This is wrong on so many levels. Why was my ex-husband

excusing his criminal conduct to my little daughter? Did he mention to her we'd been apart for years when he slashed my tires? And how scary is it for my daughter to hear from her father that abusing another person is justifiable?

At least my dad owned up to his behavior. The very first time I met him, he insisted on having a moment alone with me once we'd reached his house.

"I did something wrong to your mother, and I need to make it right," he said. I didn't want to hear about it, but he offered me no choice. "It's bothered me for a long time. It's affected you and the other kids, and I've never forgiven myself." My dad said that he'd beaten my mother, breaking her nose. "There's no excuse for what I did. I should have never done it. No one has the right to hurt another person, and I was wrong."

I remember ending the conversation as quickly as possible, but his words were somewhat of a revelation to me.

No one has the right to hurt another person. This from a man who had hurt someone and had the courage to admit it. This after years of hearing my mother tell us kids how we'd earned our injuries by our conduct.

I don't want to lecture my little girl right now, since she's just beginning to open up, but there is a lesson from her dead grandfather that I will share with her soon.

Marianthi reports that I have "crinkles" on my face that weren't there before. Meredith notes that I am paler and thinner than she remembered, and my hair has grown longer. "Your butt fell down," she says, as I get out of the shower.

They also ask more questions about our lives in Alaska. Questions about Barbara, our old roommate. Questions about their friends from school and day care. Questions about the winter snow and darkness in Alaska. They even want to know about my mother.

My mother. The girls have met my mother less than a handful of times, so I am surprised by their sudden interest. "Can we go driving with her when we get back to Alaska?" Marianthi grins, shooting a knowing glance at her sister.

Now I get it. The last time the girls saw their Alaskan grandmother was four years ago, during the weekend of my college graduation. We rode around town with her one day, the girls seated snugly in the back of her rental car. The traffic light turned green as we approached it. "Thank you, Jesus!" my mother sang out.

She said it again as we neared the second traffic light and the third. "Thank you, Jesus!"

But as we neared the fourth traffic light, it remained red for several beats.

"Goddamn sonofabitch!" Mother screeched, as she slammed on the brakes.

I was startled, but Mother appeared nonplussed, staring ahead until the light turned green. I looked at the girls' reflection in the small mirror in my visor. Their hands covered their mouths as they stifled laughter.

They may not miss her, but my daughters do remember their grandmother. And they remember their lives in Alaska.

It's Friday, three weeks after our court hearing. My anxiety has shifted into high gear. I call my attorneys with greater urgency. "Be patient, Liz," Michael Pappas tells me. "I have heard that the judge will make his ruling Tuesday of next week."

Our days are excruciatingly slow now. We fiddle with our food in the morning. Marianthi mashes her boiled egg yolks into a saucer, opens the marmalade, and mixes them together. Meredith is a better eater and finishes her toast, tea, and egg;

she listens to me trying to coax Marianthi into eating and making less of a mess. We've discontinued tutoring since the hearing is over, and I can't help but notice that the main clerk at the front desk has had his second haircut since we first moved in. This is taking way too long.

Tuesday arrives. The girls watch cartoons while I sit on the bed, willing the phone to ring. We walk to Theodora's for lunch.

"Any news, girls?"

"No. But you remember what they say in America—no news is good news, right?" We laugh insincerely, and the girls and I take our lunch back to the hotel, where more cartoons and soap operas await us.

Finally, at dinnertime, the phone rings.

"The judge has taken annual leave today. He was not available to make his ruling after all," Mr. Pappas says. "I'm sorry, Liz. I don't know what to think anymore."

Neither do I. It has to be more than a coincidence that the judge happens to have taken the day off on the day he promised to rule. Something else must be at play.

Masking my apprehension around the girls gets harder and harder. Marianthi corners me the next day at the athletic club while Mimi is in the pool with Margot and Meredith.

"Mom," she says, looking down at her feet, "I don't think this will happen or anything, but what will you do if the judge tells us we have to stay with our dad? What will you do with all of our toys in Alaska?"

This is a punch in the gut.

"I don't know, honey." My eyes fill with tears at the thought of saying good-bye to my daughters. I clear my throat and smile. "I guess I could go home and box the toys up and send them to you."

She shakes her head. "No, Dad will never let us keep

them. I want you to keep them. So you can have something to remember us by."

I turn away as tears spill silently down my cheeks.

But she isn't finished. Marianthi apologizes for lying to me before about their lives. "Daddy said he would hurt us if we told you how things are here for us."

The corrected version, she says, is that she and her sister live in what amounts to a studio apartment with their father and share the double bed with him.

She says they no longer see their relatives and that their father is prone to disappearing for a day or two without warning, leaving Marianthi in charge of feeding and caring for her rowdy younger sister. "Once, we locked ourselves out of our apartment, but a woman saw us and invited us to stay with her. We played with her daughter's toys; she was nice to us."

Why couldn't any of this have come up while we were going through the court hearings?

"And what do you eat when you're on your own?" I ask, keeping my tone even.

"I like bread and chocolate frosting," Marianthi admits, "but Meredith doesn't eat much."

No wonder Meredith is so scrawny and Marianthi's coloring and teeth look unhealthy.

Meredith, wrapped in a towel after emerging from the pool, now joins the conversation. Hearing her sister talk seems to empower her. "Daddy choked me and picked me up by my neck, like he did with our dog." *Poor baby. Poor dog.* She says their father disappears for periods of time and doesn't buy them birthday presents, instead taking for himself the birthday money that relatives have sent the girls.

Sad as it is, it is a relief to hear. They are finally talking, really talking, about their life in Greece with their father, not simply parroting back what he'd want me to hear. But I also can't assume that they will automatically want to leave that life behind and follow me.

"Girls, I have something serious to ask you. Do you think you might want to go home to Alaska with me?"

"I want to go home! I want to go to Alaska with you, Mom," Marianthi says.

Meredith's eyes well up with tears. "I'm scared. I'm afraid to leave Greece," she wails. "I told the judge I didn't want to go, Mom. I just want to visit Alaska. I'm sorry!"

Meredith has only confirmed what I've suspected, but it's hard to hear. And if it is hard for me to hear, it is devastating for her to confess.

I quickly change the subject. "What gift should I give you when you come home to Alaska?"

Marianthi wants a cat. Meredith wants a dog. And both girls agree they need a brother.

"A baby brother isn't something I can just get for you, girls," I explain. "They require a stable relationship and money. I don't have those things right now."

But the girls aren't interested in any excuses from me about why I can't deliver them a brother. They begin naming him, finally agreeing on Kounoupi.

"Kounoupi? I've never heard of that name here," I say. "Why not Nikos or Apollo—something more Greek?"

"It means *mosquito*," Marianthi tells me. "Our brother is Kounoupi."

❖ ❖ ❖

We are on week number eight at the hotel, and until I get paid from AWAIC, I will continue to eat scraps off the girls' plates for sustenance. A bite of meat here, some spinach pie crumbs there, and in the mornings my complimentary boiled eggs, which I sometimes bring back to the hotel room to nibble on during the day. My pants begin to sag, and my flagging energy levels force me to shorten my daily walks with the girls.

"It's seriously time to come up with your plan B," Mimi tells me on Friday while we're at the athletic club. It's mid-May, and I'm facing another weekend without having the court's ruling. "This is Greece. A woman can't count on justice, Liz. So what will you do if the judge rules against you? Will you really leave the girls behind?"

It's a prospect I can't fathom.

My children are being punished for my choice to leave their father. There is no way I will allow him to further destroy their childhood or our lives.

The next day, Mimi and Fern approach me again about cobbling together an alternate exit plan.

"Fern's got a male friend on the island of Kos," Mimi says. "He can meet you and pretend to be your husband so you don't stick out like a sore thumb traveling without a guy. It's a small island, and I don't think computerized passport services exist there. We can get you three on a ferry to meet up with a travel agent he knows who lives there. She's a German woman who was raked over the coals when she divorced her Greek husband, so you're in luck—she'll want to help you. And she can connect you with a boat headed for Turkey."

Turkey? That seems like such a long shot. But since the Turks and Greeks have long-standing political strife between them, we will be safe from reprisals from either the Greek authorities or Gregory. From Turkey, we will make our way back home to Alaska.

The plan has some easily foreseen wrinkles.

I won't have any way of verifying that Kos doesn't have automatic passport services until I get there. My visa, good for ninety days, has expired. The girls' passports are brand new, and mine is two years old. They speak fluent Greek and have clearly been living in Greece for some time. Greek mothers don't routinely travel alone in the smaller villages and islands with their children, so I will need to count on this unknown Greek male for help. What will he want in return? I don't have enough money to get any farther than Turkey. And I can't be sure of how the girls will endure the stress of an escape plan, given their young ages and Meredith's ambivalence about going back to America.

Just the thought of being caught en route and separated from the girls is terrifying. Being arrested once in a lifetime was enough for me. No interpreters are offered. It's not like America. No public defender is guaranteed. I could rot away in Greece or Turkey, potentially for years, and never see my daughters again if I'm apprehended while trying to leave.

But my friends are right—I can no longer bury my head in the sand and pretend the children and I are somehow guaranteed a storybook ending. We may have to move toward a plan B.

On Saturday, I'm surprised by a call from Ms. Barnes. It's good to hear from her.

"I want to invite you to a barbecue tomorrow, Liz. I've heard glowing feedback from the embassy folks who were at your hearing. We want to celebrate your victory with you tomorrow. Can you come? And just so you know, I've already planned out my outfit that I'll wear to the airport to see you guys off."

I can't believe what I'm hearing. I haven't seen this optimistic side of Ms. Barnes. She has no reason to shine me on, and she's thinking we'll be leaving soon, just after the court rules in our favor. And she's thinking this because the embassy staff, who have more legal savvy than I ever will and who were at my hearing, have told her about it. I accept the invitation, and I can't wait.

Sunday, the day of the barbecue, is May 19. It also happens to be Gregory's birthday, a fact I enjoy as I dig into some homemade brownies Ms. Barnes's coworker baked. The barbecue is outdoors, and it's a sunny, warm day. They've put out a spread of all the fare we'll soon be having in America: hot dogs, potato salad, hamburgers, potato chips, corn chips, and brownies. Food has never tasted so good. I eat enough today to make up for all of the days that I haven't. The girls love the hot dogs and potato salad best, and they play in the yard with some other children. I overhear Ms. Barnes marveling at how healthy the girls are looking already while I glance around at my new friends, quietly memorizing their faces, knowing that indeed this will be the last time I see them. We are leaving soon. They are right.

I can will myself to believe only the best. Soon, I will get the call about the judge's ruling. Soon, we will go home to America.

I'm sure I will sleep better tonight than I have in a long time. It's amazing what comfort food and good company can do. The girls are happily worn out and begin snoring almost as soon as the lights are out.

Waking up just before nine, we rush to get ready for breakfast in the lobby so we can join Mimi at the athletic club. Marianthi squashes the yolks of her boiled eggs into her cup of chamomile tea as Meredith and I wolf down our toast and jam. I've long given up curbing Marianthi's unfortunate breakfast routine. It keeps her occupied, and she doesn't listen to my protests anyhow.

I don't hear the phone ring until the front-desk manager beckons me to it. "It's your lawyer," he says, pointing at the phone.

I rush to the phone.

"Brace yourself," Michael Pappas says. "I do not have good news."

Chapter 22

THE RULING AND PLAN B

We never had a chance.

Mr. Pappas tells me that the judge sided with Gregory throughout his ruling. The judge acknowledged that the girls were kidnapped by their father and taken to Greece. "But they have now lived in Greece for two years. They speak Greek. They have friends in Greece. They have an extended family in Greece," Mr. Pappas reads. Meredith told the judge that she wants to remain in Greece. The ruling concludes that the damage to the girls' young psyches would be too great if they left Greece.

"But you are invited to come back to Greece next October and revisit the entire custody issue all over again," Mr. Pappas says.

So the Greek courts have reversed my legal custody of the children. The Hague Convention meant nothing in the entire process.

Wow. I've lost the hearing, but I can leave my kids behind and hope for better luck in five months.

"So now what?" I ask Mr. Pappas.

"Gregory will have you served with legal papers. And then you'll have seventy-two hours to return the children to their father and leave the country. But first, Liz, he'll have to find you."

I hang up the phone and burst into tears. Meredith whimpers and Marianthi throws her fork down on her plate—both girls run to me. I don't tell them what's happened, but I don't need to. They already know. We share our first family hug in years, and the very idea that it may be our last makes me cry harder.

The hotel maid follows us upstairs, wiping away her own tears and hugging us. She doesn't know what's happened, but she knows that it isn't good.

In truth, I am only half surprised, but I'm fully devastated. All the faith I put in the system. All the precious time wasted. Two years of my daughters' lives missed. All of the money generously contributed, not to mention all the debt I have accrued. All for nothing.

After the maid leaves, I call Mimi and share the news. She says nothing for a few beats. Then, as if her reset button has been pressed, she clears her throat and begins barking orders. "Pack up your room and check out now. There's no point in your spending any more money. Come to my house." I don't argue. I'm on autopilot, and the girls are only too happy to help me pack, since it means they'll get to play at Margot's.

Minutes later, Mimi opens her door to us, waving us in with a lit cigarette in one hand and the cordless phone in the other. "It's Fern," she whispers to me as I usher the girls to Margot's room.

Mimi gets off the phone. "Your turn," she says, handing it over to me. "I've called everyone I can think of."

I call Michael Kreider, Ms. Barnes, and Heather. This may be the last time I speak with any of them. Anything that I do from this point on has to happen in secret. I cannot risk bringing them down with me if I decide to escape from Greece with the girls.

While I'm on the phone, the house fills with my Athens community: Sandy, Lambros, Fern, Theodora, and Chris. After hugs are dispensed and the judge has been sufficiently cursed, it's time to review my dreaded plan B.

The children and I will take a ferry to the small island of Kos, where we will be met by Fern's Greek male friend, who will pose as the children's father. He will take us to our hotel for the night, a five-minute walk from the ferry. A German travel agent will supply us with one-way boat tickets to Turkey.

Mimi's husband, George, comes home from work and asks to speak with me privately. "I cannot be involved in this, Liz," he says, while Mimi scavenges in the cabinets to find food. "I can't. Too much can go wrong for my family if you're caught . . . If Mimi is caught, I can act angry; I can make excuses for my rogue American wife. But I am Greek and I'm the breadwinner. I'm so sorry."

Clearly, George has given it some thought. He wants to help but has far too much at stake. I tell him that I understand completely, and I do. But the fear I see reflected on his face reminds me just how risky this venture really is. I hope Fern's friend doesn't share George's sentiments. Having a man meet us in Kos will be a great relief, and once we make it to Turkey, we'll be practically home free.

Yes, the risks are obvious, but the idea of not trying is inconceivable. I think about the unbridgeable gap that existed between my dad and me after I met him at age twenty. I think about the life I led before the girls were born, living in response to what everyone else around me wanted and needed. I think about the hopes I had and still have for my daughters, and the promise I made to keep them safe. And I think about how many people across the globe have joined my efforts to bring them home.

I will act on faith. I will trust in a miracle.

Before Fern leaves, she gives me some last-minute coaching. "Level with the girls," Fern says. "You'll need them to be on your side."

I do. I break it down, plain and simple. "We've lost the court battle," I tell them both. "But I have a plan, and it may or may not work. I just need to know, girls, are you with me? Because it's okay if you're not. It's going to be scary if we have to sneak out of Greece. But that's the only way we might make it to Alaska together."

Both want to go. Finally, we are a unified team.

After lunch, I start thinking. If the Greek authorities might attempt to locate the children and me at the customs office using photos, we need to change our look. Already, a healthy tan has replaced both girls' pasty-white skin. Marianthi has lost weight, while Meredith has gained enough to cover her ribs. My medium-length curly hair has become a long, frizzy mop over these months spent in Greece. But we need to do more.

The girls and I walk to a beauty parlor down the street. One by one, we get our hair cut short. The girls giggle and play while they wait for me to get my hair tinted red. For a nominal fee, we are visibly altered.

We stay in Mimi's guest room. When I can't sleep, I lie in bed next to the girls, creating a mental image of us debarking the plane safely in Alaska. The sound of handcuffs ratcheting occasionally interrupts my perfect visual.

❈ ❈ ❈

Too soon it's time to get up. I sneak out of bed, leaving the girls to sleep a while longer. The smell of cigarette smoke greets me. Mimi is awake. Before I finish dressing, I hear a knock at the door. Theodora from the restaurant, followed by Fern and her ex-husband, Ted, and Sandy from the bakery have arrived. The mood is somber as each person says good-bye.

"Keep in touch, Liz," Sandy says. "I can't wait to hear you've arrived safely."

"I'm jealous," Theodora says, smiling broadly. "I want to go back to America. Raise your girls well there, Liz, and teach them how to be good Greeks—not like their dad."

Mimi's mother-in-law, wearing, as always, her long black dress, waits quietly for my receiving line to thin out. She mutters something in Greek and squeezes the last bit of air out of my lungs when she hugs me tightly. No words are needed.

The girls are up now, getting dressed in the bathroom. Fern grips me for a bear hug. When she releases me, I follow her eyes to Marianthi's canvas shoes on the kitchen floor. Fern picks up the left shoe and strips back the sole. "Can you get me a pen?" she asks Mimi. Fern takes a blue Bic and etches her twelve-digit phone number, complete with the country code, inside the shoe. "Look, sweetie," she tells my oldest daughter, who is already on the verge of tears as she enters the now-crowded kitchen. "This is my phone number. If anything happens to your mom, please call me, okay? But keep the number private. Secret."

Fern presses the material back over the sole of the shoe. Ingenious. She must've been a drug dealer in a previous life.

Ted speaks to the girls in Greek, carefully placing drachmas into their hands and folding their fingers back over them before giving their cheeks a final pinch. Mimi will drive us to the port. Little Margot stays behind with Mimi's mother-in-law, who follows us to the car. As we back out of the driveway, I look back at Margot and her grandmother, who is making the sign of the cross over and over. She turns back and stands on the steps, her expression serious as she wills God's blessings over us—or hexes my ex-husband. I don't break my gaze until her image becomes nothing more than a tiny black spot and then disappears altogether.

The girls are quiet during the ride. Shortly after we reach the port of Piraeus, George pulls up in his own car and walks us to the ferry. I can't believe it. He must be having a weak moment, but whatever the reason for his unexpected appearance is, I'm glad he's making an appearance. He looks deeply stressed.

Stressed doesn't begin to describe how I am feeling. We have reached the point of no return. I will say good-bye to my new friends forever and risk permanent separation from my daughters if I am arrested again. The best-case scenario requires my daughters to leave their language, their home, and their relatives behind for the second time in their young lives.

"See you in a few days!" George and Mimi call out, attempting to make our travel look usual.

We make our way onto the ferry and find our cramped cabin, where I hope we can quietly remain during the six-hour ride to Kos. I'm beat. So are the girls. We did a lot of preparation yesterday to get us to this moment. I helped the girls sift through their toys and their few clothes, choosing what to bring and what to leave behind. After we got our hair cut and I got mine highlighted, Mimi and I went to get the ferry tickets for the next day. Following our last dinner together with the Mimi's family, I got the girls ready for bed and laid a few ground rules to help us get home safely.

"No speaking Greek," I told them. "Not one word." I

tried to explain how odd it would look that fluently Greek children were traveling with their clearly American mom. "No asking for extra food or souvenirs on the ferry, either. We need to watch our money; plus, it'll put us in harm's way to speak to some nosy Greek clerk. And play in our cabin, not around the boat this one time, please. Let's just quietly rest in our room until we get to Kos, okay?"

But when we open the door to our cabin, there's no room for them to play. There's just a set of bunk beds and a few feet of floor space. We drop our bags and crawl into our beds to rest.

When dinnertime comes, I remind the girls again not to speak any Greek as we make our way downstairs to an empty table. All of the other tables are full with friendly-looking Greeks, and I avert my eyes to keep from possibly engaging any-one in conversation. Though we're surrounded by rowdy diners, the girls whisper to each other in English. I can't speak in any language. My head is swimming with the possibilities of all that might go wrong on our journey. I tune out the girls' conversa-tion as they begin counting the number of people wearing blue on the boat. Then a fight breaks out. Meredith shoves Marian-thi, who immediately reverts to Greek. I'm not sure what she says, but it ends with *Eleni*, Meredith's middle name.

The silence is deafening. All talk between the other pas-sengers ceases, their eyes now fixed on my daughters. Then a man gets up from his table and approaches my youngest. "Eleni? Did I hear someone say Eleni?" he asks.

Oh my God. People know. People already know. But how?

Meredith nods solemnly, looking at me to gauge the dam-age her sister's outburst has done.

"Eleni," he says again. "*Chronia pola!*" (Many years.)

I recognize the phrase. I had forgotten that it is the day Greeks celebrate to honor the Saint Eleni. This kind stranger is only wishing my daughter many good years.

We all smile back at him and raise our water glasses to his, while other friendly passengers wish her many years in Greek.

The ferry ride from Piraeus to the island of Kos stops at 3:00 A.M. I rouse the girls from their sleep, and Meredith begins to cry. She's so tired. Marianthi dresses quietly and grabs her bag. I collect our few other belongings, grab Meredith's hand, and guide the girls off the ferry, trying to soothe them. "We're about to get on a big boat and go to Turkey. Maybe you'll ride a camel," I tell them. I'm ready to promise anything to stop Meredith's tears. All I know about Turkey is that there are few to no Greeks and there are camels. Both girls are temporarily hushed, and I scan the dock for Fern and Ted's friend, the fake husband who will help us.

Maybe he's late. I take the girls to use the bathroom. When we return, the port is completely empty. Our savior has deserted us.

Now what?

I pull the girls close and start walking. Just as Fern said, the hotel is no more than a five-minute walk. Meredith is crying again by the time we reach it, and Marianthi is cold and begins to whine. The burst of warm air is a welcome change as we walk inside. The front-desk attendant greets us warmly and collects our passports for check-in. He picks mine up to look at it more closely in the light. "Kentucky, huh? Hey, Yianni!" he calls out to the bartender. "This girl's from Kentucky!"

Oh, crap. What does he know?

Peals of laughter from both men follow. At least someone is having fun.

Our hotel room is cozy, with a queen-sized bed topped with a thick comforter and an inviting claw-footed tub in the bathroom. Immediately, I regret not having booked an extra day here to regroup before the final leg of our journey. "Look, Mom, a swimming pool! Can my sister and I go swimming tomorrow? Pleeease?" Marianthi begs.

I am in no mood for placating children. I'm tired. I'm cold. And I'm fresh out of patience. "We're leaving this room in less than five hours," I snap. "Go to bed. *Now!*"

My daughters don't know what to make of the new witch who has seemingly inhabited their mother's body. It probably confirms their father's stories of my evil disposition. But moments after climbing into bed, they are sleeping. I will try to find my sweeter self later.

I stay up, worrying I will oversleep. Soon it is 7:00 A.M., time for the girls and me to get ready. They wake up, grumpy and disoriented. "I don't want to leeeeave," Marianthi wails. Meredith's chin begins to tremble. "Knock it off!" I bark back. The girls fall quiet. We eat our continental breakfast in the hotel lobby and wait for our ride to show up. There are no words left to speak. I cannot lie to my daughters about a rosy future I'm not sure I believe in. For all I know, I might be ruining their lives.

A few minutes before 8:00 A.M., a red car with the steering wheel on the right side pulls up to the hotel lobby. The driver looks directly at us, and we go out to join her. Out pops a very tall and striking redheaded woman, the German travel agent, who gives me a half smile as she escorts us into the car without introducing herself. I begin babbling immediately.

"I'm so afraid this won't work," I tell her. She looks at me and says nothing but drives fast toward the port. "I'm really feeling sick," I say. She stares ahead. As we get out of the car and approach customs, I try again. "I'm not sure I can do this," I say. "I feel really sick."

"I see."

I'm aggravated by her lack of response. I want her to talk me out of my fear. The boiled egg I ate for breakfast begins to make its way up my throat. I heave into a garbage can as we reach the line for customs. The travel agent calmly hands me our one-way tickets to Bodrum, Turkey, while my head is hanging over the garbage can. A few heaves later, the tickets are nowhere to be found. I have lost them. But she remains composed, seeming not to notice what a basket case I am. She puts her warm hand on my shoulder and gently urges me forward. The customs officer scrutinizes our passports and gives me a pen to sign paperwork. I wait for him to comment on the fact that my passport indicates I arrived in Greece nearly two years after my daughters, or even that my daughters speak flawless Greek while I fumble through the most basic greetings with a thick American accent. My hands are now shaking so violently that I can barely hold the pen in my hand, but I scribble my signature and hand it to him. "Are you a doctor?" he asks me gingerly.

"No," I answer weakly. "Why do you ask?"

"Because your writing is as sloppy as a doctor's!" He laughs, glancing around for approval from the onlookers, and then waves us onto the boat. "I saw your tickets before. Go on," he says. "I know you paid."

And with the wave of his hand, our lives are saved. We are really, truly, finally leaving Greece.

The children and I wave to the travel agent as we board the boat. As the boat pulls away, the girls and I look back at the shore and see that she's still watching us. We wave again, and Marianthi looks up at me.

"I knew you could do it," she tells me. "I knew that you'd never leave us behind."

"This is my best day ever," Meredith adds.

This is my best day ever, too. I am scared, but I am present, and my daughter has faith in me that I can pull this off.

We stand watching the island of Kos shrink as we sail

away. And just over forty-five minutes later, we are in Turkey. It is a whole new world.

The Aegean Sea is clean and blue, and the homes on the shores of Turkey are whitewashed, matching the white sand. As the boat closes in on the dock, I am sure that I have never seen any place so lovely. We gather our belongings. I spot a handsome man with dark hair and broad shoulders wearing a name badge on his shirt and lean over to speak. "I would please like some help making plans once we get to Turkey," I say. He looks at me and gives a slight nod. "I need a Turkish visa. I'd like help getting back home."

My stomach tightens. *What if I've spoken to the wrong person? What if he works for the Greek government? Maybe they're looking for me and the girls.*

The girls and I stand toward the back of the boat, and as we near the port, the same man I've asked for help approaches us and grabs our bags from our hands, hopping off the boat. I am stunned. Has our dream ended so quickly?

But he looks back to make sure we're following him.

My knees buckle, and I lower myself onto a bench. The man smiles, snatches the passports from my hands, and walks to the front of the customs line. A moment later, he returns with the passports, which now have Turkish visas attached to them. "Come with me," he instructs, as he leads us to a cramped kiosk.

I tell him that I am too ill to travel and need a cheap room to bunk in for a day or so, until I have the strength to travel home to America. He pulls a brochure from his desk and shows me a spacious hotel room complete with an outdoor swimming pool.

"I'm afraid I can't afford something that nice," I say, lowering my voice so the girls won't hear me.

"It is twenty-three dollars a day," he tells me.

"Perfect." The world is looking better already. He drives us through hills, stopping only to honk at men crossing the street on camels. Minutes later, we arrive at Hotel Domino, our new haven until we can complete our journey home. The girls are overjoyed. No more hiding. No more fear. We have beds and a swimming pool right outside our room.

I call Heather as soon as the girls and I finish our hotel pizza. "You're not out of the woods yet," she reminds me, after she joins me in a moment of celebration. "The authorities could block your entrance into the States at any point between Turkey and home. The sooner you get home, the better."

She's right. America is a signatory of the Hague Convention. Maybe I'll be in trouble at home for leaving Greece in violation of its new court order. I would love to stay in Turkey until I feel well, but there's no time to waste. "But the thing is," I tell Heather, "I don't have money to buy plane tickets." After all she's done for me, I loathe telling her this now.

"Don't worry about that," Heather assures me. "I've got it. You'll owe me for life, kid. You just focus on feeling better and come home."

Heather tells me she'll call Lynn, the travel agent who dated Gregory years ago, to make our reservations. And a few hours later, Lynn calls me at the hotel lobby to finalize the arrangements. We will need to get to the nearest airport to fly to Istanbul. Then we will fly to London, where Lynn has arranged a hotel room for us. We will leave the next afternoon and fly to Minnesota, where we will switch planes to return to Anchorage. Lynn tells me she's planned our whole journey meticulously, working her special magic so our reservations cannot be traced on the manifests. "We'll worry about the money later," she says. "I've got some friends from the airlines who'll want to greet you in Minnesota and help you make your connection."

We frolic for two days in Turkey as though we are tourists. The healing powers of food and rest are on my side, and we sun ourselves poolside until our color and strength return.

During our last afternoon, I beg a man giving camel rides to let the girls on so I can snap their picture. I assume he understands me when he smiles and helps them onto the camel's back. The girls begin to cry. The camel also begins to cry and then tries to shake my daughters off his back. The man smiles and stares ahead as he leads them on a walk, oblivious to the girls' screams and my wishes to get them off the animal. The ride seems to go on forever. Trailing behind, I yell up to the girls, "Trust me, you'll love this picture someday. The best memories sometimes come from bad experiences."

If I'm right, we're set for life in the memory department.

We fly to Istanbul on May 23 and arrive in London that afternoon, in time to see a few sights and get ready for our big next day. I can't call Mr. Pappas or Michael or Jim at home, or even Poppy. I have to keep our news a secret to shield them from possible trouble.

The next morning, we board a Northwest Airlines flight for Minneapolis, Minnesota. As the girls watch the in-flight movie, about a lovable pig named Babe, tears of joy and exhaustion stream down my face. Marianthi looks over at me and gives me a reassuring pat on my hand. "It's okay, Mom. It's *Babe*, isn't it?" She returns her attention immediately to the movie.

Several hours later, we arrive in Minneapolis. As we walk toward customs, an American flag welcomes us. I have never seen a sight so beautiful. Then two motherly-looking women wearing airline jackets spot us. "Lynn called us about you," one of them explains, as she throws her arms around me. "I spoke with my husband about it, and you and the girls can live in our cabin indefinitely if you need to for safety reasons," she adds, thrusting a small piece of crumpled paper with her phone number on it into my hand. "Call anytime." Both women wipe tears from their eyes. They hustle us to the front of the line to make our connecting flight, hugging us hard before wishing us well with the rest of our lives.

After we board the connecting flight, I spot the air phone in its cradle as the plane takes off, and I cannot resist the temptation. I call Heather. I call Michael Kreider. I call Jim Swanson. I call my workplace. The cost no longer matters. This is a moment that has to be shared.

So many times over the past twenty-six months, I have played the scene in my head: my two daughters and I walking off the airplane at Anchorage International Airport. Friends applaud not just our safe return but the end of their own pain and the celebration of their collective efforts. I've imagined it so many times that when it happens, it seems more like theater than real life.

As the plane's wheels touch down, I rake my fingers through the girls' hair and then mine. Just as well that we had most of it cut off in Greece. We are unwashed and bone tired, but I am determined that we will hold our tired heads upright as best we can while making this most important memory.

Allowing the other passengers to leave before us, I can't help but wonder if this is really it. Can we start to live our lives again as a family? Will we ever feel normal? Will we feel safe?

I take a deep breath. "Are you ready?"

The girls respond with weak smiles. Time to disembark.

Today is May 24, 1996. I will forever remember it as

the day that the girls and I arrived in Anchorage. We can hear excited voices well before we make our way down the long jetway that leads to the airport lobby. There are balloons everywhere. Thunderous applause and shrieks of joy come from twenty or more of our closest friends, clutching flowers and toys for the girls. They form a receiving line. The lawyers. Their wives. Faith Daycare staff. My coworkers. Heather and her husband, Hank. While I hug my way through it, the girls freeze and cling to Barbara, our old roommate. One by one, old friends approach my daughters, bending down to touch them, hand them toys, and speak their names, as if to reassure themselves that I've brought home the original ones.

It is precious. It is perfect. It is finally real.

We ride in a procession toward my home, my little fixer-upper that the girls have not yet seen, the home that will give each girl her own bedroom.

Ann Kreider and Janet Swanson, Jim Swanson's wife, have worked like little elves to paint the girls' rooms and stock them with toys. A plastic kitchenette and neatly arranged baskets of My Little Ponies, Barbies, and books cover the floor. The girls ignore our visitors, focusing instead on opening each new package and then rifling through their drawers to find their pre-abduction belongings. I sit on Meredith's bed and close my eyes, hearing our happy visitors visiting and my happy daughters chattering.

Finally, sleep comes.

Chapter 23

BACK IN ALASKA

As great as it is to wake up in my own home, I'm confused. There are two little girls peering down at me from the foot of my bed.

I can't figure out who they are, where I am, or how I got here. I have a sneaking suspicion that I know these girls. They look familiar. "Mom?" the biggest one says with a distinct accent. "Mother?" They look at me like they know me.

"Mom!" the little one says, with more edge.

Mom? And then it hits me. These girls are my daughters. We're home, at long last, and now they expect I'll take care of them.

Single parenting is tough under the best of circumstances. Let's say the primary parent gets child support and has extended family to help out; say she has a coparent who participates some of the time. Ask anyone—it's tough.

I've never had even those things. What I have now are two very traumatized little girls who have to march right back to school, speaking a language they're still relearning, because I'm flat out of leave. I'm flat out of money. And I'm flat out of my mind. My days are filled with flashbacks, and my dreams at night morph into nightmares—about Gregory, about the arrest, about having the girls ripped away, again and again and again.

But, boy, do I have a happy community. People flock to see the girls. The newspaper publishes a follow-up story, and the community in Anchorage embraces our success as their own. Faith Daycare gives the girls a scholarship to attend its after-school program, where they will be surrounded by their old friends.

I also have two grateful daughters who seem to enjoy rediscovering everything from turning on American light switches to maneuvering faucets and doing chores. They appreciate every small and large thing that I do. "Thank you for dinner," they tell me, and "Thank you for washing our clothes," and "Thank you for bringing us home." It is foreign to me, until I get more glimmers about their life in Greece and I understand how bleak it really was.

I take Meredith and Marianthi to their pediatrician. Dr. Keller is old enough to have been my pediatrician, and his staff posted the girls' missing-children's posters in their office. They are welcoming when the children return to their care. Meredith, who's filling out nicely but is a half sandwich above starvation, is weighed. When she left, she weighed a nice, round thirty-eight pounds—not heavy, but a solid four-year-old. Now, she still weighs in at thirty-eight pounds, despite having grown much taller. Her TB test is positive, as is her subsequent bubble test and the final X-ray of her lungs.

Marianthi has developed at an astonishing rate, and Dr. Keller gently tries to prepare her for the onset of early menses, despite the fact that she's not quite nine. "Your body is trying to turn you into a woman, so soon you'll get your period." He's attempting to give it a positive spin, but Marianthi shuts down.

After a pause, she looks up at him and asks, "Does this mean that I won't get to be a little girl anymore? Because I just now got my toys back."

She says it without bitterness or self-pity. Just a sincere question from a sweet child. The doctor begins to cry.

After we all get into counseling, I want to focus on new goals. Like affording the vacation to Disney World that Jim Swanson and his wife gave us airline tickets for. Like getting the girls into soccer and making good on my promise of pets. Like paying down our debt. Like going to graduate school.

I'd like to get a job with the state government, too. It's the only way I'll be able to provide the girls with health insurance. Private insurance companies won't let me get a policy for two years, stating that the children have lived in another country for two years and no one can verify what they've been exposed to.

I am turning thirty-two soon. My daughters are seven and eight years old, and we have many good things to look forward to together.

※ ※ ※

I am so fortunate to return to work at AWAIC, where my loyal coworkers have donated leave and given emotional support for the past two years. They have done my job for me during my long absences. And how do I repay them? With a greater lack of focus than ever, terrifying mood swings, and the request for a flexible schedule while I get my daughters to and from school and other appointments.

I'm mad all the time now, when I should be grateful. It catches me unaware, and I feel bad for feeling angry. But I am, for so many reasons and at so many people. I'm mad at the punk who drove my ex-husband and my girls to the airport. I'm mad at a few of the parishioners from the Orthodox church who saw the girls and their dad in Greece during holidays there and blatantly lied to me upon their return. I'm mad at the detective who refused to put Gregory in the crime computer database, and mad at the other detective, who tried to develop a close relationship with me in exchange for interdepartmental favors. I'm mad at the State Department's Office of Children's Issues, which gave me contradictory information on how to resolve the issue legally. And most of all, I'm mad at myself for enlisting so many people in the Anchorage community to assist me in my Herculean efforts at bringing the girls home legally, only to end up sneaking out of Greece with them like a thief in the night. If only I had known that my ex-husband's female lawyer in Greece is married to the judge who supervises all the other judges in the region, or that not one parent has prevailed in Greece using the Hague Convention to regain custody of a child, I would surely have made other arrangements.

How trusting in the legal system I have been.

The final straw comes when I run into Anchorage's police chief after a conference we were both attending through work. I've met him before, and he knows my face from newspaper articles. I tell him about the random call I received from APD staff recently at work, asking if my kids had been found. The caller told me that the contents of my entire investigative file have gone missing. "What do you make of this?" I ask him.

"Detective Rose probably destroyed the evidence to avoid a civil suit," he says, a little too easily for my blood. He shrugs and moves on. Now I'm even madder, and I want to sue the world.

It's Michael Kreider and Heather Flynn who bring me back to reality.

"Civil suits can last a long time, Lizzie. They're expensive and can cause you to relive the worst aspects of the experience. And there's no guarantee you won't lose and end up having to pay the other side's legal fees."

Heather fills me in on just how many people stepped in to help while I was in Greece. "I asked a lot of people I knew to write letters of support so the lawyers could give them to the court in Greece. And not a single person said no."

At the time of my arrest, Heather organized a calling tree. Callers, many of whom were staff members at the girls' day care, rang Senator Stevens's office in Washington, DC, demanding that he pressure the American embassy staff in Greece to help us. And he did just that.

"The senator told me he couldn't wait for the crisis to end, not just because he cared about what happened to you and the kids, but also because he wanted to get some other work done," Heather says, laughing.

Jim and Michael can name half a dozen clients between them who offered help. People in the midst of their own divorces, personal-injury suits, or criminal charges still thought about the future of two little girls they had never met and wanted them to reunite with their mother. We are the recipients of uncommon grace.

My therapist refers me to a psychologist, who confirms a diagnosis of post-traumatic stress disorder. My brand of crazy has a name, and it won't necessarily be a permanent part of my life.

While I get more therapeutic support, my friends increase their support of the kids and me. Jim and Janet Swanson pick the girls up from school sometimes and take them shopping and out to dinner, then allow them to spend the night. Heather's husband, Hank, also pitches in and teaches them everything little girls should know, like how to make bananas Foster, how to play poker, and how to win at poker by lying. And he and Heather include us in their Sunday dinners, where we all catch up on the week's activities and Hank wows us with his newest recipe he's trying out. His retirement suits us well.

It's springtime. It's been nearly a year since we returned. My mood and affect have stabilized. The girls and I are making progress in mending our relationships. Life is humming along nicely, yet I can't seem to shake the feeling that more bad news is headed my way.

I'm at work when the other shoe drops. "Liz, someone is here to give you something," the new secretary at AWAIC mumbles over the intercom. *Can you please be more specific?* I want to respond. I leave the time sheets I am signing on my desk to meet Someone.

A process server hands me a summons to appear in federal court. Gregory has applied under the Hague Convention for relief as the left-behind parent of abducted children. Honest to God, this feels unreal.

I take the paperwork back to my office and shut the door, then call Michael Kreider. We make an appointment to look it over with Jim Swanson after work. They pore over the documents in complete silence while I wait for some form of reassurance from them. I read magazines. I bite my nails. I study their foreheads. It feels like a very long wait before Michael looks up and clears his throat.

His weak smile says everything. "Well, kiddo, I don't know how to say this: this doesn't look so good."

"Will Gregory be coming to Alaska for the hearing?"

In unison, Jim and Michael say no. Gregory will have to remain in Greece, because of his arrest warrant. I feel light-headed. Jim looks jaundiced. Michael speaks in a measured tone.

"I think he's got a decent shot. Your Greek lawyers forgot to submit a critical piece of paperwork to the courts in Athens that first year of the girls' abduction, so the Hague Convention doesn't apply under that technicality." And though Greece has no history of following through on the Hague Convention, America follows it to the letter. Gregory's lawyers in Greece and America have filed all the right documents within a year of our return to America.

Our hearing is scheduled for late June, so we still have over a month to prepare. Michael and Jim divide the labor evenly over the next many days. While Michael seeks out the counsel of attorneys around the country who have handled abduction cases, Jim consults with local lawyers, one by one, about the details of my case. When I ask him why, since they have far less experience than he has, Jim explains that it's good "to get their input." But it isn't their input he is seeking, Jim tells me later. All of the lawyers who listen to him will be forced to decline the case themselves should Gregory attempt to retain their services. The man is a genius.

It appears as though mine may be the first case of child abduction in which the Hague Convention is used against the original plaintiff. It's not a detail I'm happy about, but it makes the case something other lawyers will be interested to help with.

The only hope we have to win our legal case hinges on the Fugitive Disentitlement Doctrine. In a nutshell, it means that Gregory's appeal process should be disallowed if the judge decides that he does not deserve to use the court's resources, since he has forfeited his right by fleeing the country after breaking the law.

Or the judge may decide that I have taken the kids illegally and rule that I have to return them to Greece.

How will I prepare the girls for this next struggle? They have been through so much already. How much more can they take?

Our therapist helps me. "Keep it simple," she tells me over the phone. "Think of it as you would a conversation with them about sex. Tell the girls only what you know they'll be able to digest. Be honest, but don't overwhelm them with too many details, or with your anxieties. Just what's needed for right now."

It's been a couple of days since I received the summons. I sit the girls down in the living room and give them the news. I believe in pulling a Band-Aid off quickly. "Girls, your dad is suing me from Greece to get custody of you. He might win."

Silence follows.

Meredith talks first. "Can we move to India?" She grabs a piece of typing paper and crayons in the junk drawer and draws a self-portrait, complete with a *bindi*, a red dot on her forehead, and a crown on her head. Marianthi looks as though she might cry but stifles herself quickly. "I think we'll win," she says brightly.

My poor little girls.

Before our hearing, I make one last-ditch effort to get assistance from the State Department's Office of Children's Issues in Washington, DC. After getting bounced to several voice mails, I hit zero and reach a human. A very young male voice answers the phone. "Can I put you on hold while I find your file, please?"

I suspect that he is actually a college intern. "Sure."

A few minutes later, he is back and ready to proceed. *Keep it matter-of-fact, Liz.* "It's just that now the Hague Convention is being used against me, and I'm the one who had custody to begin with. Is there something I can do? Can you help me?"

Long pause. I picture him muting the phone and popping a pimple while looking in the mirror. His voice cracks.

"It says here, ma'am, that your lawyers in Greece neglected to file all the proper paperwork. They missed one of the forms."

"Thanks for that. I *know*. But we're here now, and I'm wondering why I spent many thousands of dollars and two years to get my children home legally through the Hague Convention, only to have it used against me later. Who's actually in charge of overseeing how it's applied? I mean, who can I complain to? Isn't there some governing body somewhere? Someone who enforces this or applies sanctions to governments that don't follow the treaty they've signed?"

He clears his throat. "Now, that's a tough one. The Hague Convention's Civil Aspects of International Child Abduction is a voluntary treaty." It sounds like he is reading from a brochure. "It relies on each signatory to use their own honor system to implement the recommendations. And the recommendations are that each signatory agree to send abducted children back to their place of habitual residence to work out their differences. The country of habitual residence isn't an issue any government's staff would weigh in on, either. If the abductor doesn't agree to . . . well, that's a tough one."

Apparently, the treaty is like a purity ring, the kind of ring well-intentioned young girls wear when they vow to remain chaste until marriage, impressing only their equally innocent parents, who are stunned when their angels become pregnant. Unwittingly, I have become one of those naive parents, believing in the protection a precious concept provides and overlooking the obvious. The Hague Convention on International Child Abduction is a civil remedy to address a most uncivilized act.

We talk for a few more minutes, but it's a waste of time, something he notices before I do.

"Ma'am, I'm going to have to end this conversation now. But best wishes in your hearing. And if you need me to send you a booklet—"

I slam down the receiver, feeling only half guilty for terrorizing the poor kid.

By now, I know better than to believe that the courts will rule in our favor. Even Jim and Michael have encouraged me to consider moving out of the country permanently. The girls and I talk about our options as the court date nears.

"I want to move to India," Meredith reminds us at dinner one night.

"I don't want to go anywhere. I want to stay right here, where my friends and my toys are," Marianthi counters.

"You'll have toys and friends wherever you are, doll." I want to make this better for her, but how?

❧ ❧ ❧

Jim and Michael decide to have another lawyer present the case in court, since they are too personally involved and might be called on as witnesses. The third lawyer, Phil Voltare, steps in gladly to assist and offers his services pro bono.

The day of the hearing, we crowd into the federal courthouse. I'm surprised by how many people have shown up to watch. I scan the room and see Hank—always reliable, always calm. He gives me a quick wink, and I turn back, feeling reassured.

Gregory's attorney enjoys a wonderful reputation as a lawyer, and I can see why. He does a formidable job of making me look like a criminal. Plus, he's filled out his paperwork correctly, a fact he reminds the court over and over, so what else matters, right? Gregory appears telephonically and says next to nothing.

Mr. Voltare, the lawyer arguing the case on my behalf, begins his argument slowly and then picks up the tempo as he becomes more impassioned. I sit back and watch as he addresses every point Gregory's attorney has made, while reminding the judge that the girls are in my lawful custody in America, and that custody was recognized in Greece until the Hellenic court's abrupt reversal.

In the end, Judge Sedwick rules from the bench. "It is striking that the plaintiff is not in court today. . . . This case has gone on far too long."

The judge addresses the fact that the argument that I abducted the children does not have merit, as the kids were in my custody to begin with. The abductor should not be rewarded for his actions simply because he succeeded in hiding out with the children for a long period of time in Greece. Finally, he rules that ultimate custody of the children shall remain with me.

"Any further hearing granted would be unjust to the children. This matter is closed."

The court clerk bursts into tears. We are finished, once and for all. Michael and I hug our way through the receiving line that forms outside the courtroom door.

I race home to tell my daughters about the ruling. I can't help but notice how brightly the sun is shining. It's June, typically the best time of year for me, but I can't remember the last time I stopped to take a look around. From today on, I will make it a point to be more in the moment. I have to take a breather from all the work I've been doing just trying to survive.

When I get home, the girls are playing with dolls in the living room. I excuse the babysitter, and the three of us sit at the table while I explain what has happened.

I feel like I'm dreaming. The girls hug me and continue to talk and to play, but their voices are far away now. I watch them in silence.

If someone had told me that I could either leave my violent husband and then have my daughters kidnapped or stay with my violent husband and be murdered, which choice would have been the least damning for my daughters?

But that's silly. That's not how life works. I don't want any of these horrifying experiences to define my daughters' futures.

Instead, let the strength we have unearthed, the connections we have made, the travel we have enjoyed, and the grace we have experienced be what we hold on to.

Let these be my daughters' inheritance.

EPILOGUE

2016

I wish I could say that we've gone on to live happily ever after, but real life is much more complicated. Healing from trauma has been a slow and steady process for my daughters, and for me.

If you'd asked me a year or two after my daughters returned, in 1996, if they had (mostly) recovered from their experiences, I would have said yes. In my estimation, since I got them into therapy and provided a structured, safe home environment and we enjoyed a stable support network, they were on the perfect path to success. I assumed that the passage of time + counseling + a positive support system = a normal, healthy adult.

It turns out I was wrong.

We made it through the initial health challenges: Meredith's exposure to tuberculosis in Greece and Marianthi's stomach problems that appeared to stem from anxiety. Marianthi described her overall sense of guilt at not telling the flight attendants in 1994 that her father did not have permission to take her and her sister on a plane—at the ripe old age of six.

The girls flourished in school almost immediately upon their return. They even got pets and eventually came to terms with not getting the little brother they'd requested. They excelled in soccer. One was a cheerleader. Both held jobs after school when they were old enough and helped pay for their extras.

On the other hand, the girls didn't spare me a lick of pain and suffering in their teens. Both went through periods of experimental drug use. They became moody and defiant around age fifteen, and I felt as if I had very little influence. I, in turn, took it all very personally and responded in kind. When I told Meredith at sixteen that if she lived in my house, she'd have to follow my rules, she moved, renting an apartment with a coworker from Starbucks. It took six months of living on her own to realize she needed to change her ways to have the future she hoped for. Thanks to my older sister, who offered her a place to stay, Meredith relocated to her aunt's and finished her senior year in high school in New Mexico, where she eventually completed college as well.

Marianthi went to college in Washington for a time. I didn't notice it right away, but cracks started to develop in her psyche and then webbed out. She was terrified of my leaving her on campus. I told her that all kids are nervous when their parents leave them for the first time. It was only natural—a *buck up, kid; you'll be fine* kind of deal.

But she wasn't fine. By the time two semesters had passed, her anxiety had given way to full-blown mania, and the collateral damage that followed took years to repair.

Meanwhile, Meredith became physically ill with heart-stopping, gut-exploding autoimmune conditions that worked against each other to keep her in chronic pain.

And, as if that weren't enough, Marianthi's physical

health also began to deteriorate, and then Meredith was swallowed by depression and anxiety and flashbacks.

I wish I'd been more tuned in to the issues they faced. You might think I'd have empathized easily, since I, too, was a kidnapped child, but my experience was different from theirs. I found my father when I was a young adult, and it was a process I initiated. They were located as small children and abruptly brought back to the United states by me without warning.

It took a long time for me to wrap my mind around not only the aftermath of the girls' kidnapping but also their difficult return home to their former lives. A child kidnapped by a family member is abruptly uprooted from her family life, her friends, her toys, her routines. There is no closure. All normalcy simply disappears. If she's taken to another country, she loses her language and culture, too. And in order to survive, she mustn't grieve but instead align with her abductor, who often works hard to replace the child's positive memories of her left-behind parent with negative ones. Little by little. "Your dad tried to kill me," my mom insisted over and over. "Your mom locked you in a room when you were little and left you alone," Gregory told my daughters.

The abductor skillfully applies guilt to the child if the child demonstrates loss, and more guilt comes when the child learns she must lie to authorities about her life. "My mom is dead," my daughter told her new Greek teacher. There is guilt for lying to new friends made, and guilt when the child realizes she is forgetting her left-behind parent. Identity is lost. The abducted child understands that there is no one to depend on because a parent she loved took her away from the other parent she loved. Childhood, and the feeling of safety that should accompany it, has ended.

I assumed things would bounce back to near-normal upon the girls' return, but the recovery from abduction is more like a second abduction. Once again, the child loses all, without closure. My daughters lost their Greek friends, their Greek extended family, their teachers, their new culture, and their father. All the same losses, all over again. They were planted back with me, the woman who didn't protect them from being kidnapped in the first place. When people later heard of their kidnapping, their response was, "Oh. At least it was with your father," minimizing, if not discounting altogether, the girls' experiences. So then they felt self-conscious. *Just get over it* was the implied message, and I seconded the sentiment. I wanted them to be thrilled about being reunited with me and was crushed when they displayed emotions to the contrary.

Similarly, I acted as if their adult suffering were a personal affront, at least at first. *Don't I deserve some pleasant years, now that I've raised my kids on my own? Why do I have to do all of the cleanup, anyhow? Why doesn't their father get to feel the brunt of his abuse of our daughters? All I want is to see them grow up and take flight so I can be proud and then reclaim some of my life for myself.*

I am driving home one day from work when I hear Dr. Bessel van der Kolk on the radio. I have read some of his works before. Dr. van der Kolk heads the Trauma Center in Brookline, Massachusetts, and authored *The Body Keeps the Score*. He speaks about the destructive impact early traumas have on a person over the course of a lifetime.

When I was a young parent, I assumed that since I left my husband when my daughters were tiny, they wouldn't feel the full effect of being exposed to domestic violence. Likewise, when they returned from Greece, they were still little girls, so I told myself that the damage would be less impactful.

Not so, according to Dr. van der Kolk, and other brain researchers agree. Prebirth experiences—things like domestic violence and stress from poverty—affect how well a child develops language, develops connections with others, and develops physically and mentally. Trauma after birth will likely compromise that little human's physical and mental health and, if unaddressed, will shorten her life expectancy by up to twenty years.

A brutalized child develops an angry brain, Dr. van der Kolk says. "Children kept in a state of terror and fear get brains that are chronically afraid." And if a child hasn't been able to trust her parents to protect her early on, then her response to subsequent traumas is that much more magnified. The lens through which the traumatized child sees the world is changed and determines how our muscles and our stress hormones organize themselves.

The body keeps the score.

Dr. van der Kolk endorses treatment from both Eastern and Western cultures. "In the East, people move. Yoga, meditation, tai chi . . . They learn to calm their bodies." This, he says, helps move trauma out of the body. "In the West, people learn to talk and to speak the truth." Talk therapy is helpful, especially combined with movement, to help us learn to calm and nurture ourselves.

My daughters, now in their late twenties, embrace both talk and movement therapy, and I believe they will have long and meaningful lives. Meredith finished college and works as a financial analyst. She is a yoga fanatic and enjoys outdoor sports. Marianthi is working toward her degree in psychology and, like her sister, loves the outdoors. Both are smart and sassy tomboys at heart. I hope that they'll be able to fully reconnect with their family all over the globe, including their father, from whom they remain estranged after a fleeting attempt to have a normal relationship with him tanked a few years ago.

As for me, I've slowly and steadily worked my way back from being a hot mess with my own flashbacks and periods of rage to being a contented woman with an increasingly healthy lifestyle. I started with talk therapy, followed by Eye Movement Desensitization and Reprocessing (EMDR); then I earned a graduate degree in psychology and found meaningful work in state government.

I also began reconnecting with family when the girls and I got strong enough, and thanks to social media, it's been easy to stay in touch and to continue meeting more of my relatives. It's also allowed the girls to remain in contact with their Greek cousins and provided a means for their little Greek sister, born fourteen years ago, to contact them and reach out for sibling support. In her pictures, she looks like a perfect hybrid of both of my daughters, who plan to meet her.

It took well over a decade for me to climb out of debt, and there's not been a single day since when I've lost my feeling of gladness.

I've found there is an upside to having survived much turbulence. My daughters and I don't have strong attachments to things and prefer to spend our time and money on shared experiences. We've been the recipients of uncommon grace and have all made a point of paying it forward through volunteering. Each of us is passionate about culture and language, which is a good thing, since there are more than one hundred languages spoken in Anchorage alone. And we've grown more in love with Alaska, for both the wildlife and the generous people here, who take care of one another as though we are all extended family.

My life isn't perfect, but it's turned out better than I could have imagined. And despite my best efforts not to let some of the worst circumstances define it, they have. Because from them, I've learned to love writing and storytelling. I've carved out meaningful work helping people affected by trauma. I've become addicted to the adrenaline rush I get when traveling alone across the globe. And I've come to know the joy of contentment and the beauty of watching my kids blossom into adults.

My daughters may tell their own stories one day, but this is what I want them to remember of mine: once upon a time, a young mother with only pocket change, a host of bad memories, and a whole lot of love traveled the world to fight for their return, all by herself, and with the help of everyone. And they lived together, happily enough ever after, and with the knowledge that they were much more than lucky.

RESOURCES

Below are just a few organizations that offer help in the United States. Their websites provide valuable information accessible online.

For domestic violence support

The National Domestic Violence Hotline
www.thehotline.org, 1-800-799-SAFE

For Abducted Children

The National Center for Missing and Exploited Children
www.missingkids.org/, 1-800-THE LOST

The Adverse Childhood Experiences Study

www.cdc.gov/violenceprevention/acestudy/index.html

Healing from Trauma

The Trauma Center at Justice Resource Institute
www.traumacenter.org, 1-617-232-1303

ACKNOWLEDGMENTS

For those who helped me find my daughters, I thank you. Special thanks to my Alaskan lawyers and their families, Judge Philip Voland, Bonnie and Gary Hunsaker, Shelly and Ronnie Dalton, Heather Flynn and C.H. ("Hank") Rosenthal, Lynn the travel agent, Mimi and George, Maria Baskous and Dialekti Lambernakis, my Greek lawyers Michael and Panayiotis and their families, Faith Daycare and Learning Center, the staff and the board of Abused Women's Aid in Crisis (AWAIC), Ron Jones at the National Center for Missing and Exploited Children, author/ mother Betty Mahmoody, the American Consulate and Embassy Staff, *Anchorage Daily News*, Kalliope Georgiadou, and every friend, family member, or stranger who sent good intentions, prayers, and/or donations. To the supporters in Greece, in Anchorage, and everywhere in between, your kindness will never be forgotten.

To those friends in Anchorage who helped me with raising my daughters after the crisis, I thank you; My Alaskan lawyers and their families, Julie and Peter Reece, Pamela and

Dave Kelly, C.H. Rosenthal, Deen and Heather Flynn, Abed Radwan, Faith Daycare and Learning Center, Marti Guzman, and my cadre of wonderful neighbors and coworkers at various jobs, and the therapists who helped us cope with the aftermath. Long after the trauma subsided, you hung in there. We couldn't have made it without you.

To those who believed in my struggle to tell my story, I thank you. I appreciate anyone who may have proofed some or all of my writing. There are many friends who've asked me from time to time about how I'm doing with my writing, and I thank you. Special thanks goes to beta-readers and wonderful supporters Judge Ira Uhrig, Richard, Illgen, Ruth Quinlan, John McKay, and Eleanor Andrews. At She Writes Press, thank you to Brooke Warner and Cait Levin, and to publicists Crystal Patriarche and Taylor Vargecko at Sparkpoint Studio for tangible assistance that propelled this book. I owe you so much. For those who couldn't hang around long enough for me to finish my memoir, I will never forget you; my loyal cat Tana who sat dutifully by my side through the first three drafts, C.H. Rosenthal, Aunt Wanda, and my sweet niece Angie. I feel your support.

I'm grateful to the vibrant local community of writers in Anchorage like the Alaska Writer's Guild, the Kachemak Bay Writer's Conference, and 49 Writers, as well as former critique partners Debbie LaFleiche, Stacey Saunders, and Laura Carpenter. She Writes Press and the National Association of Memoir Writers have been an ongoing source of information and support.

To my daughters, I thank you for giving me a reason to learn to push back. To my siblings and to my extended family, thank you for adding dimension to my life and for your love.

ABOUT THE AUTHOR

Lizbeth Meredith is a writer with a bachelor's degree in journalism and a master's degree in psychology. She has worked as a domestic violence advocate and a child abuse investigator, and with at-risk teens as a juvenile probation supervisor. She blogs at www.lameredith.com, is a contributor to *A Girls' Guide To Travelling Alone* by Gemma Thompson, and is the author of *When Push Comes to Shove: How to Help When Someone You Love Is Being Abused*. She lives in Anchorage, Alaska near her two adult daughters.

Author photo by F/Stop Avenue

SELECTED TITLES FROM SHE WRITES PRESS

She Writes Press is an independent publishing
company founded to serve women writers everywhere.
Visit us at www.shewritespress.com.

Fourteen: A Daughter's Memoir of Adventure, Sailing, and Survival
by Leslie Johansen Nack. $16.95, 978-1-63152-941-2. A com-
ing-of-age adventure story about a young girl who comes into her
own power, fights back against abuse, becomes an accomplished
sailor, and falls in love with the ocean and the natural world.

The Full Catastrophe: A Memoir by Karen Elizabeth Lee. $16.95, 978-
1-63152-024-2. The story of a well educated, professional woman
who, after marrying the wrong kind of man—twice—finally resur-
rects her life.

Letting Go into Perfect Love: Discovering the Extraordinary After Abuse
by Gwendolyn M. Plano. $16.95, 978-1-938314-74-2. After stay-
ing in an abusive marriage for twenty-five years, Gwen Plano finally
broke free—and started down the long road toward healing.

Learning to Eat Along the Way by Margaret Bendet. $16.95, 978-1-
63152-997-9. After interviewing an Indian holy man, newspaper
reporter Margaret Bendet follows him in pursuit of enlightenment
and ends up facing demons that were inside her all along.

*Warrior Mother: A Memoir of Fierce Love, Unbearable Loss, and Rituals
that Heal* by Sheila K. Collins, PhD. $16.95, 978-1-938314-46-9.
The story of the lengths one mother goes to when two of her three
adult children are diagnosed with potentially terminal diseases.

Uncovered: How I Left Hassidic Life and Finally Came Home by Leah
Lax. $16.95, 978-1-63152-995-5. Drawn in their offers of refuge
from her troubled family and promises of eternal love, Leah Lax
becomes a Hassidic Jew—but ultimately, as a forty-something
woman, comes to reject everything she has lived for three decades
in order to be who she truly is.